THE ECONOMICS OF HUMAN BETTERMENT

OCLC

THE ECONOMICS
OF HUMAN
BETTERMENT

Edited by Kenneth E. Boulding

State University of New York Press
Albany

First published in U.S.A. by
State University of New York Press, Albany

Printed in Great Britain

For information, address State University of New York Press, State University Plaza,
Albany, N.Y., 12246

Library of Congress Cataloging in Publication Data

Main entry under title:

The Economics of human betterment.

   Includes index.
   1. Economics—Congresses.   2. Welfare state—Congresses.   3. Progress—Congresses.   4. Quality of life—
Congresses.   I. Boulding, Kenneth E. (Kenneth Ewart),
1910–   .   II. British Association for the Advancement
of Science.   Section F (Economics)   III. Title: Human
betterment.
HB21.E247   1984   330   84–3575
ISBN 0–87395–925–6
ISBN 0–87395–926–4 (pbk.)

10 9 8 7 6 5 4 3 2 1

Contents

Notes on the Contributors

Kenneth E. Boulding is Distinguished Professor of Economics, Emeritus, at the University of Colorado, Boulder, where he is also research associate in the Institute of Behavioral Science. A prolific and widely respected author, Professor Boulding's work has embraced numerous topics, including economic theory, grants economics, conflict and peace studies, evolutionary theory, general systems and the study of human knowledge and learning. He has been president of the American Economic Association, the American Association for the Advancement of Science, the International Studies Association and of many other learned societies.

David Collard is Professor of Economics at the University of Bath. He is the author of *Altruism and Economy* (1978) and of a number of papers in learned journals.

Michael Ellman is Professor of the Economics of Centrally Planned Economies and Chairman of the Department of Microeconomics at the University of Amsterdam. He is the author of *Planning in the USSR* (1973), *Socialist Planning* (1979) and *Political Economy in a Divided World* (forthcoming). He is well known for his work on planning techniques, the contribution of agriculture to economic development in the USSR and economic reform in the USSR. He is a member of the editorial board of Matekon and an associate editor of the *Cambridge Journal of Economics.*

Antony Flew is currently Professor of Philosophy in York University, Toronto, and was previously a professor at the University of Reading. He is author of *The Politics of Procrustes* (1976), *Crime or Disease?* (1973) and many other books and articles.

Jonathan Gershuny is a Senior Fellow in the Science Policy Research Unit, University of Sussex. Dr Gershuny is the author of *After Industrial Society?* (1978) and *Service Employment: Trends and Prospects in Europe* (1983).

vii

Michael Kaser is Reader in Economics at the University of Oxford and Professorial Fellow of St Antony's College. After reading economics at Cambridge and studying the Soviet and East European economies in the Foreign Office (serving as Second Secretary in the Commercial Secretariat of HM Embassy, Moscow, in 1949) he was in the Secretariat of the UN Economic Commission for Europe from 1951 until 1963. He is currently directing (with grants from the SSRC and the Shell International Petroleum Co.) research for a five-volume *Economic History of Eastern Europe 1919–1975. Soviet Economics* (1970), *Planning in East Europe* (1970) and his chapter on 'Russian Entrepreneurship' in the *Cambridge Economic History of Europe* (vol. VII, 1978) are among his many studies of economic mechanisms under central planning. He is editor (with Archie Brown) of *Soviet Policy in the 1980s* (1982)

Lim Chong-Yah is Professor of Economics and Head of the Department of Economics and Statistics, National University of Singapore. He is the author of numerous books and articles on economic theory and development and has also been active in public service in Singapore. Professor Lim is President of the Economic Society of Singapore and editor of the *Malayan Economic Review*.

Muriel Nissel is a Senior Fellow at the Policy Studies Institute. After graduating from Oxford she joined the Civil Service and was involved in economic forecasting at the Treasury and the Central Statistical Office. While at the CSO she originated and edited the first five issues of *Social Trends*. She was appointed a magistrate in 1965.

David Reisman is a Lecturer in the Department of Economics, University of Surrey. He is the author of *Adam Smith's Sociological Economics* (1976), *Richard Titmuss: Welfare and Society* (1977), *Galbraith and Market Capitalism* (1980) and *State and Welfare* (1982).

David Simpson is Research Professor at the Fraser of Allander Institute, University of Strathclyde. A graduate of the Universities of Edinburgh and Harvard, he is the author of *General Equilibrium Analysis* (1975) and *The Political Economy of Growth* (1983).

Radha Sinha is Professor of Political Economy at the University of Glasgow, where he has taught since 1964. He is the author of *World Food Problem: Consensus and Conflict* (1977), *Japan's Options for the 1980s* (1982), *Chinese Agricultural Economy* (with others) (1982) and of numerous other books and articles.

Foreword

KENNETH E. BOULDING

The enterprise to which this volume is dedicated, modest as it may be intellectually, is one of great potential significance for the human race. I have rashly called this a 'hundred-year research project' in what might be described academically as 'normative analysis'. It has two parts: first, what do we mean by things getting better rather than worse, and second, as we improve our concept of betterment, how do we in fact make decisions which lead to betterment? We are unlikely to come up with single or simple answers to either of these questions. Human valuations are very diverse; they may be co-ordinated, but they are rarely amalgamated into a single pattern. Similarly, it is very difficult to get accurate images of the immense complexity of humans and their environments, to form realistic agendas for decision and choice. Nevertheless these tasks are not hopeless, and careful scholarly investigation can improve both our images of the consequences of decision and our ability to choose among them.

When one thinks of the immense amount of human misery that has been caused by decisions that might have been made otherwise, in terms of 'war, dearth, age, agues, tyrannies, despair, law, chance', as John Donne puts it, and even chance might be reduced by greater knowledge, it is hard not to believe that the careful study of human betterment would not lead to an immense enhancement of it.

Economics should have a key role in this study. It is the discipline that concentrates most on human valuations, and on decision and choice. Welfare economics may not come out with a single answer, but it asks very good questions, and we should not be ashamed of it. Positive economics studies the consequences of decisions in an important segment of the real world, and improved knowledge of it should make bad – because ill-informed – decisions less frequent. Parts of the real world are indeed beyond economics, but economics is a good place to begin. As is *The Economics of Human Betterment*.

I welcome this volume, therefore, as a harbinger of greater hope for the future. The meeting of the British Association at which these papers were presented was a stimulating and exciting occasion, and I hope this volume will provoke in a wide circle the same quality of discussion.

Neither the meeting nor this volume would have come into being without the energy and devotion of David Reisman, the Recorder of Section F. All of us who have participated in this enterprise owe him a debt that no mere words can repay.

For myself, this return to the land of my birth and my youth was a privilege and pleasure not easy to express. Sometimes, in spite of Thomas Wolfe, one can go home again, and to find it so alive and significant was indeed a 'treasure without measure'.

Introduction

DAVID REISMAN

The Economics of Human Betterment is about three things. It is about betterment – a change or process – and thus about institutions and nations as they evolve. It is about *human* betterment – it is man and not the crocodile that God created in His own image – and thus concerned with perceived welfare, basic human needs and goals at which we not only aim but ought to aim. It is, finally, about economics – but about means the means, not means the ends – and thus asks in what way productive activities (whether free market or planned, whether in developed or in developing countries) influence essential human values and in what way they are influenced by them. Our book is not a *how to* but a *why* book. Interdisciplinary where appropriate, it is never so abstract, so formal, so deductive that it conceals what in my view must be the key point in all of economic theorising and practice – that economics is about people first and about things only in so far as they contribute to human betterment.

The book opens with Professor Boulding's Presidential Address. In it he acknowledges the current mood of pessimism concerning the GNP and other indices of well-being – but also says that wider economic and social considerations suggest to him that things *can* go from bad to better. He mentions the role of the state in economy and society and in that way alludes to one of the central questions in our book: to what extent (minimal, maximal, moderate) can the whole do what the individual parts cannot?

Human betterment is difficult to quantify, but two of our contributors show none the less how this task of measurement might be approached. Muriel Nissel presents a variety of indicators (subjective and objective, economic and social) and draws attention to work on time-use which, in fact, is taken further in the next paper, that of Jonathan Gershuny. Gershuny notes how difficult it is to interpret empirical data (as where what looks like leisure reveals itself upon closer inspection to be unpaid work), but, after allowing for

methodological difficulties, proceeds to an analysis of results collected
by himself and his colleagues. His attempt to disaggregate data by class
and sex raises the question '*Whose* human betterment?'

The next two papers are about human betterment in developed
societies. David Simpson notes the weakness of normative constraint
and self-discipline in the modern mixed economy, but does not predict
the disappearance of that compromise economic system. Michael
Kaser, writing about Soviet-type planned economies, has a great deal
to say as well about constraint and discipline, but of the external rather
than the internalised form, namely the political coercion and limitation
of choice which he finds prevalent in Eastern Europe. He notes that in
Soviet-type economies human betterment would seem to wait upon
better economic analysis; and he reflects that the social outcomes of
economic policies are themselves in command economies frequently
neglected by the authorities.

The book then turns from the Occident to the Orient and considers
three countries in two papers. Radha Sinha, writing about India and
Japan, identifies both the impact of culture upon the economy (the
case of caste in India) and of economy upon culture (witness the decay
of the invisible welfare state of the family in societies increasingly
characterised by mobility and consumption); and says that one of the
more serious costs of economic growth might be loss of social harmony. Lim Chong-Yah, writing about Singapore, shares Dr Sinha's
concern with cultural norms, but paints a more optimistic picture.
Using a wide range of indicators (reminding us in places of the kind of
criteria suggested by Mrs Nissel in her earlier paper), he says that
Singaporeans in the period since 1959 have not only benefited from a
greater number of air-conditioned cinemas, but have shown in addition a greater willingness to donate blood to help unnamed strangers.
One of the most universal indices of human betterment is, in my
opinion, the spontaneous incidence of precisely such acts of altruism
and generosity.

Indeed, it is precisely at this point that the book turns to the
problems of sharing and common well-being which occupy the last
four chapters of the volume – four chapters which raise fundamental
issues about welfare. Welfare, equality, justice and the political Good
Samaritan. Antony Flew, presenting a philosopher's perspective on
betterment, asks whether the state ought, Procrustes-like, to make us
all more equal and reminds us that perceived freedom and subjective
self-determination are to most of us an important part of human
betterment. I, in my paper on T. H. Marshall's approach to the theory

of the middle ground, raise some doubts as to whether a community becomes more caring as it becomes more wealthy and speculate on whether political democracy might not cause market values to spread into the welfare state itself. The book then proceeds to an important theoretical model of welfare by David Collard – a model which considers the links between altruism, interest and collective consumption, and reaches some surprising conclusions – and concludes with a paper by Michael Ellman depicting how the Dutch dealt with their slow rate of economic growth by scrapping a significant part of institutionalised altruism. Ellman's paper is in a sense a sad one, for it seems to indicate that, in one case at least, welfare did not temper egotism, but was instead defeated by the selfishness of the invisible hand. Perhaps, however, just as a society can have an excess of physical capital, so it can have an excess of moral capital; and perhaps, therefore, a charitable observer might want to argue that what the Dutch were doing was in truth no more than bending the bent rod so as to make it straight again. Regrettably, it is in the social sciences often far easier to argue than to prove.

*   *   *

The study of how human beings evaluate total systems is a legitimate, though difficult, field of academic endeavour. It cannot reach indisputable conclusions, but it can guard against major errors in the performing of such evaluations. If out book has a purpose, it is no more – and no less – ambitious than this.

1 How do Things go from Bad to Better? the Contribution of Economics

KENNETH E. BOULDING

'Human betterment' is one of those concepts the importance of which is in no way diminished by its vagueness. As we move from the simpler systems of the exact sciences into the study of complex systems, especially of human systems, the real world that we are studying itself becomes more and more vague. It is a great mistake to be clear in our minds about a vague reality.

By betterment I mean a process through time in which in terms of some human valuations the state of a system later in time is evaluated as superior or 'better' than the same system earlier in time. If we evaluate a human system as better today than it was yesterday, then human betterment has taken place. Human valuations are, of course, made by individual human beings. But then our images of the world of 'fact' are also in the heads of individual human beings. There is a certain prejudice in the scientific community, perhaps a hangover from logical positivism, against the study of human valuations by scholarly processes. There seems to be no justification for this. The distinction between 'facts' and 'values' is a very tenuous one. Both of them exist, if they exist as objects, in the complex structure of human nervous systems, and the processes by which our images of fact and our evaluation of these images are conducted are not very different.

It is perhaps a little difficult to say what we mean by the 'truth' of our images of value. We regard our images of fact as true if they map into a real world, some kind of a one-to-one structure. Testing is a very complex set of processes by which we are led to change our images of fact towards greater truth, or perhaps to reinforce them as true enough. A virtually similar process of testing goes on with our images of value, in that those images are 'truer' which survive testing and are reinforced by it. This process is not very different from the way in which we test and reinforce images of fact, though it is a little harder to say what our truer images of value map into. But we really cannot say this with certainty of our images of fact for, as Hume pointed out a long time ago, we can never compare directly an image with the reality, only an image with another image, so that testing is always indirect. There is no reality testing; there is only reality evidence. This is as true of science as of any other scholarly activity, or even of the processes by which we acquire the folk knowledge of everyday life.

There is a little semantic problem here as to whether there are 'things' called 'values'. This is perhaps a result of our Indo-Aryan passion for nouns. There is no doubt about there being processes of valuation and processes of learning. It seems probable that these result in structures which could be called 'values' or 'knowledge' in the human nervous system, although we do not know what these structures are or how they are coded. And it is often more useful to talk about the processes of valuation and learning with which we are all familiar.

Every human being evaluates constantly. Evaluations are the main subject of our conversations: 'How are you today?', 'How did you like such and such?', 'Do you prefer *A* to *B*?' and so on. Evaluation is also the basis of human decisions. All decisions involve an evaluation of a set of images of the future. This does not usually involve quantitative appraisals. All that is really needed is a ranking into two categories, 'best' and 'not best', and we choose the best. We should add 'best at the time', as we frequently regret decisions at a later date. We perform these evaluations when we are faced with a menu at a restaurant, a set of potential investments, a set of political policies, a set of candidates for election and so on. Valuations involved in decisions, however, are perhaps only a small part of the total evaluation process. We evaluate things all the time simply because we like to do so and we like to talk about it.

We evaluate systems of different sizes. We all evaluate the state of our own mind and body, our health, our riches, our reputation. We also evaluate larger systems – the state of our family, of our profession, of the organisations that we work with, of our local community, of our country and of the total world. The bigger the system, no doubt, the less we indulge in evaluating it. We may even evaluate the state of the solar system – indeed astronomers do. Even I think it is better for the space probes and maybe a little worse for the garbage we left on the Moon, and may become much worse if we militarise space. The theologians are not afraid to evaluate the whole universe. This is probably an activity that requires a certain humility.

We can express this by defining G (for goodness) as that which goes up when we think things are getting better and goes down when we think they are getting worse. Goodness is a stock; betterment is a flow, or change in the stock over time. Then we can postulate a goodness function:

$$G = f(\text{the relevant universe}).$$

When the relevant universe changes, if G goes up this is betterment; if it goes down it is worsening. Then we can postulate a very large number of variables in the argument of the goodness function. The first set we might describe as 'secondary values', the primary value, of course, being goodness itself. Then we write the goodness function as:

$$G = f(a, b, c, \ldots z, \ldots).$$

These secondary values – which we might call virtues or vices – are such things as adaptability, amenity, balance, beauty, bravery, congestion (a vice), conservation, conservatism (?), courageousness, death (?), delicacy, environmental quality, excitement, fashion (?), freedom, gentleness, graciousness, health, humaneness, injustice (a vice), joviality, justice, kindness, longevity (?), love, mellowness, mercy, naturalness, openness, potential, profitability, prudence, quality of life, radicalism (?), riches, stability, sustainability, tenderness, thievishness (a vice), toughness (?), ugliness (a vice), variety, vigour, violence (a vice), wealth, wisdom, wishy-washiness (a vice), x = the unknown, youthfulness, zaniness (?) – many others could be added. Some we identify as vices, a vice being defined as a secondary value an increase of which diminishes G or goodness. Some I have put question marks after because there might be differences of opinion as to whether they are virtues or vices. The unmarked ones are almost universally agreed to be virtues – that is, an increase in them increases goodness. A good many of these can be paired: beauty and ugliness, justice and injustice, riches and poverty, health and sickness. These then represent the opposite ends of a spectrum, one end of which is a virtue and the other a vice; somewhere in the middle presumably is neutral. There is a fairly universal principle, that almost any secondary value is a virtue in small quantities, but that as it increases, what might be called the 'marginal goodness', the increase in G which results from a unit increase in the secondary value, diminishes and eventually becomes zero and then negative. This might almost be called the 'parabola principle'. As we plot G vertically and the secondary value horizontally, the resulting relationship is likely to look something like a parabola, reaching a maximum and then declining. This is the basis of an old joke about 'I am courageous, you are foolhardy', 'I am thrifty, you are a skinflint', 'I am adaptable, you are a sycophant', and so on.

Each of these secondary values may have a function of their own relating them to a set of other variables, what might be called 'tertiary values' or sometimes called 'intermediate goods'. Thus, health is a function of nutrition, which itself is a function of many other variables – food input, vitamins, protein and so on; exercise, physical and personal environments, which again can be divided into a lot of other variables, and so on. The situation is confused by the fact that some tertiary goods may also have certain secondary qualities. We want food because it gives us health, but we also like food for its own sake because we enjoy eating. These are complications, however, that can be neglected for the moment. We can certainly go back to values of fourth, fifth, sixth and so on orders. We want x_1 because it increases x_2, we want x_2 because it diminishes x_3 which was a bad, we want to diminish x_3 because it increases x_4, we want x_4 because it increases x_5, we want x_5 because it increases goodness. The processes here are of great complexity and are by no means easy to describe. There is nevertheless a certain underlying simplicity to the process in its overall pattern.

Now, of course, we have to face the fact that every one of the four and a half billion human beings on the earth at the moment has a somewhat different set of valuations. How then do we co-ordinate and evaluate this great variety of valuations, which often move in different directions? Thus, a man who has just won an election can hardly be blamed for thinking that things have gone for the better; the man who has just lost it, that they have gone for the worse. Nevertheless, this immense set of diverse human valuations itself has a pattern, both as a structure at a given moment and as a process through time. These four and a half billion human valuation structures, complex as they are, are a kind of ecosystem. The valuation systems themselves are less complex than the individuals whose minds they inhabit. They interact with each other in ecological interaction and exhibit evolution in many regular patterns, which we need not dispair of perceiving, at least in part. Furthermore, just as individual members of the same species have a great deal in common, in spite of their important diversities, so human valuation structures have a great deal in common. They all start with some perception of a relevant universe. This may be no further than our own body or our own back yard, or it may include the earth as a whole. Then we perceive this relevant universe as consisting of parts, each of which is capable of at least rough evaluation. Then our overall evaluation is obtained by some process of adding up or cumulating the valuations that we place on the parts. These valuations need not be numerical. When the doctor asks the patient, 'How do you feel today?' the patient may say, 'Well, my appetite is a lot better, but the pain in my knees is a little worse. So on the whole I am a little better, thank you.' We constantly add and subtract what are essentially qualitative judgements into some kind of 'bottom line' or summary. And we do this in all the systems that we evaluate. In accounting, of course, we put numbers opposite each item of the position statement, representing a value in terms of measure of value, like the dollar or the pound. We add up these numbers, positive and negative, to get a bottom line, which is a net worth. In a looser way, however, we are always doing this for qualitative systems, and although not infrequently the answer comes out that we aren't really sure whether the system as a whole has gone for the better or for the worse, we nearly always have some idea of the range of reasonable valuations. In a world that is essentially uncertain and vague, it is actually a mistake to believe quantitative information too much. No wise businessman believes everything his accountant tells him, and he treats what the accountant has to tell him as important evidence, not as truth. In this respect he is doing something very similar to the doctor evaluating the health of a patient, or a voter evaluating the worth of two candidates for office or choosing which party to belong to, or a person deciding which, if any, church to join or ideology to espouse.

Just as ecological interaction co-ordinates the immense diversity of species, and even of individuals within species, into a single ecosystem which very frequently shows a tendency towards equilibrium in the number and size of species (populations), so social processes in the great ecosystem of the world co-ordinate the diverse valuations of different individuals. It is a little harder to tell in this case than it is in biology which individual belongs to what species, but the principle is much the same. Americans, with all their diversity, represent a certain type valuation species as compared with the Russians or even the British. The Irish Republican Army has a different valuation species from the members of the British government, and so on.

I have distinguished three major categories of what might be called 'co-ordination processes', which co-ordinate, though they do not necessarily reconcile, the different valuations of different people in different groups. The first of these is familiar to economists. It is the market and the system of interactive exchanges. It exhibits an 'invisible hand', not quite the same as Adam Smith's, which was rather special, but which co-ordinates the activities of innumerable individuals participating in production, consumption and exchange in a way that individual preferences can be satisfied without imposing too much these preferences on others. My favourite illustration of this is the old rhyme, 'She liked coffee and I liked tea and that is the reason we couldn't agree.' The rest of the rhyme suggests they became alcoholics! The market, however, as Mancur Olson has pointed out, economises agreement. If there is a market we do not have to agree. She can have coffee for breakfast and I can have tea, as indeed my wife and I do. There are limits on this process, as economists know. The poor have less capacity for satisfying their preferences than the rich. Advertising may pervert our desires and monopoly may suppress choice. But while these things do set boundaries for the system they do not destroy its very powerful validity within the boundaries, and this is an important part of the ethical case for free markets.

The market, however, cannot do everything, as even Milton Friedman has to admit. There are public goods and public bads, natural monopolies, and so on, which require government and political organisation and structures, and what might be called a 'legitimated threat system', at least in the shape of taxation. In many societies we find this in the form of conscription, which, in effect, is taxation in kind in the form of temporary slavery. Political processes and institutions, of course, differ enormously from society to society. In democratic societies we come a little closer to the market. We can't each have what we want, but we each have a right to make a fuss about it, to write to our Congressmen or to Members of Parliament, to organise pressure groups, and so on. Then decisions are made in the overall political process as a result of the interactions of the diverse valuations of the politically active, through pressure, slogans, log-rolling, and so on. In the successful democracies this works out not too badly. In dictatorships, of course, the resolution is by fiat of the dictator. It is his (or very occasionally, her) values that determine what should be done politically, and how the internal threat system should be used. Even here, though, there is a background of unacceptability which limits the behaviour even of the most brutal dictator, and, of course, there is always the benign influence of funerals as the ultimate method of dictator-removal.

The third form of co-ordination is through persuasion and what might be called the 'moral order'. Virtually every human being belongs to one or more subcultures – in the family, the church, the local community, the nation and even the world. A subculture is defined by a certain common set of value structures, often called an 'ethos'. An individual within the subculture who does not conform to this ethos will certainly be uncomfortable and will either conform to it, get out of the subculture or be thrown out of it. A scientist who is discovered to have deliberately falsified his experimental results or a professor who tries to impose his own beliefs on his students by threatening them will not last very long in the scientific or academic community.

It is the ethos of the small communities that are strongest – soldiers die for their buddies, not for their country – but the larger unit itself, like the nation-state, has an ethos which criticises the various subcultures within it, discouraging the criminal subculture, in some cases discouraging certain religious or ideological subcultures, and encouraging conformity to its own ethos. The world ethos may not be very powerful, but it does exist and nations which violate it severely will come under criticism and even ostracism, like South Africa. The national ethos changes under the impact of the world ethos. We see this in the delegitimation of empire and subsequent withdrawal from it.

There does seem to be a pattern of evolution of these ethical systems over time, although the direction is by no means always clear, and there is a good deal of backing and filling. Ethical systems, however, which clearly lead into poverty and violence, insecurity and corruption, do come under what might be called 'evolutionary criticism', and in the long run are a little less stable than those ethical systems which are more generally acknowledged to be benign. Sometimes indeed it seems to take a catastrophe to bring about this evolutionary critique of existing ethical systems, like the Irish Famine of 1846, which led to a sharp decline in birth rates; or the appalling ritual sacrifice of young men in Europe in the First World War, which eventually led to the abandonment of empires. One hopes this will not be the case in the nuclear war issue.

The co-ordinating processes seem to produce much more consensus when the changes under consideration are large. There may be wide disagreement about whether a particular artist or musician is better than another, or even about whether one politician or party is better than another. But when it comes to catastrophe, however, especially large changes that are adverse, which seem to be much more common than large changes that are favourable (for which there seems to be no word in the English language), agreement is much more widespread.

There is very widespread agreement that riches is better than poverty, although we have to allow for the concept of the filthy rich, a point beyond which an increase in riches diminishes goodness and becomes a bad rather than a good. Even though the concept of justice is extraordinarily hard to define and specify there is very widespread agreement that justice is good and injustice is bad, although whether a specific social change increases justice may not produce much agreement. Also, it is easier to identify injustice than justice. Small changes in the justice quality of a society are not very significant, but where there is gross injustice, as in the sort of things that Amnesty International worries about, agreement becomes widespread, although these processes do take time, like the long, slow delegitimation and abolition of slavery. What this suggests is that the goodness function over a good many dimensions has a flat top, rather like what is called, where I come from, a 'mesa', which is Spanish for 'table'. Optimisation on a mesa is rather silly. It doesn't matter very much where you are on the flat top. This is why religious tolerance and separation of Church and State has been such a good idea. From a social point of view there is not the slightest need to insist on conformity in religion. With a free market in religion as Adam Smith suggested, we do not have to have agreement, each can choose his or her own church – or none – according to individual needs, taste and experience. One wishes one could likewise separate nationalism from the state, let everyone choose what national group he wanted to belong to, no matter where he lived, no matter in what state he lived. But we seem to be a long way from this.

The role of economics in both the formulation of concepts of human betterment and what might be called 'normative analysis' is by no means insignificant. Any economist will recognise a certain amount of glorified economics in what has preceded in this chapter. The concept of the goodness function is, of course, our old friend the utility function in disguise, somewhat exalted. The parabola principle, of course, is the law of diminishing marginal utility. Even economists have argued that there is a law of diminishing marginal utility of riches, even though the purist school, following Hicks, finds this a little embarrassing. In the evaluation of large complex systems of many parts the rates of substitution among the parts are an important clue to how they should be valued. Economics recognises that there is a possible equilibrium price structure which stands out from all the other possibilities by the property that the relative prices conform to alternative costs – that is, essentially to rates of substitution in production of the different secondary or tertiary goods: how much of A must we give up to get a unit of B?

This is a principle which applies in a qualitative way to the evaluation of the virtues and vices. If we have to give up a lot of freedom in order to get a little more justice, we will tend to value freedom more highly and justice a little less so. We will be more tolerant of societies that sacrifice a certain amount of justice for freedom and we will be suspicious of societies which sacrifice a good deal of freedom in the name of justice. If the opportunity cost in the rate of increase in riches is an increase in inequality of substantial dimension, we will give inequality a higher rating and look with suspicion on societies that increase riches at too high a cost in equality. One of the striking things about economics and its 'uncongenial twin', accounting, is that this is almost the only place in social systems where valuations are fairly easily subject to measurement, thanks to the famous 'measuring-rod of money'. Psychologists, of course, have done a lot of measurement and sociologists have also tried their hand at it, but it seems to be hard to translate their instruments to the level of the total system, which economics can do very successfully.

The great virtue of accounting is that it does make a pretty clear distinction between stocks, as represented in the balance-sheet and position statements, and flows of the income accounts, which are essentially changes in balance-sheets. This leads to two different types of valuation of, say, a business, either in terms of net worth (the net dollar value of its stock of assets and liabilities) or in terms of a profit or loss figure, which fundamentally is the gross rate of change of net worth. Then there is also cost accounting, which deals with the throughput through the capital stock.

The state of any system can be thought of as a population of different kinds of species. Populations, however, usually have a throughput – that is, they are added to by births and in-migrations, and subtracted from by deaths and out-migrations. A good deal of demographic analysis is devoted to the implications of this, especially for things like age distributions. We somehow have to put both stocks and flows into the goodness function because future flows contribute to the value of present stocks. I have argued for many years, without much effect, that economic welfare, whatever that is, is much more dependent on the stock of capital with which we are surrounded than on the throughputs in consumption and production. I get satisfaction out of wearing my clothes, not out of wearing them out. The same goes for my automobile, my house and my furniture. On the other hand, I do enjoy eating as well as being well fed. And I enjoy learning and adding to my stock of pleasurable experiences as well as having this stock of knowledge and pleasurable memories. There is no great mathematical problem involved in all this, but it has caused a great deal of conceptual confusion to which economics has contributed, but which it has also helped to resolve.

Economics, of course, is primarily concerned with the secondary "value of 'virtue' 'riches'." We have put a lot of thought into the riches function – that is, what are the other variables which determine both the level of riches and its rate of growth? We have found that purely economic models are not sufficient for this and that in order to understand the growth of riches we have to understand a lot about psychology, child-rearing, family institutions, religion and the other elements of a society. Still there are some very simple and obvious propositions that economics produces, ignorance of which can be a severe handicap. The first is the principle that we get rich by having riches grow. If some countries are rich and some are poor today it is largely because the rich countries have been getting richer longer and faster than the poor countries.

The second principle is that growth of riches, or what is usually called 'economic development', has a great deal to do with the learning institutions of a society, both in terms of innovation – that is, the creation of new knowledge which never existed before – and imitation, which is learning what other people know. The learning culture of a society is far more significant than any other factor. Natural resources are relatively insignificant, as we can easily learn how to economise them, find them or buy them. To get richer, however, we not only have to accumulate knowledge, we have to accumulate the material and organisational embodiments of human knowledge: material capital such as buildings, machines, roads, aeroplanes; and organisational structures in terms of laws, markets, regulations, corporations, organisations of all kinds. These are as much a part of the capital structure and are as much embodiments of human learning as are computers and bulldozers.

Economists have laid a good deal of stress on the productivity of labour or human activity as a principal factor in riches and have also emphasised that in the ecology of commodities the niches for different human activities and kinds of goods constantly change in the course of development. Classical economics also had a kind of 'food chain' theory, very similar to modern ecology. Oats were fed into the farm labourer, who then produced more oats as a result than he and his family could eat. This gave us a surplus of oats, which we then fed into cloth-makers, who produced cloth, into cows who produced milk, into builders who produced buildings and so on. Similarly, iron ore is the food of iron foundries, iron the food of railroads, steel of skyscrapers and so on. Modern economics has tended to lose this very profound insight of the classical economists.

On the whole I would argue that economics has contributed more than any other social science to the concept of human betterment. A different, very interesting, yet puzzling question is whether economics as an intellectual discipline has contributed to human betterment itself – that is, has it done more good than harm to the ongoing experience of the human race? At the time of the bicentennial of Adam Smith's *Wealth of Nations* in 1976 I wrote and put on a little play, the scene being the Last Judgement, in which a hearing was held before the Recording Angel concerning whether economics did more good than harm. Testimony was obtained from Adam Smith, Ricardo, Malthus, Marx, Keynes, Schumpeter and so on. And, of course, it was not too difficult to make out a rather depressing case.

Adam Smith I think comes off pretty well. His perception that exchange is usually what today we would call a 'positive-sum-game' which makes everybody better off is a great advance over the zero-sum view of the Mercantilists. He further perceives, however, that it has certain social costs in the adverse effects of the division of labour on human character. His denunciation in Book V of the division of labour as a producer of mentally and politically crippled human beings is as powerful as any critique of the market ever made. Nevertheless, I think there is little doubt that a prejudice towards free trade is highly beneficial, that much government regulation is adverse even to its intended consequences, especially when it fosters monopoly, that there are many 'invisible hands' and unconscious processes in society making towards human betterment, and that the understanding of these can assist us in the visible hands – deliberate policy and political action.

Malthus is a particularly interesting case, as the Christian minister with the horrifying miserific vision of what might almost be called the 'invisible whip', the procreative drive which is constantly in danger of pushing us forward into irretrievable misery. And yet Malthus also saw that if you had the miserific vision, it could be avoided through the 'preventive checks' of human intelligence and foresight. Ricardo I am not so sure about. Much as I admire his superb intellectual achievement, as Keynes said: 'If only Malthus instead of Ricardo had been the parent stem from which nineteenth-century economics proceeded, what a much wiser and richer place the world would be today!'[1]

Marx, with all his genius and insight, I must confess I have to put on the negative side of the balance-sheet, not so much as an economist (his economics is not much better than Ricardo's), but for his ideology, almost a secular religion, which involved the idealisation of struggle and violence, an assumption that virtually all human relationships were either zero- or negative-sum, a total failure to understand the virtues of political freedom, a hopelessly inadequate description of the class structure of society, and an idealisation of class war, which altogether sums up to responsibility for a large amount of unnecessary human misery. He should not perhaps be blamed altogether for Stalin, for the Cultural Revolution in China, or for the appalling catastrophe of Cambodia, but he cannot wholly disclaim responsibility.

The great difference between Adam Smith and Marx is that Adam Smith knew what he liked and Marx only knew what he disliked. This 'negative cathexis', as it might be called, is the fatal flaw of radicalism. It leads into enormous pathologies. The world does seem to be divided into approachers who go towards what they like and avoiders who go away from what they don't like. Approachers resolve their dilemmas, have excellent mental health, easily form co-operative relationships and tend to have a pretty good life. Avoiders are in constant dilemmas, internal struggle and easily slip into utterly inhuman behaviour destructive of all decent human relations. One should not blame economics for this, which on the whole has enjoyed positive cathexis, being pretty clear about what it did like and going towards it. But I can certainly blame Marx for the powerful rhetoric by which he legitimated an enormously destructive aspect of human behaviour.

Then, of course, there was the Great Depression and the Keynesian Revolution. The Great Depression represented a disastrous failure of Ricardian neo-Classical economics. Marshall, with all his many virtues, never really understood that a market system could get into extreme positions which are highly pathological, as it did in 1932 and 1933. Keynes certainly did not have all the answers, but he did have some. It is no accident that both Samuelson and myself, writing of the impact of Keynes on us as young men, quote Wordsworth: 'Bliss was it in that dawn to be alive, but to be young was very heaven!'[2] I shall never forget the feeling I had, even as an undergraduate at Oxford, on reading Keynes's *Treatise on Money*; for the first time in my life the world of society and of human history began to make sense to me, which it had certainly never done in school.

If we add John R. Commons and humanistic economics (saving capitalism by making it good), and the Fabians and Sir William Beveridge as the creators of what might be called 'social capitalism',

I find it hard not to see this as inspiring a real process in human betterment, in spite of its incompleteness and difficulties, the unemployment–inflation dilemma, some excesses of government regulation, some pathologies of the grants economy and all that. The history of economic thought is the record of a very earnest attempt on the part of a very small subset of the human race to bring into human consciousness the essential characteristics of an extremely complex system. We are still not out of the woods, but compared with the threat posed to us by the breakdown of national defence in a nuclear age, and even the uncontrollability of the world ecosystem in terms of the CO_2 problem, toxic waste and so on, the contribution of economics certainly has both assets and liabilities, but my conviction is that the net worth is positive, that we have contributed quite substantially to human betterment. There is a striking contrast between the period from, say, 1919 to 1939 and the period from 1945 to date. In the first we had the disastrous peace of Versailles, so ably criticised by Keynes, the small depression of the 1920s and the Great Depression of the 1930s, culminating in the Second World War. The second period, for which economics I think can claim some credit, looks not too far from a middling golden age, in which poverty has sharply diminished in the rich countries, and even in some poorer ones, though not everywhere. Culture and higher education have spread to a much larger portion of the human race, empires have been abandoned, race relations improved in many places, a large area of stable peace established and so on. The period may end in total catastrophe, but the catastrophe will be a failure of politics and unilateral national defence, not so much of economics. This may be small consolation, but perhaps even small consolation is better than none.

Economists have something of a reputation for being cold and calculating; people who, in the phrase attributed to Oscar Wilde, 'know the price of everything and the value of nothing', people who would never dream of going barefoot in the park. As I once said: 'You wouldn't want your daughter to marry an economic man.' Certainly if we simply stop with prices and net worths and bottom lines in an accounting sense the accusation has some validity. But we do not have to stop there. I think we have a right to point out that if we do not start with something like accounting and cost–benefit analysis, relative price structures and alternative costs, substitutabilities and all these other things that economists know about, we can go very far wrong indeed in our search for the general principles of human betterment. There is no aspect of human life in which economising is not important.

Beauty is a matter of right proportions; it always involves a structure of parts and the most beautiful structure is that in which an increase in one part is not worth the diminution in other parts which it costs. Economics also points to the total folly of empire, a perfect example of a negative-sum process, which injures both the imperial power and the colonies, and the unspeakable folly of war as a negative-sum process *par excellence*, in which the human race is devoting vast resources to make itself worse off. An economic analysis of the Falkland Islands War, the cost of which could have made every Falkland Islander a millionaire, certainly reveals the very heavy burden of justification which those who made such decisions have to carry.

Where economics perhaps has failed is in the problem of the agenda of choice itself. Economists tend to assume that there is an agenda and that the only problem is to evaluate the different futures on the list and choose the best. This, however, is unrealistic. Agendas, also, are a matter of choice and bad decisions are more often a result of the failure of agendas – that is, not thinking of possible futures that we might have thought of – than they are a failure of the choice process on a given agenda. This is why the human race is sliding towards total destruction, a process certainly accelerated by the Falkland Islands War, for war is the matter of the breaking of the taboos of peace against organised destruction of life and property. And once that taboo is broken it becomes easier to break it in the future. I have no doubt Mrs Thatcher acted with the best of intentions, but I think she brought the destruction of the human race a little closer.

Economics by itself certainly cannot save us, but I cannot help thinking that compared with much ideology of all kinds, economics is a substantial asset which we can justly criticise, but of which we should not be ashamed.

NOTES

1. J. M. Keynes, *Essays in Biography* (London: Macmillan, 1933) p. 144.
2. Herbert Stein, *The Fiscal Revolution in America* (Chicago: University of Chicago Press, 1969) p. 162.

2 Indicators of Human Betterment

MURIEL NISSEL

In the 1960s, when we were said never to have had it so good, many questions were being asked, particularly by those who were already materially well-off, about how we should be measuring the quality of life. Today, when many people have never had it so bad, there is renewed interest in what kind of social impact world economic recession and the particular policies of recent governments have been having on the lives of the people of this country.

Any attempt to measure the quality of life must start with an exposition of what one is trying to assess. What, in the first place, are the fundamental values of human beings; second, precisely what is meant by the concepts used; third – if the purpose of measurement is to increase human betterment – the extent to which it is within the power of society to change the situation; and, lastly, how far it is possible to devise statistical measures or indicators which can validly and accurately reflect the quality of life.

This paper uses a descriptive approach to look at some of the issues. It shows how, during the second half of this century, economists and other social scientists moved away from the assumption that economic wellbeing is synonymous with social wellbeing to recognise more explicitly that it is but one aspect of the quality of life and economic growth no more than a means to this end.[1] The focus was more on the non-material aspects of life, particularly those areas of social concern over which governments can have some influence. In more recent years interest has shifted towards examining the importance which individuals themselves attach to particular human values and questioning the role and power of governments to change the way people live their lives.

The first half of the paper is mainly concerned with describing some

15

of the ways in which economists measure the national income and with discussing both the concepts involved and the problems of measuring them. The fumblings of economists to better define their concepts and the purpose of measurement were linked with concurrent thinking among other social scientists who were concentrating more specifically on defining and measuring wellbeing in its broader sense. The second half of the paper reviews these developments and describes the evolution of what became known as the 'social indicators' movement.

ECONOMIC WELLBEING

Material standards of living largely determine the degree to which basic needs, such as food, clothing and shelter, health and education, can be met. It is thus perhaps not surprising that the national income, as measured by the national accounts and commonly expressed by the gross national product (GNP) per capita, was long regarded as a satisfactory indication of the level of wellbeing. Although it was recognised that it did not reflect the entirety of human needs, it was assumed that any alternative more comprehensive indicator would be sufficiently closely related so that changes in the one could be identified by studying changes in the other. It is now accepted, however, that the GNP neither adequately reflects the quality of life nor is it even a particularly good indicator of economic performance. Considerable thought and discussion has consequently been devoted to formulating ideas about how it might be improved.[2] For example, in the US, Nordhaus and Tobin and others modified the GNP to prepare a Measure of Economic Welfare, and in Japan the Net National Welfare Committee set up by the Economic Council similarly used the GNP as a starting-point for estimating Net National Welfare.[3] Whereas many of the proposals have been confined to improving the usefulness of the GNP as an economic indicator, other proposals (some of which are referred to later) have gone much further and have been concerned with developing frameworks of economic growth and welfare to encompass the whole range of human activities of education and leisure as well as work and work-related activities. Much of the discussion has focused on the boundaries of final output and the meaning of the concept of utility. It has thus linked indirectly with developing ideas about indicators of human betterment and the work of other social scientists concerned with measuring wellbeing by more direct means such as social indicators.

The present system of national accounts in use in this country applies two principal criteria to the measurement of economic activity: first, that output be defined to include only goods and services bought and sold in the market and, second, that a few selected non-market activities should be included because they are analytically indistinguishable from closely related market activities. For example, although home-owners do not actually pay rent to themselves for housing services, a value is imputed based on the rents of similar housing, thus putting home-owners on a basis comparable with those who rent houses and whose payments, which come within the market criterion, are automatically included in the national accounts.

Among the more important criticisms levelled at the national accounts five are particularly important in the context of economic welfare. The first relates to the concept of national income as stopping short at the household door: goods and services produced in the market are acquired by households for final consumption, and value added within the household in the process of transforming purchased consumer goods into consumable services, such as cooking and preparing food, is not counted. The second relates to the use of inputs as surrogates for outputs for the services produced by government and non-profit-making bodies. For example, the output of publicly provided education services is valued by the inputs and no attempt is made to assess output in terms of benefits. The third criticism, under the heading of what have become known as 'regrettable necessities', relates to those expenditures, such as those on the police and the armed forces, which are necessary not for their own sake but as defensive measures. Likewise, many production processes lead to undesired outputs, or pollutants: not only is the production of these pollutants included in the national accounts but the cleaning up process may also figure if money is spent on treating them. The fourth criticism levelled at the national accounts is the inadequate distinction between current and capital flows, particularly in relation to consumer durable goods which have become increasingly important in recent decades. The failure to give due weight to this aspect of capital appreciation may have helped to disguise the growing significance of the household in the economic life of the country. From the viewpoint of the people within households, many of these consumer durable goods do not represent final consumption but are a means of increasing household productivity and hence a further stage in the economic production process. Finally, criticism of the national accounts has been extended to include the often unsatisfactory treatment of the running down of natural resources and the absence of any recognition of the value of human capital, particularly in relation to education and the resources devoted to its maintenance or improvement.

Running through these criticisms are a set of common themes, well summarised in a paper by Juster, Courant and Dow, entitled 'A Theoretical Framework for the Measurement of Well-being'.[4] The first is the need for a better measure of the division between current benefit flows and provision for future benefit flows: the second is that more attention needs to be paid to measurement systems that provide better measures of material wellbeing even if they throw less light on the costs of resource inputs: and the third is the importance of incorporating a variety of unpriced activities into economic accounting systems in a more systematic way.

All of these suggestions imply an accounting system with a greater focus on estimation and imputation and a lesser focus on recorded transactions relating to observed behaviour. It is therefore perhaps not surprising that the existing system of national accounts has been staunchly defended and that the weight of authority of the Statistical Commission of the United Nations Economic and Social Council has been put behind technical improvement rather than radical reform and adding to the usefulness of the existing accounts in a modest way by developing social accounting matrices and including material on the distribution income and wealth.[5] There are, however, certain studies in progress elsewhere, such as that of the National Bureau of Economic Research in New York[6] and the Living Standards Measurement Study launched by the World Bank in 1980,[7] which adopt a more radical approach. The latter is concerned both with developing and redefining concepts and with how to move to the empirical stage of collecting data, its ultimate purpose being to assess living standards of different groups within and between nations. More recently, in the paper referred to above, published in 1981, Juster, Courant and Dow have set out a theoretical framework for the measurement of wellbeing which is concerned with two basic factors: the amount of available human time, and the stock of wealth inherited from the past. Wealth is defined very broadly to cover not only the conventional tangible assets familiar to economists, but also intangible human and other assets, stocks of organisational capital reflected by networks of social support systems (the family, the neighbourhood), stocks of environmental assets (the sun and air) and stocks of socio-political assets (security, freedom of choice). Human time covers market work, household production, leisure and biological maintenance.

TIME USE

Most of the proposed theoretical frameworks of welfare measurement recognise that time spent on different types of activity must be an integral part of the material collected to implement their proposals. For example, most of the proposals go beyond measurement of paid work to include unpaid work, leisure, education, training, etc. Time, like money, has a value, but with the unique characteristic of being limited for every individual to twenty-four hours a day. It has a marginal utility and opportunity cost. The activities of daily life can be measured in terms of time and choices are made about the way it is allocated between them. Some activities may be given more time, but, given the overall twenty-four-hour constraint, this must be at the expense of time which would otherwise be devoted to something else. The ways these choices are made are value-laden and significant social indicators. The development of a system based on expenditure of units of time, rather than units of money, opens up interesting possibilities for its potential use in relation to indicators of human betterment. For example, it might be feasible to construct a framework which shows the trade-off between x years and good health, y years free of burglary and z years of full-time education.

Collecting information about time use by means of time diaries has been carried out extensively in many countries. For example, a major twelve-country international study, co-ordinated by Szalai, was undertaken in 1965.[8] Many of the participating countries, including those from the Eastern Bloc, have followed up the 1965 study with further surveys. Thus, in the USA, the Institute of Social Research at the University of Michigan (ISR) carried out a follow-up survey in 1975 and again in 1981. The UK did not participate in the Szalai survey, but the BBC have for many years carried out comprehensive surveys for programme planning purposes and J. Gershuny, at the University of Sussex Science Policy Research Unit (SPRU), has recently been recoding and classifying activities in the BBC surveys to make them compatible with the system adopted for the international study conducted in 1965.

The figures in Table 2.1, which subdivide time use into five main categories, are taken from the SPRU study for the UK and from the survey by the ISR at Ann Arbor for the US.[10]

An important feature of the figures is the high proportion, some 40 per cent, of total work time accounted for by unpaid work. This type of work includes the many activities, such as looking after the elderly and

Table 2.1   *Time use by main activity*

	Percentages of total time use	
	UK 1974/5	US 1975
	Population aged 16 and under 65	Population aged 18 and under 65
Work – paid (including breaks and travelling)	17	19
– unpaid (housework, childcare, shopping, DIY, etc.)	13	12
Personal care (including meals and travel associated with family and personal care)	47	13
Sleep		33
Free time (including education and leisure travel)*	25	23

*The correspondence between the two sets of figures is close and the broad allocation is as set out in Figure 2.1.

the handicapped, which if done in an institution rather than in the home would figure in the national accounts. It adds greatly to the quality of life and any indicator of economic as well as social welfare must take account of it. It is, however, non-market activity and if a money value is to be imputed to it to integrate it with the national accounts there immediately arise all the conceptual problems of how this should be done.

THE SYSTEM OF SOCIAL AND DEMOGRAPHIC STATISTICS

The problems of agreeing and formulating a satisfactory conceptual framework and the difficulties of collecting the necessary data, par-

* It should be noted that the classification adopted in the international time budget surveys of 1965 equates leisure with the residual 'free time' remaining after other more essential activities have been carried out. In present circumstances of high levels of unemployment the existence of unwanted and purposeless free time gives a different meaning to this way of classifying leisure and forces a rethinking of the purpose and basis of the classification and a reassessment of the social and individual significance of activities, particularly their causal ties and functional implications.

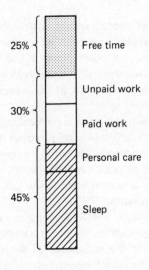

FIGURE 2.1

ticularly about time use, prompted the search for a simpler means of overcoming some of the more evident shortcomings of the conventional national accounts. For measuring economic and social welfare, it is important to recognise and accept that the accounts measure what they set out to measure, the flow of goods and services in the market economy, and as such they are self-balancing in an accounting sense, but the dynamics of change come largely from outside and an understanding of the social and environmental forces which bear upon economic and social development requires that the accounts be complemented by supplementary data. One such approach, based on the initial work of Richard Stone, was the attempt to develop a System of Social and Demographic Statistics (SSDS) which would provide information on human 'stocks and flows' for sets of subsystems in society.[11] The system called for a comprehensive data base involving unified concepts, definitions and classifications. The data for each subsystem could then be linked to the corresponding economic stock and flow data in the system of national accounts. Time use accounts, for example, would be treated as a subsystem.

Summary social indicators were regarded as an integral part of SSDS. Social scientists, such as Sir Claus Moser who was head of the Government Statistical Service in this country, were looking for ways of establishing a structural framework which would help to identify social interactions and establish causal links.[12] Within this framework, social indicators would play a part similar to economic indicators in the economic field. Likewise, Dudley Seers at the Institute of Development Studies at the University of Sussex explored ways of modifying the SSDS approach by using years of life-expectancy for integrating social indicators of years spent in various states of activity, demography, health, etc. This approach was particularly useful for comparing different countries and different groups within them and for monitoring social conditions over time. Thus, for a person born now in the UK his expected duration in both unemployment and poverty could be compared with that of a person born in the UK twenty years ago or a person born now in Sri Lanka.[13]

In the event, although SSDS may have helped statisticians to develop standard classifications for social statistics, the various subsystems which were to be the substance of the system and the social indicators which they required were never developed and the overall structure remained a framework rather than a system of social statistics. Only the French, who developed sets of satellite accounts, came near to implementing a comparable system.[14]

THE OECD SOCIAL INDICATORS PROGRAMME

Meanwhile the main thrust of the social indicators movement in the 1960s was devoted to developing indicators of a descriptive and normative type designed to help governments and others to measure more directly changes in social conditions and to make more rational and informed policy choices. The approach was firmly outcome-orientated and shifted away from the attempt to develop explanatory and predictive models towards measurement of benefits and states of wellbeing.

Many institutions and organisations were involved in putting forward and developing proposals.[15] One of the principal programmes was that of the Organization for Economic Co-operation and Development (OECD), which recognised from the outset that the significance of social indicators lay in their normative function and that the first step was to set goals towards which social statistics should be pointed. The early stages of the programme concentrated on identifying the main areas of social concern. A social concern was described as denoting 'an identifiable and definable aspiration or concern of fundamental and direct importance to human wellbeing as opposed to a matter of instrumental or indirect importance to wellbeing' and the criteria for selection were the present or potential interest to member governments.[16] Despite the varying political complexion of the different governments there was a surprising degree of consensus about the goal or direction of movement of the indicators. In some subject areas, however, it was less easy to determine whether movements up or down are 'good' or 'bad'. The birth-rate, for example, may have very different implications for China and for Australia. Likewise, improvements in some areas, such as education, is usually only feasible at the expense of devoting fewer resources to other areas, such as housing, and different governments will have different objectives at different times depending on the level of living standards prevailing and on the values underlying their political programmes.

The OECD programme was necessarily confined to those areas which were of political interest and over which governments had some direct control. For this purpose there was no point in developing indicators about the quality of the climate or even of family life. The programme identified eight main areas of concern for which it should seek indicators: health, education and learning, employment and the quality of working life, time and leisure, command over goods and services, the physical environment, the social environment and personal safety. These eight areas were then subdivided into some 30 to 40 subconcerns for each of which a particular indicator was specified. The list is set out in Table 2.2 below.

TABLE 2.2 *The OECD list of social indicators*

Social concern	Indicator
Health	
Length of life	– Life-expectancy
	– Perinatal mortality rate
Healthfulness of life	– Short-term disability
	– Long-term disability
Education and learning	
Use of educational facilities	– Regular education experience
	– Adult education
Learning	– Literacy rate
Employment and quality of working life	
Availability of employment	– Unemployment rate
	– Involuntary part-time work
	– Discouraged workers

TABLE 2.2   *(continued)*

Social concern	Indicator
Quality of working life	– Average working hours
	– Travel time to work
	– Paid annual leave
	– A typical work schedule
	– Distribution of earnings
	– Fatal occupational injuries
	– Work environment nuisances
Time and leisure	
Use of time	– Free time
	– Free-time activities
Command over goods and services	
Income	– Distribution of income
	– Low income
	– Material deprivation
Wealth	– Distribution of wealth
Physical environment	
Housing conditions	– Indoor dwelling-space
	– Access to outdoor space
	– Basic amenities
Accessibility to services	– Proximity of selected services
Environmental nuisances	– Exposure to air pollutants
	– Exposure to noise
Social environment	
Social attachment	– Suicide rate
Personal safety	
Exposure to risk	– Fatal injuries
	– Serious injuries
Perceived threat	– Fear for personal safety

In addition to the selection of a balanced set of indicators within each fundamental concern, the development of the relevant indicators had also to take account of the need to disaggregate between different groups of people living under different circumstances. For example, a country with a low average infant mortality rate and a high material standard of living may comprise within it subsections of the population, perhaps certain ethnic groups or people living in certain areas, who are particularly deprived and living below generally acceptable standards. The distributional aspect of income and wealth is a problem familiar to economists, and it is no less of a problem for social scientists grappling with the problems of social indicators.

IMPLEMENTATION OF THE PROGRAMME: THE UK

The designers of the programme were faced with the reality of what statistical material individual countries might be able and willing to provide. In many cases the choice was between a desired indicator which could validly represent the concept in mind but which was statistically unreliable or difficult or impracticable to collect and a less satisfactory indicator drawn from a statistically reliable and well-established series. The sources of the well-established series very often spring from information collected in the course of administering services and the statistics thus better describe the services provided than the people they are designed to help. A more satisfactory way of gathering information about individuals and households, particularly the distribution of wellbeing across different population groups, can be by means of multi-purpose surveys and, as part of the OECD programme, a special questionnaire was designed for use by member countries to provide a standard data base for international comparisons. Several countries made extensive use of the questionnaire and others incorporated substantial parts of it into surveys which they were carrying out for other purposes. The UK did not collaborate in this part of the programme, but many of the statistical series already available provide a fair approximation to some of the proposed indicators. Table 2.3 sets out a selection of them.

Table 2.3 tells some kind of story. Over the past two decades most of the indicators – health, education, leisure time, income, housing – suggest that the quality of life has been improving. Those for employment, the distribution of income and personal safety from crime show something rather different. The table, however, says very little about the impact on different groups of people. Even if the information were available, which for the most part it is not, disaggregation in any detail soon becomes unmanageable, at least for summary purposes, and calls for something more in the nature of a full-scale social report, such as the UK Central Statistical Office annual publication, *Social Trends*, the periodic US publication, *Social Indicators*, or the French *Données Sociales*.[17]

TABLE 2.3 *Social indicators*

	1961	1971	1981
Health			
Expectation of life – years (UK)			
Males – at birth	68	69	70
– aged 20	50	51	52
– aged 60	15	15	16
Females – at birth	74	75	76
– aged 20	56	57	58
– aged 60	19	20	20
Perinatal mortality[1]			
– per 1000 live and still births	33	23	13
Temporary disability[2] – average number			
of days per person (GB)	..	16	22
Education and learning			
Pupils in school at age 17			
– per cent of age group (UK)	9	21	24
Employment and quality of working life			
Unemployment (UK)			
– per cent registered	1½	3½	10½
Activity rates – per cent (GB)			
– Males	86	81	77
– Females	37	43	47
Hours worked (GB)			
– full-time male manual workers	48	45	44
Accidents at work – deaths – '000s (E & W)	1.1	0.8	0.5[3]
Earnings – average per week – £s (GB)			
– Males	..	29[4]	137
– Females	..	16[4]	91
– as per cent of median			
Males – upper quartile	..	128[4]	130
– lower quartile	..	79[4]	79
Females – upper quartile	..	129[4]	130
– lower quartile	..	80[4]	81
Time and leisure			
UK paid holidays – male manual workers (UK)			
– per cent receiving			
two weeks and under	97	28	..
between two and three weeks	2	5	..
three weeks and under four	1	67	13
four weeks and over	..	..	87
Command over goods and services			
Real household disposable income per head			
(1975 = 100) (UK)	75	90	111

27

TABLE 2.3   *(continued)*

	1961	*1971*	*1981*
Final income[5]–per cent of shares going to			
– top one-fifth of households (UK)	..	37½[6]	39
– bottom two-fifths of households (UK)	..	20½[6]	19½
Numbers receiving Supplementary Benefit			
(millions) (GB)	1.9[7]	3.0	3.7
Marketable wealth (UK)			
– per cent owned by most wealthy			
1 per cent	33[8]	31	23
50 per cent	97[8]	97	94
Physical environment			
Households–per cent with (GB)			
– over one person per room	..	7	4
– lacking or sharing bath/shower	27	12	3
– lacking or sharing inside WC	..	15	4
– central heating	..	34	59
Pollution–million tonnes (UK)			
– smoke emission from coal combustion	1.6	0.6	0.3
– sulphur dioxide emission from fuel			
combustion	5.7	5.9	4.3
Social environment			
Suicides–numbers (UK)	5600[9]	4308	5016
Personal safety			
Road accidents–deaths–'000s (GB)	6.9	7.7	5.8
Home accidents–deaths–'000s (GB)	8.1	7.0	6.2[10]
Criminal offences recorded by the police (E & W)			
– violence against the person	..	47.0	100.2
– burglary	..	451.5	723.2

[1] Deaths under one week plus stillbirths.
[2] Restriction of normal activity because of illness or injury at any time in the two weeks before interview.
[3] 1978.
[4] 1970.
[5] Disposal income plus an imputed allowance for publicly provided benefits in kind.
[6] 1976.
[7] National Assistance.
[8] 1966.
[9] 1963.
[10] 1980.

SOURCE   *Social Trends:* various issues (Central Statistical Office).

CONCEPTUAL AND MEASUREMENT PROBLEMS

The very attempt to draw up a table demonstrates the inadequacy of available statistics to sum up, except in a very general way, the effect of social change on the quality of life. It pinpoints the two major problems with which those concerned with the development of social indicators continually found themselves confronted – defining the concepts and finding appropriate measures to represent them either from existing statistics or by collecting new ones. Health, for example, is both difficult to define and to represent statistically. Health as a positive concept might be regarded as a state of complete physical, mental and social wellbeing. It is normally thought of, however, as absence of disease or illness. Even this way of thinking presents problems. First, it is difficult to derive universally valid norms of physical functioning because what is normal for one person may not be for another, or for the same person at a different age or in different circumstances. Blood-pressure is an example: some people with 'high' blood-pressure are perfectly well according to other organic signs as well as not experiencing any symptoms commonly associated with hypertension. Second, disease may be present without causing pain, distress, disability or death to the person concerned, who might describe herself as perfectly healthy. Likewise, it is perfectly possible to feel ill without being diseased: an objective assessment might describe such a person as healthy whereas the individual's perception is different.[18]

Most of the indicators listed in Table 2.3, and to a somewhat lesser extent those proposed by the OECD in Table 2.2, are poor measures of the qualities they set out to represent. Expectation of life, infant deaths and disability reflect mortality and morbidity, not positive health. Years of schooling are not synonymous with education nor do numbers of persons per room or income per head reflect the quality of life within the households concerned. The concepts themselves are often complex and cannot be adequately measured by simple indicators. Although in theory it might seem desirable to select one indicator to represent the general concepts of health or education, it is not feasible in practice. In the absence of the ideal indicator embracing the broad concept, it is inevitably necessary to fall back on a series of indicators representing different aspects of the area of concern and then possibly to combine them into an aggregate index.

The process of combination opens up a whole new set of problems. Combining social indicators, whatever the level of aggregation, implies a weighting based on some system of values and the difficulties of reaching consensus are manifold. Unlike economic indicators there is no unifying thread of monetary values underlying the weighting of social indicators. Despite the many values which people hold in common there are as many value systems as there are individuals and even within the same family the priority which each member would choose to give to expenditure on health as against education or leisure will most likely differ according to their sex and age. The problems of reaching agreement amongst communities and countries which are far from homogeneous are yet more difficult and it thus becomes impossible to devise a generally accepted aggregate index or social indicator representing the quality of life as a whole which can be set alongside economic indicators such as the GNP.

None the less, some system of weighting which might be used to compile a quality of life indicator is implicit in the policies pursued by individual governments. Indeed, the very choice of sets of social indicators for particular areas of social concern in itself involves value-laden decisions. Much of the early development work on social indicators was related to government needs and the indicators selected were those thought by those in power to reflect the needs and values of the people being governed. For this purpose they were based on objective conditions: they did not describe how the people who were recipients of these policies themselves viewed the policies.

The weakness of this approach became increasingly apparent. However objectively desirable spacious well-equipped houses with gardens may seem, the ultimate success of housing policies is as perceived by the people who live in the house in relation to their expectations, aspirations, attitudes and values. It could well be that space and physical conditions are not the primary factors and that such psychological considerations as familiarity with the neighbourhood, proximity of friends and social status of the area contribute more to satisfaction or dissatisfaction with the way people feel about the place in which they live. In this sense, objective conditions are 'intermediate' social indicators while subjective measures register 'final output'.[19] Linked with the increasing questioning of the significance of objective social indicators was the recognition that government policies themselves, and many of the statistics needed to monitor them, were often more concerned with means than with the final outputs which were one of the principal objectives of the social indicators movement.

In this context it is interesting to note the shifting attitude of government itself as reflected in some of the questions asked in the General Household Survey. This multi-purpose household survey contains sets of questions on population, housing, employment, education, health, leisure and participation. The section on health originally contained questions on short- and long-term disability related to restricted activity and days of incapacity due to acute and chronic illness. The usefulness and reliability of the information to measure change over time was found to be limited and the questions were dropped in favour of others giving more emphasis to the effect of health problems on people's lives.[20] According to the 1977 report on the survey, 'the proportions reporting illness were small, even though it was known from other studies that much larger proportions were concerned about their health; although health is one of the most important areas in an individual's life, little was being learnt about the health difficulties and problems of the majority of the population'.

The growing appreciation of the importance of people's perceptions shifted the emphasis of the social indicators movement away from objective measurement towards what became known as subjective social indicators. The change of emphasis led to a rethinking of the fundamental concepts underlying human betterment and a reappraisal of the areas of concern, or domains, which go to make up the quality of life. The areas of concern selected for measurement by objective social indicators, such as those chosen by the OECD and shown in Table 2.2, were developed from pragmatic criteria, not from abstract theory or elaborate statistical data systems beyond the realistic potential of government statistical agencies. Since they were explicitly policy-related and comprised only those social conditions which were readily susceptible to government manipulation they necessarily left out major areas of concern, such as family life, marriage and friendship, which are the basis of much of human happiness. The framework of domains selected for representation by subjective indicators, however, set out to cover the whole spectrum of human needs. Much of the development work had its roots in the work of Cantril[21] and of Abraham Maslow[22] in the 1950s and early 1960s which involved interviewing people from various countries to determine what aspects of life they found important and where they scaled their personal standing in the present and future. Maslow classified five levels of human need: physiological needs (hunger, thirst, sleep, shelter, sex, etc.), safety, interpersonal relationships (love, affection and belongingness), esteem (self-respect, self-esteem and the esteem of others, including prestige, status and dominance) and self-fulfilment (including the need for aesthetic beauty and knowledge as ends in themselves).

The main practical work on subjective social indicators in this country was carried out by the Social Science Research Council (SSRC) Survey Unit under Mark Abrams,[23] and later by Knox[24] at the University of Dundee. This work followed the lead given in the US by Angus Campbell, Frank Andrews, Stephen Withey and others at the Institute of Social Research in the University of Michigan.[25] The surveys undertaken in this country and in the US were concerned with establishing the importance of the various domains, or aspects of life, to the overall quality of life and the satisfaction accorded to them. The difficulties of interpretation were recognised from the outset. Satisfaction is a personal experience and this experience varies from person to person. Moreover the importance attached to and the levels of satisfaction with different aspects of life vary from time to time according to circumstances, such as the absolute and relative levels which prevail. People who start from a low absolute level of wellbeing are more likely to be satisfied with improvements in general conditions than those who already start from a higher level, and those who live side by side with others who have much better living conditions than they do themselves are more likely to be dissatisfied than those in a society where there is more equality. Moreover, if people are already well satisfied with a particular aspect of their lives, such as personal safety and religious toleration, they are less likely to appreciate its positive value and to cite it as an area of concern. This particular problem was reflected in the shifting of the rank order of the various domains in the different studies. Family life, marriage and friendship, however, followed by health and job, predominate as the most important aspects of life with education, religion and material standards of living often trailing a long way behind.

FUTURE DEVELOPMENTS

Social indicator developments in recent years have continued to concentrate on people's attitudes to their living conditions. In Great Britain an important new annual survey of social attitudes has recently been put into the field by Social and Community Planning Research (SCPR), and a first report is now expected. This work partly builds on and extends work done earlier at SCPR on evaluating community preferences by interviewing groups of people and asking them to play a priority evaluation or trade-off preference 'game' using an electronic device built for that purpose.[24] The new survey contains four basic sections. The first is concerned with political attitudes, including semi-constitutional issues such as the monarchy, the House of Lords and voting systems, the second with economic and labour market issues, the third with some of the major government social expenditure programmes and the fourth with attitudes towards religion, race, sex, crime, etc. Additionally there is a separate self-completion question-naire on some of the current sensitive issues such as divorce, abortion, euthanasia, nuclear power, trade unions, etc. There is also under way at the international level a comprehensive comparative study of funda-mental human values. This study, which began in 1978, originally set out to analyse and describe the moral and social values prevailing in Europe, but now covers more than twenty countries including Eastern Europe as well as the Far East, Middle East, and North and South America. It covers attitudes towards religion, work, neighbours, fami-ly, health, children, politics and a wide range of other social issues. Preliminary results from the material so far collected, for which the initial processing in being done by Gallup in London, already reveals something of the wide diversity of values both between countries and between different groups within countries.[27]

What is the future of indicators of human betterment? Interest in defining the concepts underlying the quality of life and in finding means to measure them began during the 1950s and reached its peak during the late 1960s and 1970s. This coincided with a period follow-ing sustained economic growth in Western Europe and North Ameri-ca. Most people in these countries had sufficient of the basic necessities of life to allow them to concentrate on improving the quality of life in its wider sense. It was a period, too, when governments had interceded to an extent never before experienced to provide income support, health, education and social services and to establish what became known as the welfare state. Moreover, there was a belief that govern-ments were powerful and could substantially influence the economic and social life of their citizens. In the succeeding years scepticism about governments as the best arbiters of the needs of people helped to shift interest in social indicators from objective to more subjective meas-ures based on the perceptions and attitudes of those who were on the receiving end of government policies. Today there is not only less faith in the ability of governments to provide what is needed, but many governments no longer see their role as one of intervention in the social fabric of the country. They thus see no need for indicators of human betterment. Indeed, it might be fair to say that the era of liberalism and concern for the individual is past, albeit temporarily, and that governments today are increasingly concerned with maintaining power and extending political influence throughout the fabric of society. Though not immune to social attitudes and to the views people hold about the policies they pursue, they are not anxious to disseminate information which might be used to criticise these policies. To avoid these dangers it is very important for independent organisations to develop monitoring systems to analyse and interpret such statistical material as governments make available and to collect information themselves to monitor social change and assess it in terms of the quality of life.

Furthermore this vigilance must extend to continuous reassessment of the reality underlying the concepts of human betterment and to the search for a better understanding of how society works. It means in particular integrating social factors, which provide the dynamics of change, into economic models and accounting systems to discover how best to improve economic and social welfare in its broadest sense.

NOTES

1. J. K. Galbraith, *The Affluent Society* (London: Hamish Hamilton, 1948); Fred Hirsch, *Social Limits to Growth* (London: Routledge & Kegan Paul, 1977).
2. Milton Moss (ed.), *The Measurement of Economic and Social Performance*, Studies in Income and Wealth, no. 38 (New York: National Bureau of Economic Research, 1973).
3. William D. Nordhaus and James Tobin, 'Is Growth Obsolete?', *Economic Growth*, Fiftieth Anniversary Colloquium V (New York: NBER, 1972).
4. F. Thomas Juster, Paul N. Courant and Greg K. Dow, 'A Theoretical Framework for the Measurement of Well-being', *Review of Income and Wealth*, series 27, no. 1 (Mar. 1981).
5. United Nations, *The Feasibility of Welfare Orientated Measures to Complement the National Accounts and Balances* (Economic and Social Council E/CN 3/477, 1946); United Nations, *A System of National Accounts*, Studies in Methods, series F, no. 2, rev. 3 (New York: United Nations, 1968); United Nations, *A Draft Complementary System of Statistics on the Distribution of Income and Wealth* (Economic and Social Council E/CN 3/400, 1969).
6. Richard and Nancy Ruggles, *The Measurement of Economic and Social Performance*, International Association for Research into Income and Wealth: Fourteenth General Conference (Finland, 1975).
7. Christiaan Grootaert, 'The Conceptual Basis of Measures of Household Welfare and their Implied Survey Data Requirements', *Review of Income and Wealth*, series 29, no. 1 (Mar. 1983).
8. A. Szalai (ed.), *The Use of Time* (The Hague: Mouton, 1972).

9. J. I. Gershuny and G. S. Thomas, 'Changing Times: Activity Patterns in the UK', unpublished (University of Sussex, 1981).

10. John P. Robinson, *Changes in Americans' Use of Time: 1965–1975. A Progress Report* (Cleveland, Ohio: Communications Research Centre, 1977).

11. United Nations, *A System of Demographic, Manpower and Social Statistics: Series, Classifications and Social Indicators*, ST/STAT 49 (New York: UN Secretariat, 1971); United Nations, *System of Social and Demographic Statistics (SSDS)*, E/CN3/450 (New York: UN Secretariat, 1974).

12. Sir Claus Moser, 'Social Indicators – Systems, Methods and Problems', *Review of Income and Wealth*, series 19, no. 2 (June 1973).

13. Dudley Seers, 'Life Expectancy as an Integrating Concept in Social and Demographic Analysis and Planning', *Review of Income and Wealth*, series 23, no. 3 (Sep. 1977).

14. Philippe Pommier, 'Social Expenditure: Socialisation of Expenditure? The French Experiment with Satellite Accounts', *Review of Income and Wealth*, series 27, no. 4 (Dec. 1981).

15. The literature on the development of social indicators is widespread and varied. The movement even spawned its own regular quarterly journal, *Social Indicators*, ed. by Alex C. Michalos. See in particular E. Sheldon and W. E. Moore (eds), *Indicators of Social Change* (New York: Russell Sage Foundation, 1968); Michael Carley, *Social Measurement and Social Indicators* (London: George Allen & Unwin, 1981); Denis F. Johnston, 'Social Indicators and Social Forecasting', in Jib Fowles (ed.), *Handbook of Futures Research* (Westpoint Conn: Greenwood Press, 1978).

16. OECD Working Party on Social Indicators, *Measuring Social Well-being: A Progress Report on the Development of Social Indicators*, Programme Series 3 (Paris: OECD, 1976); OECD Working Party on Social Indicators, *The OECD List of Social Indicators*, Programme Series 5 (Paris: OECD, 1982).

17. UK Central Statistical Office, *Social Trends* (London: HMSO 1970 *et seq*); US Department of Commerce, *Social Indicators 1973* (US Govt Printing Offices, 1973); Institut National de la Statistique et des Études Économiques, *Données Sociales* (Paris, 1973).

18. Roy A. Carr-Hill, 'Indicators of Health and of Inequalities in Health' (Aberdeen: MRC Medical Sociology Unit, May 1983), unpublished paper.

19. Juster, Courant and Dow, op. cit.

20. Office of Population Censuses and Surveys, *General Household Survey 1977* (London: HMSO, 1979).

21. H. Cantril, *Pattern of Human Concerns* (New Brunswick, N.J.: Rutgers University Press, 1965).

22. A. Maslow, *Motivation and Personality* (New York: Harper, 1954 and 1970).

23. M. Abrams, 'Subjective Social Indicators', in *Social Trends*, no. 4, ed. M. Nissel (London, HMSO, 1973); M. Abrams, 'Social Indicators and Quality of Life Studies', paper presented to the Conference on Social Indicators in Planning and Policy, Regional Studies Association (London, 1978).

24. P. L. Knox, 'Social Priorities for Social Indicators', Occasional Paper no. 4, Dept of Geography, University of Dundee (1976).
25. Angus Campbell and Philip E. Converse (eds), *The Human Meaning of Social Change* (New York: Russell Sage Foundation, 1972); E. M. Andrews and S. B. Withey, *Social Indicators of Well-being* (New York: Plenum Press, 1976).
26. G. Hoinville, 'Evaluating Community Preferences', *Environment and Planning,* vol. 3 (London: Pion, 1971).
27. Gordon Heald, 'A Comparison between American, European and Japanese Values', unpublished paper presented to the World Association for Public Opinion Research Annual Meeting' (Maryland, 1982).

3 Growth, Social Innovation and Time Use

JONATHAN GERSHUNY

INTRODUCTION

I am going to talk about two competing views of the consequences of economic growth for human wellbeing. I shall consider the thesis of the late Professor Fred Hirsch, that there are 'social limits' to growth; that past some particular level of economic development, economic growth does not add to, and may even diminish, human welfare.[1] And I shall introduce a somewhat contradictory argument, that through a particular sort of technical change, through a *change in the way commodities are consumed*, human welfare – or at least the welfare of some humans – can indeed be improved.[2]

The argument relies on a distinction between two different sorts of technical change. The first of these is the conventional one: technical change associated with the productive economy. Innovations here lead to an increase in the efficiency of production of particular commodities, or to an improvement in their performance, or even to the development of new commodities for sale to final consumer. This sort of technical change is normally implicated in economic growth; within Hirsch's thesis this first sort of technical change leads merely to a purposeless proliferation of consumer gadgets.

The second sort of technical change is not considered by Hirsch. This is change, over time, in the ways in which people seek to satisfy their needs. Instead of achieving domestic comforts through the agency of paid servants they buy and use domestic equipment. Instead of purchasing transport they buy motor-cars; instead of theatres, television. We might think of this second category as a sort of *social innovation*, a change in the mode of provision of services, a change in the techniques and organisation of materials, equipment and time so as to provide for needs in new ways.

I shall argue that this second sort of technical change provides the meaning for what is to Hirsch a meaningless elaboration in the range of commodities for sale. It enables new patterns of activity, which have had the consequence of redistributing welfare between the classes and the sexes. The argument which follows is in part theoretical, suggesting some new analytical categories which call the Hirsch thesis into question. But ultimately the issue is in large part an empirical one. It depends on the answer to the question of what people do with the new products that growth permits them to buy.

For this reason I shall try to substantiate my argument, not from conventional economic data, but from an unconventional, sociological source: estimates of change in time-use patterns from the 1930s to the 1970s. Rather to my surprise, part of what emerges does support Hirsch's thesis, in so far as it shows that growth over this period had the result of reducing some groups' access to particular sorts of services that they previously enjoyed. But nevertheless I shall suggest that these costs cannot be viewed as 'limits' to growth since, through the process of social innovation, other groups gained access to services that were previously unavailable to them. In short, Hirsch's arguments point us, not towards limits, but towards a particular sort of *redistributive consequence of economic growth*.

THE SOCIAL LIMITS THESIS

Hirsch's argument rests on what is in effect a theory of consumption, which distinguishes between the different sorts of satisfaction that an individual derives from different sorts of commodities. Commodities which satisfy the more basic human needs – e.g. for nourishment – give satisfaction strictly in relation to their *intrinsic characteristics*. So food, to a man on the breadline, is valued for its inherent nutritive qualities. The only constraint on the possibilities for economic growth to increase the supply of this sort of commodity is physical scarcity – ultimately the Malthusian scarcity of land to produce food. The Club of Rome's original 'limits to growth' argument related to physical scarcity in this sense. But when we turn to commodities which satisfy what might be considered luxury requirements, we observe that characteristics other than the intrinsic qualities become important determinants of the satisfaction they generate. *Extrinsic characteristics* are now important – specifically the social context of the use of the commodities.

Hirsch identifies two ways in which the social context impinges on the satisfaction derived from the use of commodities. There are constraints which result from *congestion*: thus the satisfaction derived from a motor-car is limited by the state of crowding on the roads (which in turn reflects the number of other people who have cars); or to choose another, more abstract, of Hirsch's examples, the sort of job which may be obtained with a particular level of educational qualification depends on the number of other people who have attained that level. Of course the supply of a commodity to other people does not *necessarily* diminish the satisfaction that an individual derives from consumption. On the contrary the car-owner needs some other car-owners in order to justify the construction of motor-roads: the well-educated individual gets the best economic return from his education in a society that has a sufficient level of general education to maintain an efficient modern economy. In these cases the social context of consumption constrains satisfaction only when the commodities are *over*-supplied.

But Hirsch points to a second category, of cases where *any* increase in the supply of the commodity to others decreases the satisfaction derived by the individual. There is some satisfaction derived in, say, the possession of an Old Master painting, entirely extrinsic to the painting itself, that may be actually diminished by the discovery of a lost hoard of that Master's works. There is a class of benefit derived by the owner of the only weekend cottage on the shores of an isolated lake that is lost by the construction, however discreetly, of even one more cottage on the lake. Social cachet that depends on the *exclusivity of possession* of commodities is necessarily diminished by any increase in the supply of such commodities.

These two categories add up, in Hirsch's account, to a new sort of constraint on the possibilities for economic growth to add to human wellbeing. In addition to the Malthusian physical constraints there is a new range of Hirschian *social constraints*. We can all build ladders and stand on them, we cannot all stand on each other's shoulders.

So far I can see no objection. There clearly are some classes of satisfaction which depend on exclusivity and cannot logically be extended through any process of economic growth (or indeed by any mechanism whatsoever). But how numerous are these cases? What part of economic growth can be attributed to the vain attempt to evade Hirschian scarcity? And how do we evaluate the cases where the extension of supply of a commodity both reduces the level of 'extrinsic characteristic-related' satisfaction (i.e. its exclusivity) – and yet at the same time increases the level of 'intrinsic characteristic-related' satisfaction (i.e. the real material benefits to its individual consumers)? It is in the answers to these questions that I am forced to part company with Professor Hirsch.

Hirsch argues that, once basic needs are satisfied, we wish to take an increasing proportion of our consumption in the form of commodities which give satisfaction as a result of their extrinsic characteristics. Hirsch describes these as 'positional goods' – commodities which we purchase because of the status conferred by their possession. But positions in a social hierarchy are inherently scarce. Seeking status through the possession of material goods, argues Hirsch, is a necessarily self-defeating activity. Some sorts of commodities are not essentially limited in number. For some material goods – particularly manufactured products – economic growth can mean that more people can possess them. But if the purpose of the acquisition of the commodity is the achievement of the social status that possession of it confers, then acquiring it through a general process of economic growth must necessarily defeat this purpose – since what one individual of a particular social status can buy with his increased income, can now also be bought by every other individual with that status. And, meantime, higher status individuals can buy other goods which are still out of reach of the lower-status individuals. Growth serves simply to devalue the positional connotation of possession of particular goods.

And other of the commodities that we demand as we get richer are more limited in supply, at least in the sense that increasing their numbers decreases the utility derived from them. I have already mentioned Hirsch's example of an increase in the number of motorcars on a given road system, which, past a certain point, reduces people's standards of transport because of traffic jams. Personal services are a particularly important case here. As we get richer we want to spend more on such services; it is commonly accepted, however, that services are not susceptible to productivity growth – but service wages nevertheless grow in line with those in other sectors, and service prices rise relative to the general level. So economic growth may mean that we spend a larger proportion of our money on services, but we actually consume less services.

Hirsch extends a powerful metaphor, borrowed from the sociologists Michael Young and Peter Willmott, of a developing economy as a marching column of men and women. From time to time the vanguard wheels to right or left; one by one the following ranks wheel on the same spot. The spacing between the ranks represents the income distribution, it remains essentially unchanged; yet, to Young and

TABLE 3.1 *Purposes of household and government final expenditure, classified by function and by type of commodity*

'Function' classification	*'Commodity' classification*		
	Primary and manufactured goods	*Marketed services*	*Non-marketed services*
A. Food, drink, tobacco	Food, drink, tobacco (D1)	—	—
B. Shelter, clothing	Rent, fuel and power, clothing and footwear (D2, D3)	Personal cars and effects (D81)	Housing and community amenities (sewers, etc.) (G6)
C. Domestic functions	Furniture, furnishings, appliances, utensils and repairs to these (D41 to D44)	Household operation and domestic services (D45, D46)	Social security and welfare services (G5)
D. Entertainment	Equipment, accessories, and repairs to these, books, etc. (D71, D73)	Entertainment, recreation, cultural, hotels, cafés, etc., packaged tours (D72, D83, D84)	Recreational, cultural and religious services (G7)
E. Transport, communications	Personal transport equipment and operation (D61, D62)	Purchased transport and communications services (D63, D64)	Roads, waterways, communications, and their administration subsidies (G8.5, G8.6, G8.7)

Functions provided mainly by households

Functions provided mainly by governments

Function			
F. Education	—	Purchased education (D74)	Public education (G3)
G. Medical functions	Medical and pharmaceutical products and appliances (D51, D52)	Purchased medical services, medical insurance service charges (D53, D54, D55)	Public health services (G4)
H. Other government functions	—	—	General public services, and economic services excluding transport and communications (G1, G8.1 to G8.4, G8.8)
I. Defence	—	—	Defence (G2)
J. Function not elsewhere specified	Goods n.e.s. (D82)	Services n.e.s. (D85, D86)	Other public services n.e.s. (G9)

ESA Classifications and Coding of the Purposes of Final Consumption of Households (ESA, 1979, table 7). (The same as table 6.1, SNA, UN, New York, 1968.)

ESA Classification and Coding of the Purpose of General Government (ESA, 1979, table 8. (The same as table 5.3, SNA, New York, 1968.)

References in parentheses to classifications of the European System of Integrated Economic Accounts (ESA).

Willmott, this is progress – each rank does advance in material terms. Hirsch's rebuttal is, of course, that if the purpose is to *advance relative to the ranks ahead*, then no real progress has been made. And in so far as the increase in production leads to congestion and the dilution of exclusivity – the gaps between the ranks may actually get larger as the rearguard struggle across ground broken up by the marching feet of the forward ranks.

Why then do we persist in wanting economic growth? Hirsch explains this in the form of an individualist fallacy: *each* individual thinks that the common will support one more goat – but if *every* individual pastures an extra goat then the whole flock will starve. 'Taking part in the scramble [for advancement] is fully rational for any individual in his own actions, since he never confronts the distinction between what is available as a result of getting ahead of others and what is available from a general advance shared by all.' So this is growth, to Hirsch; the individually rational pursuing the collectively unachievable.

AN ALTERNATIVE THEORY OF CONSUMPTION

It seems to me that Hirsch's error lies in his theory of consumption, specifically in his linking of the satisfaction of particular 'needs' to the purchase of particular commodities. It seems to me more useful to think of 'needs' as being requirements for something rather more abstract: for the particular *consequences that result from the use of particular commodities* – I shall refer to these, for reasons which will soon become apparent, as 'final service functions'. We do not have needs for particular commodities; rather we have certain requirements which might be satisfied in various *different* ways; particular 'final service functions' may be met by *different combinations of commodities.*

We can describe the association between particular final service functions and the particular sets of commodities which go to satisfy them in a quite comprehensive fashion. Table 3.1 outlines an example of such a classificatory exercise, using the expenditure categories of the European System of National Accounts. It identifies nine service functions – nutritional, shelter, domestic, entertainment, transport, educational, medical, governmental and other – though, of course, this list could be either longer or shorter depending on the purpose.[3]

Each item of final consumption, purchased by households or directly provided by collective agencies such as governments or charities, can be classified as relating to one of these functions (investment expenditure is treated as intermediate output for these purposes). Obviously relating to each of the final functions will be a number of very different sorts of commodities. There will be finished final services, privately purchased or furnished collectively, which provide for the final function directly, and there will be various other commodities – materials, consumer durables, material infrastructure, intermediate services – which provide for similar functions indirectly: they are used in what I have elsewhere termed the 'informal' production of services: economic activity outside the measured money economy, producing the final services we actually consume.[4] Thus, to satisfy the 'transport' function, for example, we employ a mixture of final services produced in the money economy – buses and trains and taxis – and final services produced informally – car or bicycle travel – which employ products (i.e. cars and bicycles) from the formal economy as intermediate inputs to the final transport service function. We either buy final services, or buy goods and make the services ourselves.

Over extended periods of time we can see, in the distribution of final expenditure classified in the manner outlined in Table 3.1, two quite different classes of systematic change. First we can see a change in the distribution of expenditure by 'final services function'. We see, throughout the developed world, a shift in the balance of expenditure away from the more basic categories of nutrition and shelter, towards the more luxury categories of domestic services, entertainment, transport, education and medicine. Table 3.2 provides evidence of these changes in a number of European countries during the 1970s.

This is, of course, quite in accord with Hirsch's argument. Basic needs being satisfied, we want sophisticated services. Hirsch argues, however, that these sophisticated services are in necessarily short supply. We cannot all have domestic servants, professional musicians entertaining us in our drawing-rooms, personal chauffeurs. But could equivalent final service functions not be provided for by other means? At this point we have to consider then a second class of systematic change in expenditure patterns over time.

In addition to the shift towards the satisfaction of the more sophisticated final service functions, we may also see a shift away from the purchase of some particular finished final services, towards expenditure on materials, consumer durables, intermediate services.

TABLE 3.2 Changes in the distribution of total household consumption

	Germany		Holland		UK		Belgium		Italy		Direction of change		
	Early 1970s Total	Late 1970s Total	Early 1970s Total	Late 1970s Total	Early 1970s Total	Late 1970s Total	Early 1970s Total	Late 1970s Total	Early 1970s Total	Late 1970s Total	−	0	+
A. Food	21.4	19.7	20.0	19.2	21.8	19.4	23.7	19.8	33.4	30.5	5	0	0
B. Shelter	14.0	13.0	13.6	11.6	13.0	13.1	13.7	13.9	14.2	14.1	4	0	1
C. Domestic	10.8	10.6	10.6	9.0	7.6	8.2	11.9	12.4	7.2	7.4	2	0	3
D. Entertainment	11.7	11.9	8.2	10.0	16.1	16.9	11.7	11.4	12.3	13.5	1	0	4
E. Transport	11.4	13.2	7.5	10.2	12.1	12.7	10.8	11.3	9.8	10.2	0	0	5
F. Education	5.2	5.8	9.6	9.9	7.8	7.9	8.6	9.8	6.6	7.4	0	0	5
G. Medicine	9.8	12.1	8.8	8.9	6.4	6.8	6.4	8.2	4.6	5.6	0	0	5
H. Other Government	7.6	6.0	—	—	4.6	4.7	4.3	4.1	6.7	6.4	3	1	1
I. Defence	5.2	4.5	5.6	4.2	7.5	6.7	5.6	5.1	3.2	2.9	5	0	0
J. Other	2.9	3.2	16.1	17.0	3.1	3.7	3.3	4.0	2.0	2.0	0	1	4
Total	100.0	100.0	100.0	100.0	100.0	100.0	100.0	100.0	100.0	100.0			

This reflects a *change in the mode of provision for particular needs*. As the relative costs, and the technical performances, of alternative means for providing for particular functions change, so households change the technical means they use to satisfy them. Table 3.3 shows, for the 1970s, a shift in general away from the purchase of final services in the domestic, entertainment and transport functions. (The changes shown here are admittedly not very large – in the more fragmentary evidence for the 1950s and 1960s, when most of these changes in the mode of service provision were happening at their fastest, the changes would show up as rather more substantial.) We have, over the last period of economic growth, increasingly used cars instead of purchased transport services, washing-machines instead of laundries and so on.

The growing demand for the satisfaction of these domestic, entertainment and transport functions did indeed have a Hirschian effect on the availability and quality of the finished final services associated with these functions. The prices of these final services rose: overall consumption of them declined. This is clearly what Hirsch describes as 'congestion'; the increased effective demand eventually leads to a reduction in output as prices rise; quality falls and customers go elsewhere. And some people – precisely those people who were previously in a position to purchase the final services and now are not – will certainly feel themselves worse-off as a result.

But the question we must ask ourselves is: what is the overall balance of consequences between those who are worse-off and those who are better-off? Because others who previously were ill-provided with these service functions are now better-provided. Admittedly the extrinsic characteristics that previously attached to the satisfaction of the particular function have been degraded.

But is the *only* reason that we want sophisticated services, that the nobs on the hill have them? Presumably we would place *some* value on having the clean and convenient housing, the frequent changes of clothing, the occasional changes of scene, the regular access to entertainment that is enabled by the self-serviced, consumer-durable-owning mode of service provision – even though access to these service functions does not imply the social status that it did when we purchased them directly in the form of marketed final services.

An extension of the same argument applies to those more luxurious final service functions which have not in the past been subject to innovations in their mode of provision. The postwar decades saw an expansion in the provision of educational and medical services. But we would certainly not consider that the current level of provision of these

TABLE 3.3 % of household expenditure on each function devoted to final services

Service %		Food	Shelter	Domestic	Entertainment	Transport	Education	Medicine
Belgium	1970	0	8	33	73	23	–	75
	1979	0	7	26	63	17	–	3
Denmark	1970	0	6	33	55	25	0	35
	1979	0	4	25	46	29	0	36
France	1970	0	5	32	77	19	100	78
	1979	0	6	25	61	22	100	79
Germany	1970	–	–	–	–	27	–	–
	1979	–	–	–	–	26	–	–
Holland	1970	0	8	18	42	26	100	92
	1979	0	5	18	34	24	100	87
Ireland	1970	0	3	30	51	26	100	38
	1979	0	6	26	48	18	100	38
Italy	1970	0	11	39	71	27	100	50
	1979	0	11	38	65	27	100	59
UK	1970	0	5	26	76	34	100	37
	1979	0	5	26	72	34	100	43
Direction of Change								
Towards services		0	2	0	0	2	0	3
No change		7	3	2	0	2	6	2
Away from services		0	2	5	7	4	0	2

is satisfactory. And it is rather difficult, at least in countries like Britain, to see how the levels of provision could be substantially improved by simple extensions to the existing system. Clearly we have Hirschian congestion here: to provide all the educational and medical services we might conceivably want we would all have to *be* doctors or teachers. An impasse?

Not necessarily: just as we had, in the 1950s and 1960s, innovations in the mode of provision for domestic and transport and entertainment services, based on a particular set of technologies developed in the 1930s and before (the fractional horse-power electric motor, the valve, the television tube, the internal-combustion machine), so we might imagine future innovations in the mode of provision of educational and medical services, involving technologies we have already developed (the microcomputer, the video recorder, the satellite and fibre-optics telecommunications links). The Open University is a harbinger, though we have hardly started to consider the variety of possible social forms that such social innovations might take. Of course, there will be negative effects, just as there were in the historical examples. The new modes of provision will tend to price some particular sorts of personal services in these categories beyond the pockets of all but a diminishing number of plutocrats. The hour-long supervision of one undergraduate by one university professor may disappear, as we adopt some of the techniques of the Open University. But can we really justify the persistence of a society which provides this sort of education – to 5 per cent of its population?

HISTORICAL CHANGES IN THE USE OF TIME

So far I have not introduced any direct evidence about how people use the products they purchase. I have suggested that we buy goods in order to satisfy particular final service functions, and I have cited evidence of an historical change in expenditure patterns from which we may infer the development of innovative ways of satisfying some of these service functions. But to take the argument further we must look directly at what people actually do. To be able to say that people use the goods they purchase to produce final service functions, we must look directly at what work they do *outside* those hours they spend working in the *money economy*. and we must consider what the consequences of those changes have been for leisure time.

To this end a group at the Science Policy Research Unit of the

University of Sussex has for some years been putting together a collection of data on time-use patterns, largely by reconstructing surveys carried out by earlier researchers.

What follows is drawn from this data set. I should at this point add a caution: the very earliest data, from 1937, are not very reliable – the sample is a small one (about 600 day-diaries) and is in no sense randomly chosen from the population. However we have no reason to suspect that the sample is radically unrepresentative, at least with respect to the particular data that I shall present here – the results have a certain plausibility, and the very large differences between the earlier and the much more reliable later data (2500 and 3500 cases, randomly sampled) seem unlikely to have come about as a result of bias in the earlier sample,

DOMESTIC WORK TIME

What would we expect to have happened to unpaid work time – spent in housework, cooking, etc. – over the period from the 1930s to the 1970s, on the basis of Hirsch's argument? We have seen , at least over the latter part of this period, the spread of a wide range of gadgets relating to domestic work – vacuum cleaners, washing-machines and all sorts of kitchen equipment. We would expect – and Hirsch does in fact predict – that domestic work time should increase. We buy these gadgets to 'keep up with the Jones's' – or rather, vainly trying to get ahead of them – and then we must spend our time using the things. In fact, quite a lot of the available evidence about change in domestic time use does actually support this prediction. For example, a detailed reconstruction of old time-use surveys carried out by Robinson and Converse[5] has revealed that housework time has on average increased for both employed and non-employed women between the 1930s and the 1960s.

It seems quite likely that we can generalise from this result. An analysis of the data on housework from the multinational time budget survey carried out under the auspices of UNESCO during the mid-1960s leads to the following conclusion:[6]

There is little sign ... that the gains from an abundant labour saving technology receive much translation into leisure. Variations in time devoted to household obligations across our sites are not spectacu-larly large – roughly plus or minus thirty per cent around a mean value – and in any event correlate with household technology only very weakly. Indeed, if it were possible to take account of additional amounts of housework accomplished by paid household help (registered in our data as formal work rather than as housework) which is most prevalent in those Western countries enjoying most labour saving consumer durables, then there might well be a fully counter-intuitive relationship across the sites between the efficiency of household technology and amounts of time given over to household obligations.

This is the 'domestic labour paradox': 'labour-saving devices' appear to increase the amount of domestic work. From Hirsch's point of view, of course, this is not at all 'counter-intuitive'. This is simply evidence of 'social congestion' in the domain of time use. But when we consider more recent data for the 1960s and 1970s, from the US (which parallel our UK findings, and other results from Holland and Norway), we find that latterly housework time has been quite substantially declining.[7]

In fact, if, rather than seeing the diffusion of this sort of equipment as a sort of status-seeking, we view it instead as a process of household investment, in equipment which households use to produce 'domestic service functions' we can arrive at a rather more plausible explanation. From this perspective we would say that the effect of the acquisition of new equipment depends on the relationship between the rate of growth of *productivity* of work time in the household enabled by the new gadgets, and the rate of growth of household *output* induced by this higher productivity. If the growth in ouput is higher than the growth of productivity, then household work time will increase; if, on the other hand, the growth of productivity accruing from new domestic equipment is high and at the same time people become satiated with the services produced by this equipment, the amount of domestic work time may decline. By thinking about the problem with a little more care we can develop a quite determinate model which predicts over different historical periods, first increases in domestic work time, and then decreases.

We have some grounds for expecting the productivity of particular items of domestic equipment to develop along a specific path. We derive this from the notion of the 'product cycle'; initially when a new piece of domestic equipment first provides a viable and attractive alternative mode of provision for a particular function, the market for the class of equipment grows quickly, and demand for it is not particularly sensitive to differences in performance between 'makes' – since *any* version of the gadget enables a considerable advance on the previous means of achieving the same end-result. Under these conditions manufacturers will concentrate on enlarging their own production facilities, confident that due to the expanding market they will be able to sell their product irrespective of the details of its performance relative to its competitors.

But as the market grows past a certain point its rate of expansion will start to decline. As more and more households switch to the new mode of provision of the particular service, so the market for the products used in this mode approach saturation. Manufacturers are now in a more competitive situation and they will compete with each other partly on the basis of the price of the product – and partly in terms of its performance. So there is now a motive for improving the 'productivity' of the equipment. To put the point more concretely, we might take the homely example of the washing-machine. The first, top-loading electric washing-machine involved quite a lot of ancillary labour, and sold very easily, particularly as their price declined; but as the market for them approached saturation, the competition, particularly for the 'replacement market', centred around performance, and specifically around automation, the reduction of the amount of labour involved in their use. So the domestic productivity of the washing-machine initially grew slowly, but subsequently increased its rate of growth.

Now combine this pattern of evolution of the machine's productive efficiency with a diminishing marginal utility of the material product derived from the use of the equipment. To continue our 'clothes-washing' example; initially the increased efficiency inherent to the innovative mode of provision may have led to a very big increase in the number of clothes being washed. Perhaps the rate of increase in the size of the wash was even bigger than the increase in domestic productivity accruing from the change from the traditional wash boiler to the electric machine – so the time spent by the household in clothes-washing would increase. Or if the clean laundry had previously been acquired in the form of a purchased service, then certainly we should expect an increase in domestic work time. But needs for clean clothes are not inexhaustible, and we might ultimately expect the rate of growth of productivity of the washing-machine (or rather the rate of decline in domestic work time required for a washing-machine load) to exceed the rate of growth of the quantity of clothes to be washed – so the work time decreases.

Figure 3.1 gives a graphical interpretation of this argument.

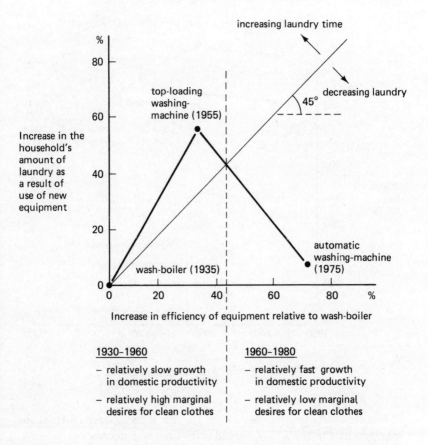

FIGURE 3.1 *Domestic output, domestic productivity and domestic work time:*
the hypothetical case of the washing-machine

In short, for any particular class of domestic machinery, we can
expect two different processes to take place: a declining marginal
utility for the particular sort of service it gives rise to; and an increasing
rate of improvement in its productive efficiency. Putting the two
processes together, we might draw a general conclusion as to the effect
of social innovation on unpaid work-time. The change in the mode of
provision for the particular service may initially increase domestic
work time, as more households engage in the productive activity, and
as the absolute output of the final service increases. And subsequently,
as the rate of change in the society's mode of provision is reduced, as
the efficiency of the domestic capital equipment increases, and with a

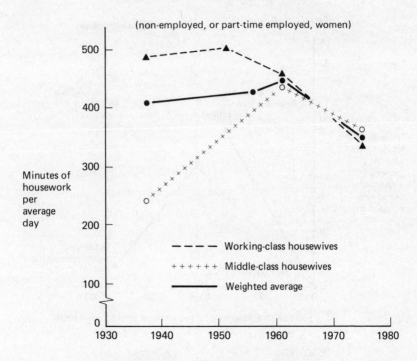

FIGURE 3.2   *Housewives' domestic work*

diminishing marginal utility of the specific income derived from the equipment, the amount of unpaid work time may decrease.

In fact the real situation is even more complicated than this theoretical model would suggest. Figure 3.2 shows the estimate of the evolution of housewives' housework time in the UK derived from our data series. The time spent in housework does seem to follow the trajectory that is suggested by the 'product cycle' model – giving us the interpretation that at first (i.e. in Figure 3.2 between 1937 and 1961) output of domestic services grows faster than domestic productivity, and subsequently domestic productivity outstrips output – which would yield the initial increase and subsequent decline in the 'weighted average' curve.

But when we disaggregate the data into the two social classes, we notice a new effect. Certainly, in both cases we find the initial rise and subsequent decline of work time characteristic of the 'product cycle' explanation.

But in addition we find a striking process of convergence between the classes. In the 1930s it seems that middle-class housewives did something like half the working-class housewives' total of housework. By 1961 the difference between the two classes was insignificant. The middle-class housewives' increase in housework was accordingly very much faster than the working-class housewives'. What explains this difference? Presumably the explanation is not that the output of domestic services grew very much faster in middle- than in working-class households – but rather that middle-class households lost their servants.

In the very steep rise in the middle-class curve over this period we have a reflection of what used to be known as 'the servant problem'.

So the full range of effects of domestic technology on housework over this period of time are probably as follows: for working-class households, the diffusion of the technology leads initially to a very substantial rate of increase in the quality and quantity of domestic services – output at first rising faster than domestic productivity, but, as the markets for the basic equipment became saturated, productivity growth gradually rises to overtake output growth; for middle-class households, output perhaps grew more slowly, but the mode of provision changed, from a predominantly 'serviced' (i.e. purchased) basis to a 'self-serviced basis'.

We might note that part of these effects correspond to Hirsch's predictions. The purchased domestic services which were once enjoyed by the middle classes have been crowded out, by phenomena associated with economic growth. The increased domestic work time that results from this change must undoubtedly be accounted as a cost.

But to set against this cost there are clear benefits to working-class households. Working-class households certainly did not enjoy lower standards of domestic amenity in the 1970s than in the 1930s, and clearly the amount of time spent in domestic work declined dramatically over the period. So, overall, a loss to the middle classes, a gain to the working.

LEISURE TIME

What would Hirsch's argument lead us to expect about leisure time? His major prediction in this field is of the overcrowding of leisure time. He quotes with approval, for instance, the passage from Staffan Linder's book *The Harried Leisure Class*, which describes the predicament of the citizen of the high-consumption society who must attempt to cope simultaneously with his Brazilian coffee, his French brandy, his

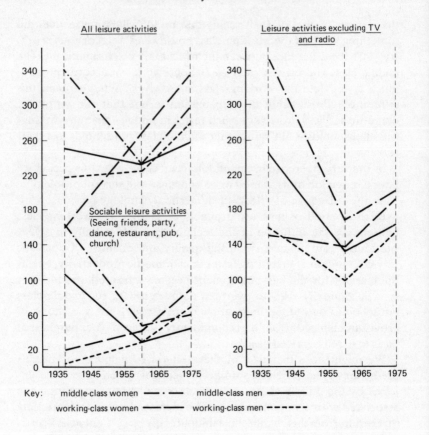

FIGURE 3.3   *Changes in leisure activities 1937–75 (adults with children)*

Dutch cigar, his German concerto on his Japanese stereo system, and his Swedish wife. Our time budget data set is not sufficiently detailed, unfortunately, to allow us to look at the intensity of leisure-time use in anything like this detail! But we can consider two other sorts of issue: the change in the overall allocation of time to leisure pursuits, and the distribution of this between some general categories of leisure activity.

Figure 3.3 gives the overall pattern of change in leisure time over the period, for four groups: for employed men with children, in the middle class and the working class, and for non-employed women with children, again in the middle and working classes. The changes are again quite striking.

In the first period, between 1937 and 1961, middle-class women had an enormous reduction in their leisure time, from 346 minutes per average day, to 272 minutes (this corresponds to their even larger increase in domestic work time). And even the very substantial increase in their leisure between 1961 and 1975 leaves them with about a half-hour less leisure per day than they had in 1937. By contrast, working-class women had a very substantial increase of leisure time through the whole period; while in 1937 they had just about half as much leisure time as the middle-class group (reflecting the fact that they did about twice as much housework) by 1975 they had a substantially larger total of leisure time than their middle-class peers. The men show a similar pattern, though the differentials between the classes were in 1937, and remained in 1975, smaller than those between working- and middle-class women.

It might be objected, on the basis of these aggregates, that the changes simply reflect the growth of television watching. But it should be remembered that the same period that has seen the birth and maturity of television, has seen the virtual death of radio listening as a primary activity. In our 1937 sample, for example, the working-class men with children appear to have spent about an hour and a quarter listening to the radio – that is, listening to the radio as a 'first activity' – on an average day. As Figure 3.3 demonstrates, though television watching has undoubtedly become the major leisure activity, nevertheless leisure time *excluding radio and television* has risen for all groups since 1961. And though the middle-class non-radio and non-television leisure time has fallen dramatically over the whole period, the equivalent statistic for working-class men shows only a very small overall fall, and for women shows a very substantial increase. Furthermore, while sociable activities (visiting friends, going to parties, dances or pubs) has fallen overall for the middle classes over the period, this total for both working-class men and working-class women has shown a steady rise through both of the periods for which we have data.

CONCLUSION: THE REDISTRIBUTIVE EFFECTS OF GROWTH

Let me try to pull together the various sorts of evidence I have presented.

1. With respect to expenditure we have seen within some particular service functions, a shift away from the purchase of services, and towards the purchase of goods – which I interpreted as a move from a more 'serviced' to a more 'self-serviced' mode of provision for those functions.
2. In the evidence on unpaid work time, the growth in expenditure on goods – in effect equipment for self-servicing – seems to have reduced the unpaid work load on working-class households, and has undoubtedly improved their conditions. But the same set of changes lost the middle classes their servants, and certainly very much reduced the wellbeing of middle-class women.
3. As regards leisure time we can say quite unequivocally that the position of working-class people has been improved – but we are much less clear about the overall consequences for the middle classes.

Where does this leave us? Clearly, despite the costs to the middle classes, we cannot talk of 'limits' to the benefits from economic growth – since the majority of the population (i.e. the working classes) have done well out of the process.

What we can say is that there is a change in the relative positions of the classes. Even if the distribution of money incomes between the classes remains constant, the change from 'serviced' to 'self-serviced' modes of provision for particular needs, means that at least with respect to those particular needs, the real welfare of the less well-off has improved, both absolutely and relative to the better-off. Even where there is no redistribution of income, where economic growth involves the sort of social innovation I have described, it may well have the effect of redistributing welfare within the society. It may be this effect of growth – the imposition of costs, or relative costs, disproportionately on the middle classes – that explains why Hirsch's book found such ready acceptance . . . at least among his mainly middle-class readers.

NOTES

1. F. Hirsch, *Social Limits to Growth* (London: Routledge & Kegan Paul, 1977).
2. This argument is covered in more detail in J. I. Gershuny and I. D. Miles, *The New Service Economy* (London: Frances Pinter, 1983); J. I. Gershuny, *Social Innovation and the Division of Labour* (Oxford: Oxford University Press, 1983).

3. This analysis, and the data presented in Tables 3.1–3.3, are discussed in more detail in pp. 95–120 of Gershuny and Miles, op. cit.
4. Ibid. chap. 3.
5. Taken from J. P. Robinson and P. E. Converse, 'Social Change Reflected in the Use of Time', in A. Campbell and P. E. Converse (eds), *The Human Meaning of Social Change* (New York: Russell Sage, 1972).
6. J. P. Robinson, P. E. Converse, A. Szalai, 'Every Day Life in Twelve Countries', in A. Szalai (ed.), *The Use of Time* (The Hague, Mouton, 1972).
7. J. P. Robinson, *Changes in American Use of Time: 1965–1975* (Communications Research Centre, Cleveland State University, 1977); W. P. Knulst, *Een Week Tijd* (Sociaal en Cultureel Planbureau, 's Gravenhage, Netherlands, 1977).

4 Technology, Communications, Economics and Progress

DAVID SIMPSON

The scope of the topics which form the title of this chapter is extraordinarily ambitious. I hasten to say that I am not bold enough to have chosen this myself, but it does at least suggest the appropriate analytical framework within which I, as an economist, should treat this subject.[1] That framework is provided by the classical theory of long-term economic growth or economic progress. Unlike its neo-classical counterpart – the theory of steady-state growth – the range of variables in the classical theory is broad enough to encompass the diverse topics proposed, and its methods – those of political economy – are sufficiently flexible to handle the major issues which arise. Of course the adequacy of the treatment of the topic depends entirely upon the author, but at least he is not crippled from the start by the necessity of working within an analytical strait-jacket which compels him to disregard some of the more important variables simply because they are not easily or usefully quantifiable.

The classical tradition in the treatment of economic growth contains such distinguished names as Adam Smith, Karl Marx, Allyn Young and Joseph Schumpeter. The point of departure in this paper is the most recent exponent of that tradition, Schumpeter, and it will be necessary to begin with a brief summary of his contribution to our understanding of how a modern advanced economy works. This is followed by an account of Schumpeter's predictions of how such an economy could be expected to develop, in particular the trends which he anticipated in attitudes, institutions and forms of organisation. The next section of the paper suggests reasons why the post-war trends in the advanced economy, correctly foreseen by Schumpeter, may now be slowing down, even arrested, and if not reversed at least changed in direction. There is first a political reason – the desire to preserve the present degree of individual choice, second, an economic reason: the unwinding of the present level of the division of labour, and third, a technical reason: the nature and rate of progress in technology, particularly, although not only, in the field of communications technology. Finally, this paper concludes with some reflections on the nature of present tendencies in economic institutions and attitudes and how they may be related to the question of human betterment.

SCHUMPETER'S ANALYSIS OF ECONOMIC PROGRESS

Schumpeter is perhaps best known for his early contribution *The Theory of Economic Development*, published in the year 1912. However it is on his later work, notably *Capitalism, Socialism and Democracy* (first published in 1942) that I wish to dwell. Here, he expressly approves the correctness of the Marxist vision that capitalism will eventually be replaced by socialism. Schumpeter followed Marx in believing that this change would be brought about by factors endogenous to the capitalist system itself, although he advanced very different reasons from Marx for the disappearance of capitalism. In his view there would be a steady and gradual decomposition: a 'quenching of capitalist attitudes and institutions'. This idea has echoes of Marx's view that capitalism carries within itself the seeds of its own destruction, but whereas in Marx's case destruction comes about in an abrupt and violent collision between material and political forces, in Schumpeter's view destruction is slow and moves through intangibles. The transition is painless and indeed the date of transition may not be clearly marked.[2] In both cases, however, capitalism is destroyed by its own success.

The biggest single factor in the decline of capitalism is the decline in the motivation of the entrepreneur. The modern corporation, itself a product of the capitalist process, 'socialises the bourgeois mind'. The modern corporation executive acquires something of the psychology of the salaried employee working in a bureaucratic organisation. The increasing size of firms knocks out the notion of property or of freedom of contract: the figure of the proprietor, and with it the specifically proprietory interest, vanishes from the picture. The labour contract is impersonal, stereotyped and bureaucratic. 'The capitalist process takes the life out of the idea of property.' In Schumpeter's view the increasing concentration of firms means that the political structure of society is profoundly changed by the elimination of a host of small and medium-sized firms.

In the last year of his life, 1949, Schumpeter looked at developments in the economies of the UK[3] and the US[4] and perceived the continuation of the tendencies which he had identified in 1942. Indeed, he went so far as to predict the trend of events in the following decades.

He foresaw that what he called 'social democracy' (or the mixed economy as we should now call it), or again, 'operating the capitalist engine in the labour interest', could only be a transient phase in the economic organisation of advanced society since it lacked the discipline of the forces prevailing in the traditional market economy or the sanctions of a Soviet-type planned economy. Activities which no longer have an economically useful function are automatically eliminated by competition in the market economy. In the command economy, when recognised, they are eliminated by decree. But in a mixed economy it is frequently possible for those who have a vested interest in uneconomic activities to use the political process to protect and thus to perpetuate such activities.

For its long-term survival the mixed economy would therefore have to rely on individual self-denial. Agents would have to act in the interests of the economy as a whole, rather than in their own material interest. But to an extent not envisaged even by Schumpeter, in the modern consumer society of the advanced countries of the world (the OECD countries), self-indulgence has taken the place of self-discipline and self-denial. It should be emphasised that this is not just a question of the consumption of private goods. There is an equally insistent demand for the collective provision of goods such as medical care, education and defence services, as well as the whole range of social security benefits, as indicated by the continuing budget problems of the advanced countries. Consequently it appears unlikely that the mixed economy could survive for long as a viable form of economic organisation. Faced with an increasing proportion of uneconomic activities, the political pressures for change would become irresistible.

Thus Schumpeter anticipated that there would be a gradual drift – a deterioration in his opinion – of the market economy towards a planned economy. There would be no sharp upheaval, no discontinuity of events in practice, but for the analytically minded observer he suggested that the watershed in this transition from capitalism to socialism would be marked by what he called 'the socialisation of the labour market', which we should today call the establishment and acceptance of a permanent statutory incomes policy.

Since the Second World War there have been significant developments in the organisation of the economies of the advanced countries, common to all of them. Apart from the historically high rate of growth in output there has been an increasing concentration in the size distribution of firms, notably in the manufacturing industries, the growth of corporate forms of organisation at the expense of the family firm, nationalisation of many sectors of the economy, great expansion of state provision of medicine, education and social services, various experiments in the introduction of incomes policy, and in general a greater degree of intervention and regulation by governments in the market economy than ever before.

While Schumpeter seems correctly to have anticipated the trends in the advanced countries in the thirty years following his death, when we look today at the situation through his analysis it seems as if these trends are in the process of being arrested. Schumpeter himself would not have been surprised. He was at pains to emphasise that he was making no dogmatic predictions concerning the long-run and that any tendency could be halted or even reversed at any time. In this respect Schumpeter's view of historical evolution is similar to that of his fellow Austrians, and quite distinct from Marxist determinism.

There are three major reasons why it seems that the post-war drift towards a planned economy in the advanced countries may have been stopped. First of all, the citizens of the advanced countries have had the learning experience of more than thirty years of this drift. While they have welcomed the collective provision of such commodities as medical and defence services and they have pressed for the extension of the range of social security benefits so that few governments of these countries have escaped apparently intractable budget balancing problems they have also experienced the consequences of certain movements in the direction of a planned economy, viz. the establishment of state monopolies, the growth of the central government bureaucracy and the extension of personal taxation and government controls and regulations relating to their personal economic activity.

In particular, most of the advanced countries have experienced since the Second War periods of statutory restraint on wages and sometimes other incomes, whether under the name of pay pauses, pay freezes, wage guidelines or whatever. While all of these attempts have been temporary, they have been generally unpopular[5] (their success in terms of their unstated objective of lowering the real wage is a matter of academic debate). At least in the UK neither major political party has dared to declare that, if elected, they would adopt such policies. Groups of people, like individuals, do undergo a learning process. Indeed, it may be said that one of the characteristics of the democratic political process is that it is a learning process. The conclusion that I would draw from the history of the past thirty years in the advanced countries is that the population of these countries have decided that incomes policies are an unacceptable restriction on their individual freedom to bargain in the labour market, and that a truly major economic catastrophe leading to a continuing foreseeable decline in their living standards would be necessary before they would be willing to surrender the degree of freedom which they enjoy at present in the labour market. A similar 'learning process' argument applies to their political attitude to state monopolies, the bureaucracy, taxation and controls. While people are eager to have the benefits of the welfare state, they have learned through painful experience that there may be corresponding costs, and they are politically concerned that these should be minimised.

UNWINDING THE DIVISION OF LABOUR

Since before the time of Adam Smith the progress of the advanced countries has proceeded by means of an ever-increasing degree of specialisation or division of labour. Indeed the whole economic development of both the advanced and the developing countries can be regarded as an unfolding of the degree of the division of labour as traditional activities are broken up into increasingly specialised functions to form new industries. Technical progress is intimately related to this process, since, together with the size of the market, it provides the opportunity for taking the division of labour one step further. All this was the subject of the Presidential Address to Section F of the 1928 meeting of the British Association in Glasgow.[6]

As the division of labour proceeds further, however, its costs increase while its benefits become less apparent. In the advanced countries today there is what Galbraith has called a 'diminishing urgency of wants', brought about by a combination of higher levels of consumption of privately purchased material goods and services together with a high level of collective provision of goods and services including widespread social security benefits. It is easy to see therefore why the benefits of further extensions of the division of labour, namely high material output, should become less important.

The costs of increasing the division of labour are several. First there is the familiar problem of alienation. By means of specialisation in technical progress a worker is typically denied a creative work-role. This of course can be mitigated by the fact that technical progress has been able to eliminate many dirty, menial, dangerous and physically exhausting tasks, and that the conferment of increased status together with higher real wages may compensate for the loss of self-esteem which the worker might otherwise suffer. Second, as the division of labour is extended, there are an increasing number of intermediaries between the primary stage of production and the point of final consumption. Since intermediation invariably involves a human agent, and since the price of labour rises relative to other commodities in the course of economic development, it follows that, for most com-modities, the total transactions costs, when summed over each stage of intermediation, become over time an increasing proportion of the total costs of production.

Third, the ever-extending chain of interdependence which arises from specialisation in a money economy increases the vulnerability of the whole system to disturbance, since the chain is only as strong as its weakest link. The uncertainty which is enhanced by this circumstance dampens risk-taking and thus investment.

Fourth, there are the social as well as the economic costs of the disturbance induced by a further step in the division of labour: these include the costs of unemployment and retraining as well as job-search.

The diminishing utility and increasing costs of continuing further extensions of the divisions of labour in the advanced countries suggest that the process may be slowing down or even coming to a halt. This is not to say that specialisation in a technical sense is diminishing; there are after all many new products and new processes coming into existence, but rather that a smaller and smaller proportion of the total supply of labour is being supplied to the labour market.[7]

It is not simply a question of increased time being devoted to leisure; it is that an increased amount of labour is being applied outside the market, to creative and satisfying forms of work inside or outside the home, including voluntary work and public interest activities, as well as DIY, recreational work, and hobbies.

The shrinking of the market economy and the development of the home economy have a number of important implications. First of all it permits the individual to opt out of much organised economic activity. This will make less likely the realisation of the classical forms of socialism. Attitudes are likely to change towards more self-sufficiency of the family or household group if not the individual (a reversion to peasant-like attitudes). A planned economy assumes a high degree of the division of labour within society. Without such an extensive division of labour, planning must be less comprehensive and control less complete.

Second, it implies a greater stability for the household or family unit. The 'home economy' may involve several members of the household in co-operative activity which is productive, but not necessarily all of which is destined for the market. This may not only have a favourable effect on youth unemployment, but equally importantly restores the unity of labour, of which the division of labour is so destructive, together with the psychological benefits which go with it.

THE EFFECT OF NEW TECHNOLOGIES

As indicated above, the tendency of the market economy to shrink at the expense of the home economy is being reinforced by new developments in the field of technology, particularly in the field of communications, but also to a lesser extent in the field of energy. These developments are making possible the territorial decentralisation of production, so that work for the market may increasingly be performed in the individual household or in small family firms rather than within such agglomerations as factories and cities. This again makes a movement towards socialism less likely. It is after all a highly centralised form of economic organisation, and it may not be accidental that planned economies have had the greatest difficulty in coping with such highly decentralised industries as peasant agriculture, where the household is the decision-unit.

We noted above Schumpeter's prediction that the increasing concentration of the size of the firm would shift the political balance of society in the direction of socialist attitudes and towards a planned economy. But if, in fact, this process of the elimination of small firms is now being reversed[8] then one should expect to find, following his view, that the political balance would move away from socialist attitudes and towards a greater reluctance to accept the central planning of economic activity.

The decline in the relative importance of large-scale factory production could also account for a major shift in attitudes. Many economic historians believe that a major element creating feelings of social class hostility was the way in which workers were concentrated in factories and were housed in associated blocks of dwellings whether privately, or later, publicly owned. If these processes are now being reversed, then one should expect, likewise, the abatement of such feelings.

Other developments in communications technology point in a similar direction. They convey the possibility of the individual shopping, carrying out financial transactions and, even, working from his own home.

As well as the decentralisation of production from larger to smaller units of production (in the extreme case, the household) there is also the possibility of territorial decentralisation of production, a process for which there is already much evidence. There is the continuing drift of population from the cities to the country. Much attention has been paid to the ensuing problems of the declining inner cities, with attendant social problems. However, these influences on attitudes may be overshadowed in their consequences by the broader changes in political attitudes throughout society.

These tendencies we have just identified are the consequences of the specific form or nature of contemporary technical change. There are also some consequences of the speed of contemporary technical change, which in some industries at least is apparently accelerating. In the great debate[9] in the 1930s about the feasibility of establishing a planned economy, the telling point was made by Hayek that it would be technically impossible for a central planning authority to acquire all the information necessary to carry out correct economic decisions as to the quantity and price of each commodity to be produced. This debate was carried out within the theoretical framework, common to both sides, of a static general equilibrium model, i.e. the basic parameters of information concerning wants, resources and technology pertaining to or available to every household and firm in a hypothetical economy were assumed to be unchanging. Recent developments in communications technology might make it possible to overcome Hayek's objection, at any rate for not too large an economy and for unchanging information. But while the technical problems of data transmission and analysis may be said to have been solved, the problem of the collection of fragmentary and uncertain information, whose dimensions are themselves changing, remains.

THE RESPONSE OF INSTITUTIONS TO CHANGES IN TECHNOLOGY

The response of most institutions to the pressures of change is to resist them. The classical argument in favour of the market economy as a form of organisation is not that it realises or approximates static allocative efficiency (the neo-classical argument), but that it makes such resistance on the part of institutions unavailing. This was Adam Smith's recipe for economic growth. It may be said that the success of the advanced countries in their economic development since the eighteenth century has been due to the flexibility of firms in response to the pressures of change. Whereas in earlier times pressures upon firms for change largely came from the opening of new territories and the development of consumer demand, it now comes primarily from technical progress. The role of institutions in the process of economic growth is just the same in the developing countries and in the planned economies as it is in the advanced countries. In his authoritative quantitative analysis of the barriers to economic growth in the developing countries Leontief concluded that the effective constraints were not physical ones, such as a scarcity of resources, but institutional ones.[10] Again it is worth noting that the principal obstacles to the growth of the contemporary Soviet economy appear to be institutional ones.

Menger identified two kinds of institutional change: there were those which were the result of human action, but not human design, to which he gave the word 'organic'. Pragmatic institutions, on the other hand, were those which were generated as the result of legislation or other purposeful collective agreement. As an example of organic processes of institutional change brought about by changes in technology we have already noticed the decentralising effects of changes in communications and energy technology. This will affect such institutions as the family and the town. But new technology is having its effect not only on communications between production units, but within them as well. The increasing automation of the control and organisation of the whole manufacturing process, as well as of individual tasks within it, is bringing about not simply a reduction in the direct labour force, but the enhancement of the advantages of batch production of a variety of products at the expense of economies of scale of mass production of standardised units as well as the redundancy of traditional craft apprenticeships. These changes can be expected to have far-reaching effects on the attitudes and organisation of the workforce and upon the optimal size and organisation of firms.

So far as pragmatic changes are concerned the development of new communications technology (such as satellites, cables and cassettes) has broken the natural monopoly[11] which the pre-existing state of the art had conferred on the communications industry in the advanced countries. These recent changes have caused the US government to legislate for the break-up of the hitherto publicly regulated but privately owned monopoly AT & T. The response of the British government has been rather different. It is now in the process of legislating to turn the British communications industry from a publicly owned to a privately owned monopoly. It is not effectively ending the monopoly as such. Whatever may be said in favour of the particular arrangements in the US nothing at all can be said in favour of the British legislation, since it is based on an apparent failure to distinguish between the form of organisation of an industry (i.e. a monopoly or competitive supply) on the one hand, and the form of ownership (i.e. private or public) on the other. It may not be too fanciful to attribute this misunderstanding to the absence of a generally accepted contemporary theory of growth for an advanced economy.[12]

Progress in information technology, together with human preferences for greater independence, point to some characteristics, which we have just outlined, of the successor state to the mixed economy. However, these and other developments in technology are also likely to increase the role of government as the provider of security. At the same time large corporations (whether publicly or privately owned) will continue to exist in many sectors of productive activity, where economies of scale and agglomeration justify them. The economic institutions of the successor state are therefore likely to be pluralistic, with strong political rivalry between the bureaucracy of government and of the large corporations on the one hand, and small to medium-sized firms, the home economy and perhaps the black economy, on the other. The bureaucracy will represent pressures for protection, self-interest and resistance to change, while the other sectors of society will represent pressures for freedom and flexibility in the widest senses of those words.

CONCLUSIONS

What does all this mean in terms of human betterment? In the nineteenth and early twentieth centuries the prevailing form of economic organisation – the market economy – permitted the realisation of the potential for technical progress, with resulting benefits of higher living standards in the advanced countries. This material progress was not achieved without considerable costs, which flowed directly from the form of organisation itself. Now however, it is possible, following the transitional state of the mixed economy, to envisage a successor state in which the population of the advanced countries will not only have been freed from material poverty, but will also have been freed from the organisational constraints which were necessary to overcome that poverty. While the successor state may be centralised as to its security aspects, in the field of production and consumption (i.e. economic activity) it will be highly decentralised, with consequent benefits for the family and community life.

The notion of economic transition as a turnpike was introduced to us by Dorfman, Samuelson and Solow. Their analysis was confined to strictly quantifiable data concerning capital stock and the composition of output in a growing economy. We can employ a similar metaphor more loosely to describe the progress of human society from the pre-industrial to the post-industrial period. In order to achieve rapid economic growth in the industrial era it was necessary for household independence to be sacrificed so that the advantages of higher productivity obtainable through the extension of the division of labour could be achieved. At the end of the turnpike, once the material benefits of higher productivity have been achieved, households (labour supply units) may be able to revert to the degree of independence which they formerly possessed.

In principle, therefore, we should expect to find that institutional forms could evolve in the successor state to the mixed economy which will make possible the realisation of the traditional aspirations of Western civilisation for the entire population of the advanced countries. Whether this dramatic potential will be realised is, of course, another question.

This is a question which I should have preferred to leave unanswered, were it not for the fact that human betterment is the theme of this year's Economics Section. I therefore feel obliged to make a few remarks on this question by way of conclusion. Those who have thought and written about the human condition can fairly easily be divided into one or another of two classes. There are those who believe that human misery is the product of circumstances external to the individual human being, and that therefore, given some appropriate form of economic and social organisation, the Kingdom of Heaven can be built upon earth. In the simplest form of this view, material poverty is by far the greatest, if not the only, burden on humanity, and it follows that the lifting of this burden will usher in an age of universal human happiness. Into this class fall Marx and Rousseau.

Into the second class fall all those who believe that the removal of the burden of poverty will merely make way for other human problems to come to the fore. It is a view expressed by such writers as Forster, Orwell and Huxley. All of these writers foresee that the developments in technology which make possible the abolition of material poverty in human societies will eventually destroy 'every vestige of humanity' (in Gerver's words)[13] in the citizens of these societies. More recently the economist Mishan has reiterated such views.

Although few who have experienced them would claim that the availability of eighty television channels represents any contribution to human betterment (rather the reverse, it seems) it is possible to err too much on the side of pessimism. In Pakistan, for example, it is reported that those citizens with TV sets ignore the government-inspired propaganda which dominates all the broadcast channels, and use the sets simply to play their video cassettes, which are freely available.

My own view is that the net effect of new developments in communications technology within our evolving political and economic system will be a liberating one, which will alleviate the lot of most people.

NOTES AND REFERENCES

1. I am grateful to Robert Crawford and James Walker for their comments on an earlier draft of this paper.
2. See page 60.
3. See the Preface to the third English edition of *Capitalism, Socialism, and Democracy* (London, George Allen & Unwin Ltd, 1949).
4. See J. A. Schumpeter, 'The March into Socialism', *American Economic Review* (May 1950).
5. While opinion surveys have indicated that the majority of respondents are in favour of incomes policies, I suspect that they really wish the restraints to be applied to members of the labour force other than themselves. Ironically the trade unions have been the strongest source of opposition to incomes policies in the UK. In this respect they are blocking the road to socialism.
6. A. Young, 'Increasing Returns and Economic Progress', *Economic Journal* (December 1928).
7. When the supply of labour is measured by hours offered through a working life, the reduction in the supply in the UK between 1870 and 1980 is almost 50 per cent. See Sir Bruce Williams, 'Technology Policy and Employment', Discussion Paper, The Technical Change Centre (London, 1983).

8. It may be asked, what is the empirical evidence for the assertion that a process of deconcentration is under way? The general literature is inconclusive and the evidence which I can offer is only fragmentary. While I would concede that many of the older manufacturing industries may be becoming more concentrated, this process must surely be outweighed by the growth of small firms in the services sector. Despite the recession and the uncertain investment outlook at the present time the formation of new companies in Scotland (virtually all of them small companies) is at an all-time high. It seems, too, as if the size distribution of establishments or workplaces may be becoming less concentrated.

9. O. Lange and F. M. Taylor, *On the Economic Theory of Socialism* (Minneapolis: University of Minnesota Press, 1938). F. A. Hayek (ed.), *Collectivist Economic Planning* (London: G. Routledge & Sons, 1935).

10. W. Leontief (ed.), *The Future of the World Economy* (New York: Oxford University Press, 1977).

11. Rothbard and others believe that the only true monopoly is one which is protected by state legislation, since all unprotected 'natural' monopolies will, in time, be eliminated by the competition of alternative modes or technologies. The critical question is: how long will this time period be?

12. See D. Simpson, *The Political Economy of Growth* (Oxford: Basil Blackwell, 1983) chap. 3.

13. I am grateful to Dr Elisabeth Gerver for drawing to my attention E. M. Forster's short story *The Machine Stops*, from which a quotation appears in her as yet unpublished paper.

5 Human Betterment in a Planned Economy – the Case of the Soviet Union

MICHAEL KASER

WEIGHING THE SOCIAL COST OF ECONOMIC PROGRESS

Economics is a necessary but not a sufficient discipline to assess human betterment. Its insufficiency needs no further justification after three decades of Western criticism of gross national product (GNP) as a measure of development and many compilations of 'social indicators'. There is ample evidence, moreover, in the chapters by Dr Sinha and Mrs Nissel in this volume. But our ability to measure 'betterment' is even more flawed with regard to the East – the tolerable misnomer for countries with Communist parties in sole control. With the Soviet Union as the case study, this chapter examines three characteristics which affect our assessment.

First, in comparison with a market system, planning – and above all Soviet central planning – involves more choice on behalf of the individual than by the individual. As Kenneth Boulding says, a market 'economises agreement'; Lenin's democratic centralism on the other hand must override agreement.

Second, there are remarkably few measures of social outcomes in the USSR, either planned or incidental, and the coercion applied for political reasons involves negative welfare. A Western democracy suffers negative welfare – unemployment, pollution or mugging could be cited – but it would cease to be democratic if it introduced the police state of Stalin or Hitler.

Third, the USSR has hitherto made little use of economics to assess efficiency and welfare, but in the 1960s and 1970s two other mechanisms came to be tolerated: neither enjoyed the wholehearted favour of the Party bureaucracy, but they did offer a way of getting the desired 'bill of goods' produced without a conspicuous waste of resources. One was to harness the computer and mathematical techniques to the planning process, the other was to allow more scope to strictly personal initiative through a parallel market, permitting a 'second economy' to operate alongside, and in the interstices of the Plan. Both may now be at risk under Chernenko, who may also have quashed Andropov's call for a revival of economics.

Professor Flew's 'Procrustean ideal', elsewhere in this book, applies to the USSR because the social welfare function was chosen by the state for, not by negotiation with, those affected, who could be gratuitously injured (or even killed) in the process. Stalin – a group of Soviet economists wrote in April 1983 – introduced 'a social system in which the people were consistently regarded as "screws" in the economic mechanism, and they behaved almost as obediently'.[1]

SOCIAL INDICATORS IN SOVIET PLANNING

The Soviet government, first, formulates its highly centralised plans as instructions to subordinates to produce or to distribute goods and services; it may, like other administrations, have certain social outcomes in mind when establishing its targets, but, because all subordinates' success is measured by target achievement, any social outcome is an incidental, not an objective. Soviet plan fulfilment and statistical reports reflect overwhelming preoccupation with intermediate flows of goods and services rather than with final welfare. Partly because it plans no social outcomes the Soviet government publishes few social measurements, a second problem in judging the betterment process. That many social indicators have improved since the Revolution is undeniable: mortality has been cut by two-thirds; life-expectancy at birth has doubled; all children attend secondary school without fees; there is universal literacy; and little sex or racial discrimination; social security provides against temporary or permanent loss of earnings (though one in five live below the official poverty line); medical care is universal and gratis; the number of public lending libraries has decupled; against the two thousand bookshops of pre-Revolution Russia, there are now 17 500, among them the largest bookshop in Europe, and from the 1500 newspapers and periodicals in 1913 there are over 13 000 today.[2] But if the 'psychic income' derived from these gains is large it must be offset by the compulsion, coercion and choice-restriction for which the Soviet regime is notorious. Can one measure the 'psychic losses' occasioned by the mass terror of Stalin's time, the persecution of religion under Khrushchev or the confinement of dissidents in mental hospitals under Brezhnev? Could one allow any positive outcome on applying the tenet that the end does not justify the means? Stalin was not alone in making bedfellows of Procrustes and Marx, but it must be granted that the brutal conformity which he exacted did bring tangible economic growth, whereas the similar periods under Mao in China and under Pol Pot in Kampuchea were economically retrogressive.[3]

On two counts the Soviet period of coercive industrialisation – from the murderous collectivisation and man-made famine of the early 1930s to the emptying of the mass prison camps in the mid-1950s – must be adjudged negative as human betterment. First, against the social gains already listed must be set losses in life and personal welfare. From the very tangible economic gains – the establishment of an industrial and military power second only to the US – must be deducted the waste of natural resources and of agricultural potential – Tsarist Russia was an exporter of grain and dairy products, but the USSR is far from feeding itself. Stalin achieved his top-priority targets in heavy industry, but the real wage of the 1920s was not regained until the 1950s. Second, the country would have industrialised under a market regime, as testified by industrial and agricultural growth from the 1890s to the Revolution, and by the early restoration of the pre-Revolutionary level under the quasi-market 'New Economic Policy' of the 1920s. Japan and Russia had about the same GNP per capita in 1913, but despite its immensely greater natural resources the USSR today ranks lower than Japan. An econometric study of two smaller, and hence statistically more amenable, East European countries (industrialised Czechoslovakia and less-developed Romania) suggests that alternative strategies would have yielded faster growth.[4]

Stalin's 'errors' are still castigated in Soviet official circles today (though less than in the aftermath of Khrushchev's famous 'Secret Speech' to the 1956 Party Congress), but for them to call the net outcome negative would strike at the roots of Party self-righteousness. It is for this reason that the present leadership will never denounce collectivisation, though it is already doing much to modify the harm which it inflicted on Soviet farming. At the more routine level, Soviet statistical reporting continues to place overwhelming emphasis on the production of physical commodities, and pays scant attention to social indicators.

Until quite recently the annual communiqués on plan fulfilment issued by the USSR Central Statistical Office contained only three such indicators – birth- and death-rates and the statement that 'as previously, there is no unemployment in the USSR'. It is of course right to draw attention to the assurance of some sort of employment as a social 'good' while the West has partly to offset its higher living standards with a social 'bad'.[5] Even so, full employment and demographic growth are poor surrogates for the social conditions which the Statistical Office should record. In fact its annual report cites only six items of social data – all inputs not outcomes: educational enrolments and the numbers of scientists and technicians, of physicians and sanatoria, and of libraries and cinemas; all other returns are economic.[6] The full statistical abstract[7] yields little more in the social field. Birth- and death-rates are still given, but the policy of earlier editions to include series on infantile mortality, marriage and divorce has been suppressed; health care institutions and personnel are enumerated, but the only morbidity or mortality rates given are those for seven communicable diseases which, as a member of the World Health Organization, the USSR is obliged to publish; the abstract reveals nothing on abortion (though the average Soviet woman is said to undergo five during her reproductive years). There are ample statistics of cultural establishments and of education, literacy and publishing; it would be unrealistic to expect data on the work of the censorship (Glavlit) or on crime, but the data collected on leisure time could be systematically presented.[8] There is something on housing facilities (82 per cent of public-sector urban dwellings have a bath and 59 per cent have a hot-water supply), and on sport (78 million regular participants); a short section on environmental protection has recently been added.

The foregoing is enough to demonstrate that published statistics are too meagre for a non-official analyst to evaluate betterment through social indicators; it also demonstrates the bias in planning and reporting that favours economic at the expense of social targets. What the State Planning Committee actually employs as targets is published, even if the statistics on them remain closely guarded secrets.[9] The Planning Committee's instructions for the current Five-year Plan period (1981–5) include no social indicators whatever. Only one (no. 23) of 26 chapters deals, as its title states, with 'Drawing up the integrated plan of social development and the raising of the people's level of living' and it is a catalogue of money outlays and operational orders.[10]

THE ABROGATION OF ECONOMICS

Maurice Dobb defended Stalin's growth strategy in its choice of a single social and economic package at low cost, whereas a market offered a wider range of social and economic benefits but at a high cost. Thus for the same resources the Russians could obtain a bundle of communal services and uniform consumers' goods, but a market would supply many fewer heterogeneous goods.[11]

If a choice is to be exercised among such 'bundles', account has to be taken of the relative preferences of the individuals concerned and the degree to which the economic process satisfies them. This is not a call for the optimality of Pareto nor the suboptimality of Lipsey and Lancaster's 'second best': the President of this Section over thirty years ago wrote:

> Instead of a relatively simple problem of climbing the preference mountain along the opportunity fence until we reach the highest point – which is the essential principle of maximising behaviour and of welfare economics – we find ourselves climbing a quaking jelly of a mountain that dips and sags as we walk across it, along a nightmarish fence which shifts and wavers as we walk beside it.[12]

It merely requires the measurement of opportunity cost, namely, that the planner ordering social preferences and the individual laying out his expenditure should each be aware of what he forgoes when making any specific choice. Until Brezhnev died the Soviet government found no place in policy-making for economics as we define it in the West. The rehabilitation of the discipline by Andropov to his Party Central Committee in June 1983 gave ground for anticipating more rational selection in the future.

The ideological defence of mass coercion was the Party's declared certainty in its own self-righteousness, to the point that some victims of the 'Great Terror' believed that their false confessions were in the interests of the Party line. Stalinist self-righteousness in economics had first a crude and then a more sophisticated form. The crude form was the simple declaration that economics did not exist as a science applicable to a socialist government: the state allocated resources and determined distribution by fiat. The leading Russian economist of the time, Academician Stanislav Strumilin, was denounced as 'counter-revolutionary' in 1937 – the peak year of the Purges – for proposing that 'the basic objective of production is consumption'.[13] In those days the Soviet authorities patently had scant regard for 'human betterment' for the worker and peasant either as producer or consumer.

On the eve of the Second World War the rapid turnover of Ministers due to the Purges threw up a talented young economist as chairman of the State Planning Commission: Nikolai Voznesensky was in his mid-thirties when appointed in late 1938; he became a Deputy Premier within a few months. He prevailed upon Stalin to permit a series of private meetings of economists, from which emerged an assertive version of economic laws.[14] A 'law of value' was declared acceptable for socialism in 1943 and Stalin enunciated a 'Fundamental Economic Law of Socialism' in 1952. This has an unexceptionable objective of 'betterment', but yields no economic criteria for its attainment: 'the securing of the maximum satisfaction of the constantly rising material and cultural requirements of the whole of society through the continuous expansion and perfection of socialist production on the basis of the highest technology'.[15] No guidance is afforded either on the choice of technique and other imputs nor on the mix of outputs which would afford 'maximum satisfaction'. Stalin's other 'economic laws' were 'planning rules' institutionalising a high rate of accumulation (that is, new investment and a part of defence expenditure), but without formulating how that accumulation could be scaled to a rate of time discount. Moreover, not only was any rate of interest ideologically condemned, but also obsolescence: no logical choice among investment variants to attain the same eventual consumption was hence feasible.

It is an open question whether Voznesensky would have prevailed upon Stalin to rationalise decision-making in that direction. He was certainly aware of the need for a consistent set of prices. He wiped out the war-time inflationary overhang by a currency reform in December 1947 and introduced a retail-price list which for the only time under Soviet central planning actually cleared the market. We know this because in 1948, and for that year alone, food prices in the peasant markets were identical to official retail prices; from 1929 to the present they have invariably been above the prices in state shops, where shortages and queues have demonstrated the inconsistency of pricing to consumer-good production plans. On 1 January 1949 he applied a new list of wholesale prices which replaced the quite obsolete '1926/7 prices' and largely eliminated subsidies.[16] Far from being gratified by these reforms, Stalin arrested Voznesensky in early 1949, had him executed the following year, and reversed both measures. From March 1949 he began a series of annual retail price reductions which disequilibrated the supply–demand relationship and in January 1950 and July 1952 did the same for wholesale prices. These actions he justified by a reversal of Say's Law that 'supply creates its own demand' – that is that demand should always exceed supply in a state of permanent repressed inflation. He also threw domestic prices further out of line with foreign prices by substantially revaluing the rouble in 1950.

Stalin's death saved the USSR from another mass purge – the wave had begun to be whipped up with his 'Doctors' Plot' – and from the exacerbation of pricing policy, which was halted in 1955 at both retail and wholesale levels. It took longer (until 1960) for the rouble to be devalued to something approaching average purchasing-power parity, but since no attempt was made to bring wholesale-price relativities into line with those on world markets the USSR remains alone among East European states in having no linkage between foreign trade and domestic prices.[17]

Khrushchev, courageously denouncing many of (though not all) Stalin's excesses made no fundamental concessions to economics. He authorised the use of a form of interest rate in the choice of capital projects and the incorporation of obsolescence into depreciation charges, but, like Stalin, he wanted the state to have no truck with economic choice. Whereas Stalin masked that lack of criteria by shortage (the seller's market), Khrushchev's smokescreen was abundance (a buyer's market). The 1961 Programme of the Communist Party sought 'Communism in our generation', that is, an abundance of consumers' goods that would eliminate the need for choice and, in the interim, an extension of collective consumption at the expense of personally chosen purchases. The vision of betterment through abundance had suitable antecedents. Engels invoked the need for an abundance of consumers' goods and services to justify the abolition of private property: 'Society will have at its disposal such a quantity of products that distribution among its members will be equitable and satisfactory. The division of society into various antagonistic classes will then become superfluous.'[18] In the *Communist Manifesto* he and Marx called for the centralisation of 'all instruments of production in the hands of the State, ... and to increase the total of productive forces as rapidly as possible'.[19] Lenin posited 'the planned organization of the social and productive mechanism to ensure the welfare and harmonious development of all members of society'.[20]

The Marxian and Soviet objective of abundance satisfies materialist ethics and avoids the allocative problem of normative economics. As Nove has recently put it:

Abundance removes conflict over resource allocation, since by definition there is enough for everyone, and so there are no mutually-exclusive choices, no opportunity is forgone and therefore there is no opportunity cost.... The task of planning becomes one of simple routine; the role of economics is virtually eliminated.[21]

Before abundance is attained the Communist state distributes 'according to need'; before the Communist state, the socialist state orders society such that distribution is 'according to work'. In both forms it is the state, not a market, which sets the parameters of distribution.

Even when Khrushchev relaunched abundance in the Party Programme, the chief Party ideologue, Mikhail Suslov, voiced regret that economics had been so downgraded under Stalin. He wrote in 1962 that 'a major divorce from reality, from the practical needs of socialist development, took place also in economics'.[22] But he and the rest of the leadership could not, or would not, overcome the obstacles to economic rationality that persisted when the greatest hindrance, the whim of a dictator, had gone: these obstacles were Marxist theory and Soviet bureaucracy.

Marx was a macroeconomist: capitalist profit and competition were instruments of economic growth as well as of the exploitation of labour. The *Communist Manifesto* (1848) could not have put it more clearly:

The bourgeoisie cannot exist without constantly revolutionizing the instruments of production, and thereby the relations of production. ... Constant revolutionizing of production ... the need of a constantly expanding market for its products chases the bourgeoisie over the whole surface of the globe. It must nestle everywhere, settle everywhere, establish connections everywhere.... The feudal relations of property become no longer compatible with the already developed productive forces.... They had to be burst asunder; they were burst asunder. Into their place stepped free competition, accompanied by ... the economic and political sway of the bourgeois class.

But Marx had no theory of the capitalist firm – still less one of the socialist enterprise – because his theory of value had place neither for utility nor for any non-labour factor of production. He wrote in volume I of *Capital*:

The exchange of commodities is evidently an act characterized by a total abstraction from use-value.... If then we leave out of consideration the use-value of commodities, they have only one common property left, that of being products of labour.

Later, in volume III, Marx was to pose his famous and still controversial 'transformation problem' of values into prices:

Capitalist profit-seeking brings about such a proportion of supply to demand that the average profit in the various spheres of production becomes the same, so that values are converted into prices of production.[23]

Stalin was not so naïve as to take Marx literally in this respect; rather he took over, with many other concepts, Evgeny Preobrazhensky's view in *New Economics*, which sought to

counterpose to commodity production, socialist planned production; to the market, the accounting of socialist society; to value and price, the labour costs of production; to the commodity, the product. ...Instead of the law of prices of production, we have in our economy a price policy dictated by the task of obtaining each year a definite accumulation fund for the state economy as a whole.[24]

Single-factor pricing persisted in the state production sector until 1967, when Kosygin's economic reform included a charge for capital in wholesale prices, but because capital assets were themselves valued in labour costs, the resultant price relativities remained uniquely determined by supply.[25] Even the latest price reform (1982) allows only sporadic entry to determination by relative scarcities, that is by admitting opportunity costs.

The terms of the 'betterment' objective the extant Party Programme, that drafted under Khrushchev in 1961, is no more evaluative of opportunity cost than was Stalin's Fundamental Economic Law of Socialism:

The aim of communism is the ever-fuller satisfaction of the growing national and cultural needs of the people by an uninterrupted development of social production.

One of Andropov's first declarations was that a new Party Programme was needed.

The Party as an ideological force did not abandon a Procrustean ideal. The objective of Communism remained 'distribution according to need' with no mechanism other than the state foreseen to determine such need (short of unbelievable abundance); collective consumption was perceived as superior to a privately purchased mix; and hopes for the shaping of 'Soviet man' continued to be formulated. But the practical issues had to be faced of the post-Stalin economic priorities – not a consumerist society, but one in which human betterment was genuinely sought both as a goal in 'competitive co-existence' with capitalism and to offer as incentives amid weak work motivation and disastrously poor labour productivity. The Soviet citizen could no longer be 'screwed' into his allotted place either as producer or as consumer.

ANDROPOV'S QUALIFIED REHABILITATION OF ECONOMICS

Andropov's call for a new Programme was made to the Party Central Committee in June 1983, but his speech was more notable for his admission that the objectives of a planned economy cannot, at least as yet, be formulated as 'economic laws of socialism'. This is a contradiction to Stalin, though not in so many words.

> Frankly speaking, we have not yet studied properly the society in which we live and work, and have not yet fully revealed the laws governing its development, particularly economic ones. This is why we have to act at times empirically, so to speak, by the quite irrational trial and error method.[26]

Andropov had begun his speech by calling for

> a new considerably higher standard of ideological and theoretical work, in the sphere of social sciences and above all economics

and may have felt freer to criticise the past because the ideologue of the social sciences, Suslov, had died in 1982. The message was clear enough: he had given a new lease to the study of economics in the USSR. It is still a limited lease and is especially set about with constraints when 'betterment' is in issue. Such was evident at the June Central Committee session when Konstantin Chernenko (Andropov's rival in the Brezhnev succession, and now with power to block many of Andropov's reform measures) attacked the two Soviet research institutes that have done most to analyse what the Soviet citizen really wants – the Institute of Sociology and the Central Economic Mathematical Institute (TsEMI). Chernenko took the two bodies to task to check their normal reaction to Andropov's new licence, for sociological research even within the political monolith could help to define a 'social preference function' and the economics institute had already done a great deal to reconcile consumer satisfaction with 'planners' sovereignty'.[27] Chernenko was warning, with the two least-ideological institutes in social science as scapegoats, that Andropov's new economics should not go too far.

The June Central Committee meeting as a whole demonstrated the limits on Andropov's freedom of action. The session was convened to discuss 'Topical questions of the Party's ideological and mass-political work': to strengthen ideology is to weaken independence of thought. The session did not consider the modest agricultural liberalisation which a Party Secretary, Mikhail Gorbachev, had announced in March as already decided upon by the Politbureau; it gave no hint of the industrial reform which one of Andropov's consultants (Oleg Bogomolov) had revealed in March was under study by an inter-departmental committee, and on which experiments were soon to be permitted. One has only to consider the immense vested interests created by the bureaucratic state and the command economy to appreciate the cause of Andropov's caution. In his own ideological manifesto (an article in February 1983 on Marx's Centenary) he warned that any change must be well prepared, that 'to run ahead means to put forward unfeasible tasks' and that there is not the slightest question of dismantling 'public collective ownership, which has been firmly established and has proven its advantages'.[28]

PLANS WITHOUT MARKET-CLEARING PRICES

Those who would understand the Soviet economy have always had to keep in balance two startlingly contradictory aspects of its performance. It is an economy perpetually in crisis, wasteful and inefficient in the use of resources, bureaucratically musclebound in efforts to innovate technologically and institutionally, and scandalously callous and inept in meeting the Soviet population's consumption wants. Despite all this, its growth performance has been impressive. Lurching though its progress seems, it overcomes crises rather than allowing them to accumulate to the point of collapse.[29]

Robert Campbell expresses the Soviet power of survival without the pricing mechanism which market systems employ for economic cohesion. At the opposite extreme to that 'decentralized solution' is the 'completely centralized solution'.

The phrase 'perfect computation' as symmetric to 'perfect competition' is due to Peter Wiles. As he explains, 'the possibility of perfectly computing, from a single centre, every detail of an economy remains in my opinion real, and worth discussing', but he immediately goes on to point out that 20 million commodity-types (the estimate of Soviet economists) would have to be computed as to 'prices or outputs or both' and that elasticities would also have to be dictated since 'in a command economy we cannot, of course, by definition, speak of elasticities since price is not the causative variable'.[30] For the leadership, however, even a partial planning solution ('suboptimal' in the technical sense) assures central control: it renders the Plan a more efficient instrument of the Party but bypasses the political dangers of devolving effective authority to technicians or managers.

The establishment in 1963 of the Central Economic Mathematical Institute in the USSR Academy of Sciences provided the first men and materials for such planning and a phrase in Brezhnev's speech to the 1966 Party Congress furnished approval from the top. Even in the mathematical formulation of planning problems some of Stalin's prejudice had first to be cleared away. Cybernetics, the conceptual basis for computerising any management process, had been described as 'a tool of the reactionary bourgeoisie and inimical to Marxism'[31] as late as 1954, but two years later Leonid Kantorovich (later to become the first Soviet Nobel Laureate in economics) was able to present to a seminar on cybernetics a paper entitled 'Mathematical Methods in Economic Planning'. A decree of March 1966 on the development of automatic management systems and on the utilisation of computer technology in planning signalled the formal start to what Michael Ellman then called 'the mathematical revolution'.[32]

In the event no 'revolution' took place, and the Soviet system still operates on a balance of opposing, but self-regulating forces,

the one inducing a seller's market, the other a buyers' market.... Quasi-automatic increments in plan targets constitute an inbuilt mechanism for tightening demand for inputs, and at the same time an assurance that all outputs will be absorbed, since they can be stored against further upward clicks of the ratchet. ... The opportunity for the enterprise manager to trade-off his degrees of response to taut plans or ratchets furnishes the matching mechanism at microeconomic level. It explains why swollen intermediate consumption, waste and unused capacity – symptoms of a buyers' market – co-exist with their opposites – derivatives of a sellers' market.[33]

The present writer's analysis some years ago was a precursor of the elegantly developed concept of countervailing pressures and suctions whereby Kornai explains 'the shortage economy',[34] but an economy which does not clear the determined quantities at the going prices must be suboptimal.

A genuine market can, if competitive, approach optimality, and a 'second economy' has massively expanded in parallel to the official channels of exchange since Stalin's death.[35] But since such non-official markets form a spectrum from the wholly licit to the illegal,[36] some are now in danger of extinction under the drive against bribery, corruption and managerial indiscipline.

The 'second economy' performs within the USSR the function of the Western economies in Soviet external relations: it can demonstrate a market clearing price, although in neither the domestic nor the foreign case does it show that price which would obtain if all Soviet transactions were decontrolled. Nevertheless, the prevailing 'shortage economy' conveys incorrect information to planners and hides true consumer preferences. The Soviet authorities have always appreciated that an equilibrium is practicable between the quantities of consumers' goods and services which they plan to put on offer and the purchasing power which could buy them. If the balance can be struck, macroeconomic repressed inflation could be avoided. Stalin's permanent 'repressed inflation' is no longer a doctrine and it was as an evil that Andropov admitted (in his June 1983 speech) that it still exists today. Nevertheless avoidance of microeconomic inflation arising from the mis-match of specific goods and prices has now become the more important task for the Soviet planners. The queues and shortages for the ordinary buyer, and the preferential supplies for the bureaucracy, are measures of the inadequacy whereby the USSR today fails to minimise the use of its potential for personal welfare. It is the system which is at fault: the Soviet citizen can neither choose with his vote nor buy with his earnings the options for his own betterment.

NOTES AND REFERENCES

1. Paper for a confidential seminar organised by the USSR Academy of Sciences, the Economic Department of the Central Committee of the CPSU and the USSR State Planning Committee, reported in the West by Dushko Doder of the *Washington Post*. Summaries were published in the *New York Herald Tribune* and *The Guardian* of 4 August and *The Times*, 6 August 1983.

2. For these and other social outcomes, and an assessment of their quality, see A. H. Brown, J. Fennell, M. Kaser and H. T. Willetts (eds), *The Cambridge Encyclopedia of Russia and the Soviet Union* (Cambridge: Cambridge University Press, 1982).

3. The extent of the economic damage wreaked during the Great Leap and the Cultural Revolution is only gradually becoming known; see especially Roderick MacFarquhar, *The Origins of the Cultural Revolution*, vol. II (Oxford: Oxford University Press, 1983). Dr Sinha pointed out at the meeting that much of the information about losses under Mao is due to a government which is anxious to discredit him; Stalin has not been criticised in the USSR in this regard. A report by the government of Kampuchea (*Press Bulletin* no. 8, 30 August 1983, p. 8, Vietnamese Embassy, London) estimated that 2.74 million people have been killed and 634 000 houses and 5800 schools have been destroyed under the Pol Pot regime.

4. Simulation studies of Czechoslovakia and Romania by J. Brada, M. Jackson and A. King in C. K. Wilber and K. P. Jameson (eds), *Socialist Models of Development* (Oxford: Pergamon Press, 1981).

5. On the other hand job security and overfull employment weakens poor labour discipline, which the Andropov administration was trying to reinforce: a resolution of 6 August 1983 promised 'tougher measures against absentee and other persistent offenders against labour discipline'. Between 1961 and 1970 under the so-called 'anti-parasite' law any able-bodied citizen of working age could be sentenced to 2–5 years' exile if judged not in regular employment. On the social injustice arising see the memoir of one such exile, Andrei Amalryk, *Involuntary Journey to Siberia* (London: Collins, 1970).

6. This is the tally of the latest, wholly typical, annual plan fulfilment report, that of 1982, published in *Ekonomicheskaya gazeta*, no. 5 (1983) pp. 11–14.

7. The latest abstract includes (tendentiously chosen) earlier years to commemorate the 60th Anniversary of the USSR, *Narodnoe khozyaistvo SSSR 1922–1982* (Moscow, 1982).

8. Samples published elsewhere than in the official annual indicate, for example, that Soviet fathers spend $4\frac{1}{2}$ times as much time on child care as US fathers (J. Berliner, *Journal of Comparative Economics*, 7 (1983) p. 137).

9. Penalties for the unauthorised transmission of state statistics were draconian in Stalin's time, and are severe under the extant statute (*Vedomosti Verkhovnogo Soveta*, no. 1, 1959).

10. *Metodicheskie ukazaniya k razrabotke gosudarstvennykh planov ekonomicheskogo i sotsial'nogo razvitiya SSSR* (Moscow, 1980), reproducing State Planning Committee Instruction no. 63 of 31 March 1980. The five sections of chap. 23 are household income and expenditure, retail trade, consumer and municipal services, education and training and health services. There is also a chapter (18) on measures for environmental protection.

11. Maurice Dobb, *Soviet Economic Development since 1917* (London: Routledge & Kegan Paul, 1948), pp. 5–6; but the same approach without coercion can be found in John Kenneth Galbraith, *Economic Development in Perspective* (London: Oxford University Press, 1962) chaps III and IV.

12. Kenneth Boulding, 'Welfare economics', in B. F. Haley (ed.), *A Survey of Contemporary Economics* (Homewood, Ill., 1952) ch. 1. Of the non-Paretian literature see particularly Charles Rowley and Alan Peacock, *Welfare Economics: a Liberal Restatement* (Oxford: Martin Robertson, 1975) chap. 10.

13. S. Strumilin in *Planovoe khozyaistvo*, no. 4, 1937, cited and commented upon by J. Miller, *Soviet Studies*, iv (1953) p. 412; on the denunciation see A. Zauberman, *Review of Economic Studies*, xvi (1948) no. 39, p. 1.

14. The present author has unravelled the evolution of this change in *Annuaire de l'U.R.S.S., 1965* (Paris, 1965) pp. 555–69 and in 'The Stalinist "planning rules"', *Soviet Studies*, xiv (1962) pp. 109–31.

15. J. V. Stalin, 'Economic problems of Socialism in the USSR', *Bolshevik*, no. 18, 1952.

16. The present author was the first outsider to perceive the significance of this reform, 'Soviet planning and the price mechanism', *Economic Journal* (1950) pp. 81–91.

17. The divorce between home and traded price-relativities is commonly known by the East German term *Preisausgleich*; between 1967 and 1978 each East European state has applied an 'internal rate of exchange' to convert foreign earnings or outlays to producers' or buyers' receipts or costs (with another rate for non-commercial transactions), while Hungary has gone further and has a unitary rate of exchange.

18. F. Engels, *Principles of Communism* (1947), trans. J. E. Elliott, *Marx and Engels on Economics, Politics and Society* (Santa Monica, Calif: Goodyear, 1981) p. 459.

19. K. Marx and F. Engels, *Collected Works*, vol. 6, p. 504.

20. V. I. Lenin, 'On the Draft Party Programme' (1917), *Sochineniya*, 4th ed., vol. 24, p. 481.

21. Alec Nove, *The Economics of Feasible Socialism* (London: Allen & Unwin, 1983) p. 15.

22. *Kommunist*, no. 3 (1962) p. 21, cited by the present writer in 'Welfare criteria in Soviet planning', in Jane Degras (ed.), *Soviet Planning* (Oxford: Basil Blackwell, 1964) pp. 144–72, which considers the state of welfare economics in the USSR at the time.

23. For the context of these quotations and an illuminating commentary, see Elliott, op. cit. pp. 79 and 197.

24. Evgeny Preobrazhensky, *The New Economics*, trans. Brian Pearce, with

an introduction by Alec Nove (London: Oxford University Press, 1965) pp. 162 and 201; the Russian original was published in 1926.

25. Nove, op. cit. pp. 20–45, deals succinctly with the legacy of Marx on Soviet price theory; a fuller theoretical exposition is in G. Hardach, D. Karras and B. Fine, *A Short History of Socialist Economic Thought* (London: Edward Arnold, 1979).

26. *Pravda*, 16 June 1983.

27. Some of the work of TsEMI in analysing consumer behaviour is translated in Martin Cave, Alastair McAuley and Judith Thornton (eds), *New Trends in Soviet Economics* (New York: M. Sharpe, 1982). In editorial commentaries McAuley points to the Institute's acceptance of marginal utility theory and Cave to its insistence of defining an objective function for optimal planning.

28. Yu. Andropov, *Kommunist*, no. 3, 1983.

29. R. W. Campbell in R. F. Byrnes (ed.), *After Brezhnev* (Bloomington, Ind.: Indiana University Press, 1983) p. 68

30. P. J. D. Wiles, *Economic Institutions Compared* (Oxford: Basil Blackwell, 1977) pp. 274–7.

31. Cited by M. Cave, *Computers and Economic Planning: The Soviet Experience* (Cambridge; Cambridge University Press, 1980) p. 1.

32. See M. Ellman, *Soviet Planning Today* (Cambridge, Cambridge University Press, 1971), and *Planning Problems in the USSR* (Cambridge, Cambridge University Press, 1973).

33. M. Kaser, *Soviet Economics* (London and New York: Weidenfeld & Nicolson, 1970) pp. 223–4.

34. Janos Kornai, *The Economics of Shortage*, 2 vols (Amsterdam: North Holland, 1980).

35. The two principal papers are Gregory Grossman, 'The "second economy" of the USSR', *Problems of Communism* (1977) no. 5, pp. 25–40, and Aron Katsenelinboigen, 'Coloured markets in the USSR', *Soviet Studies*, xxix (1977) no. 1, pp. 62–85.

36. For a brief categorisation see the present writer's 'Economic policy' in A. H. Brown and M. Kaser (eds), *Soviet Policy for the 1980s* (London: Macmillan, 1982) pp. 190–1.

6 Culture and Economy: Human Betterment in India and Japan

RADHA SINHA

INTRODUCTION

> Numbers are a wonderful aid to clear thinking, but they defeat their purpose if we read more into them than what, in fact, they contain. Our preoccupation with economic problems and economic indicators of welfare is partly explained by their quantitative and quantifiable nature. Economic quantification is attractive and useful, but we must not let it seduce us into attaching more significance to the measure of quantity and to what is quantified than they deserve. The national income is, at the very best, an index of economic welfare, and economic welfare is a very small part and often a very poor indicator of human welfare.
>
> TIBOR SCITOVSKY in *The Joyless Economy* (1976) p. 145

The growing disillusionment, as symbolised in Scitovsky's statement quoted above, with the quantitative measures of economic betterment such as the gross domestic product or per capita income, etc., has led in recent years to a search for a set of social indicators which together with the quantifiable measures of economic output could serve as an index of human betterment. However, as a result of ambiguity in concepts and the impossibility of quantifying the qualitative differences between social consumption (items such as education, health) under differing circumstances, any judgement of inter-temporal comparisons of the state of human welfare becomes difficult, if not impossible.

Apart from the technical aspect of quantification there is a more fundamental problem which Hirsch calls the 'adding-up' problem. 'Opportunities for economic advance, as they present themselves serially to one person after another, do not constitute equivalent opportunities for economic advance by all. What each of us can achieve, all cannot.'[1] Environmental pollution and congestion are the typical examples of competition for limited opportunities by individuals leading to hidden costs for others and for oneself. If the individual valuations and the resulting benefits do not add up, the connection between individual and aggregate cannot be taken as granted.[2] In such a case the practice of expressing human welfare in terms of aggregates (or averages) of economic output and social amenities becomes highly suspect. Since no better measure of economic and social welfare is available yet, the present paper starts with some economic and social indicators and draws attention to some of the new problems generated by the very success of the efforts towards economic betterment.

INDICES OF ECONOMIC ADVANCE

On any conventional measures of economic advancement the Japanese achievements have become legendary. Within a few decades of the defeat in the Pacific War which killed nearly 2.8 million people and destroyed the major part of her economic and industrial base, she has emerged as an economy with the second largest gross domestic product (GDP) in the non-Communist world. Her share of the world total output as reflected by the sum total of the GDPs of all countries has now increased from a modest 3 per cent in 1955 to around 10 per cent in 1978, against nearly 7 per cent for West Germany, 5 per cent for France and only 3 per cent for the UK. Her per capita income (at US $9890 is almost 25 per cent higher than that of the UK (Table 6.1 – see p. 89). Her share in the world exports stands next only to the USA and West Germany. Similarly, the value added in her manufacturing is nearly 3.5 times that of the UK. In terms of manufacturing of individual products her production of crude steel in 1979 was second to the USA (Table 6.2). However in 1980 it had already overtaken the USA in steel output.[3] The Japanese production of cement in 1979 was substantially higher than that of the USA. In motor-vehicles, by 1980 Japan had overtaken the USA as the largest producer. Both in terms of the total output of key manufacturing industries and the diversified base of the industrial structure, Japan has emerged as an industrial giant. This is no mean achievement considering the fact that Japan does not possess any raw material or fuel in significant quantities. Her import dependence for raw materials, fuel and significant part of her food is much higher than most industrialised countries of the West.

TABLE 6.1 *Selected economic indicators, 1980*

	India	Japan	USA	France	UK	*West Germany*
Land area (thousand square km.)	3288	372	9363	547	245	249
Population (millions)	673.2	116.8	227.7	53.5	55.9	60.9
GDP (at market price) (billion US $)	142.0	1040.0	2587.1	651.9	522.9	819.1
Share in the world GNP[1]	1.2	10.0	21.8	4.9	3.2	6.6
GNP per capita (US $)	240	9890	11360	11730	7920	13590
Domestic investment (% of GDP)	23	32	18	23	16	25
Value added in manufacturing (billion 1975 US $)	15.6	207.6	448.2	109.1	59.6	184.1
Merchandise export f.o.b. (billion US $)	6.7	129.2	216.7	111.3	115.4	192.9
Merchandise imports c.i.f. (billion US $)	12.9	140.5	255.7	134.9	120.1	188.0

SOURCES The World Bank (1982) *World Development Report 1982*; and OECD, *Economic Surveys: Japan.*

TABLE 6.2 *Selected indicators of industrial strength, 1978*

	India	Japan	USA	France	UK	West Germany
Coal[1] (million metric tons)	101.3	19.0	566.7	21.1	123.6	90.1
Brown coal and lignite (million metric tons)[2]	3.6	0.4	32.3	—	—	123.6
Crude petroleum (million metric tons)	11.3	0.5	429.2	1.2	52.9	5.1
Natural gas (teracalories)	12 598	27 870	4 839 103	63 059	362 617	171 966
Iron ore (Fe content) (million metric tons)	24.5	0.4	50.5	10.3	1.1	0.5
Pig iron (million metric tons)	9.7	88.1	179.5	18.5	11.6	30.4
Crude steel (million metric tons)	10.0	102.1	124.3	22.8	20.3	41.3
Cement (million metric tons)	19.6	84.9	77.5	28.2	15.9	34.0

Newsprint (million metric tons) (1979)	0.04	2.6	3.7	0.3	0.4	0.6
Synthetic rubber (million metric tons)	0.03	1.0	2.6	0.5	0.3	0.4
Nitrogenous fertilisers[3] (million metric tons)	2.2	1.5	11.8	1.8	1.3	1.5
Sugar (million metric tons)	7.1	0.6	5.1[4]	3.7	1.1	3.0
Radio receivers (millions)	1.9	18.8	10.3	3.0	0.9[2]	4.6
Television receivers (millions)	—	13.9	9.3	1.9	2.4	4.2
Motor vehicles passenger cars (million)	0.05	6.0	9.2	3.6	1.2	3.9
Commercial vehicles (millions)	0.05	3.3	3.3	0.5	0.4	0.3

[1] Anthracite, bituminous and semi-bituminous only.
[2] 1977.
[3] Production in terms of nitrogen.
[4] Data for Puerto Rico included.

SOURCE UN (1981) 1979/80 *Statistical Yearbook.*

Contrary to the Japanese experience, India, on any conventional measure of economic betterment, continues to be a poor country. With nearly one-sixth of the world population it has only 1 per cent of the world's GDP. Her per capita income is one of the lowest in the world (Table 6.1). Although her industrial base is much wider the value-added in manufacturing in India is only 8 per cent of that of Japan and her export trade only 5 per cent of that of Japan. In comparing Japan and India one must not lose sight of the fact that, at her independence, India was both in terms of the industries and the infrastructure much less developed than Japan.

Except for pig iron, cotton yarn and cotton fabric India's production of industrial items in 1948 was much less than that of Japan (Table 6.5).[4] Even the war-devastated Japanese industrial structure was much more diversified than that of India. Any meaningful diversification of the industrial sector in India had to wait until the Second World War when the cessation of supplies from the UK gave fillip to the Indian industries. Among the developing countries India had a significantly developed system of roads and railways but yet on the eve of independence, she was better off than the war-devastated Japan only in terms of railway mileage. Her road mileage was only a third of that of Japan. Coastal shipping was in its infancy and the entire inland navigation system was traditional. Thus, India had inherited a rather feeble economy from the British rulers. In some ways the British had left India politically more divided than they had captured it. The country's partition into three major political divisions (India, West Pakistan and East Pakistan) together with the 612 'native' states with their legal and political status undefined left India in a political chaos, the price of which she has continued to pay in terms of wars and political differences with Pakistan and Bangladesh. Some of these 'native' states in terms of economic, social and political developments compared favourably with the British Provinces (that part of India which was directly ruled by the British) but the vast majority of these states were ruled by feudal autocrats. These 'native' states often lacked the basic essentials of modernisation in terms of education, health, justice as well as the physical infrastructure such as roads and railways. Given the rudimentary conditions of such 'native' states, the unification of India, and raising the standards of the administration, justice and welfare in the 'native' states to the standards of the British Provinces was a feat.

Notwithstanding the underdeveloped economic base and the political problems in the wake of the partition of the country, conventional quantitative measures of Indian success are many. Indian agriculture over nearly three decades since the independence has grown by around 3 per cent per annum against only about 0.5 per cent between 1900 and 1939. Population growth of 2 per cent (in 1960s around 2.5 per cent) has certainly exacerbated some of the economic problems, but it (population growth) must be taken as a sign of the success resulting from the extension of public health and sanitation facilities. Industrial and manufacturing output has grown over the three decades ranging between 6 per cent and 9 per cent. Achievements in the field of infrastructure (i.e. roads, railways, irrigation) are remarkable. The educational, scientific and technological base of the country has been strengthened considerably. Thus on almost all conventional economic indicators India has done reasonably well, particularly in view of the political shambles she was in on the eve of her independence.

DISTRIBUTION OF INCOME AND WEALTH

Notwithstanding the limitations of such estimates the distribution of income in India is somewhat more unequal than in Japan or any other developed country. The share of the poor (i.e. 20 per cent of the households) at around 7 per cent compares favourably with the USA and France at around 5 per cent, but the share of the households in the upper income brackets is much larger in India than any of the de-veloped countries included in Table 6.6. The Gini-coefficient of income distribution estimated by various sources is around 0.4, but the Gini-coefficient for land-holding around 0.6 suggests a much higher inequality in the ownership of wealth, particularly land. Even in this respect (i.e. inequality in the ownership of land) the Indian situation is much better than those of Latin American countries where (except for Cuba, Peru and Nicaragua) the Gini-coefficient is as high as 0.8 or even higher. Nevertheless, as a result of very low levels of per capita income in India, a significant proportion of population is below the 'poverty-line'. An official estimate based on the Indian National Sample Survey (NSS) suggests that, in 1973–4, around 46 per cent of the total population were below the 'poverty line', while the Indian Planning Commission suggested 48 per cent of the rural population and 41 per cent urban population being in such a category in 1977–8.[5] Even the more conservative estimates place the proportion of popula-tion below the 'poverty line' between 15 to 25 per cent. Thus even on conservative estimates, the number of people living below the 'poverty

TABLE 6.3 *Selected social indicators*

	India	Japan	USA	France	Italy	UK	West Germany
Calories per capita per day (1975–7)	1996[1]	2840	3537	3458	3462	3305	3362
Proportion of calories from vegetable sources (%)	95.7	81.3	63.3	63.0	77.5	62.2	61.2
Protein per capita per day (1975–7) (g.)	46.2	86.5	106.2	102.7	98.2	91.6	85.3
Proportion of protein from vegetable sources (%)	91.6	51.6	31.5	36.0	54.4	39.0	36.1
Energy consumption per capita (1978) (kg. of coal equivalent)	177	3825	11374	4368	3230	5212	6015
Population per physician (1977)	3630	850	580	610	490	750	490
Population per nursing person (1977)	5700	290	150	170	330	300	260
Life-expectancy at birth (1978) (years)	52	76	73	73	73	73	72
Infant mortality rate (1978)	123	10	14	11	18	14	15

Number enrolled in higher education as percentage of population aged 20–24 years (1976)	8	29	56	24	27	19	25
Number enrolled in secondary school as percentage of age group (15–19) (1977)	27	93	93	83	73	82	84
Newsprint consumption per capita (1977) (kg.)	0.34	20.3	41.6	11.0	3.8	25.9	19.4
Television sets per 1000 inhabitants (1977) (no.)	1	239[2]	571[2]	274[3]	224	324	308
Radio receivers per 1000 inhabitants (1976) (nos)	38	530	1882[1]	330	232	706	329
Telephones per 100 inhabitants (1977) (nos)	40	424	744	329	285	415	374
Passenger cars per 1000 inhabitants (1977) (nos)	1	173	505[2]	314	289	255[2]	326

[1] 1977–9.
[2] 1975.
[3] 1976.

SOURCES FAO (1980) *FAO Production Year Book, 1979*; The World Bank (1980) *World Development Report 1980*; UN (1979) *Statistical Yearbook, 1978*; *OECD Economic Surveys: Japan*, and *Far Eastern Economic Review, Asia 1982 Year Book.*

line' would be significantly over 100 million, underlining the immensity of the human problems. The majority of the poor come from the socially underprivileged groups such as the 'harijans' (the untouchables), the tribals and the castes low down the traditional social hierarchy. Clearly, the constitutional provision of 'positive discrimination' – giving preferential treatment to the underprivileged groups – has been effective only partially. Such groups have not yet received their fair share in economic, social and political spheres and it is common knowledge that even now 'high caste' Hindu landowners often in league with the police and the civil service are burning them and their villages. Repugnant as it is, such recurring clashes between the socially privileged and the underprivileged itself is a sign of dynamic social change generated by the constitutional provisions for positive discrimination. The 'harijans' now conscious of their constitutional rights refuse to work for unjust wages and do not take their deprivation as something inevitable. This threatens to undermine the traditional privileges of the so-called upper classes. But the fact remains that the underprivileged groups continue to suffer immense deprivation.

SOCIAL INDICATORS

On most social indicators (Table 6.3) Japan's recent record is quite respectable. Japanese nutritional and health standards compare favourably with other developed countries (Table 6.3). Her average consumption of calories and protein, though somewhat lower than the USA and the Western European countries are more than adequate to meet the nutritional standards. The per capita availability of doctors in Japan is less than those for the other developed countries included in Table 6.3 but the expectation of life at birth in Japan is the highest while the infantile mortality rates are the lowest of the five developed countries. In terms of higher education Japan is definitely behind the USA, but not the Western European countries. In terms of the ownership of consumer durables Japan is well ahead of the Western European countries, but not the USA. Recent surveys indicate that nearly 98 per cent of households own colour television, 56 per cent stereos, 52 per cent cars and 99 per cent refrigerators and washing-machines.[6]

In terms of social indicators India continues to be poor. Expectation of life at birth of 52 years is still low on world standards. Infant mortality is high. Literacy rates, proportion of population receiving secondary and higher education and the number of doctors and nurses per thousand of population are extremely low. Similarly, the possession of means of communication (and possibly education) such as television, radios and telephones are extremely low on world standards. In any case averages in these respects are rather meaningless. The distribution of social amenities such as health and education as well as the ownership of durable consumer goods are extremely skewed.

The standard of housing, roads and drainage and domestic sanitary facilities continue to be inadequate on Western standards in India, but also in Japan in spite of the material prosperity of the latter. Both countries, like most developed countries, suffer from serious environmental problems. There is a growing recognition of these problems in both countries and as a result of concerted effort, the situation in Japan in this respect is distinctly better now than it was in the early 1970s. However, in India, the recognition of the seriousness of the environmental problem is not as widespread. On the other hand lack of resources also prevents any serious effort to solve such problems.

EMERGING SOCIAL PROBLEMS

Both in India and Japan the breakdown of the traditional social cohesion and family ties is already creating serious problems for the children and the aged and the poorer sections of the population. It has been recognised for a long time that economic progress undermines such a social cohesion. Adam Smith has commented on this tendency in *The Theory of Moral Sentiments* in the following words:

in all countries where the authority of law is not alone sufficient to give perfect security to every member of the state, all the different branches of the same family commonly choose to live in the neighbourhood of one another. Their association is frequently necessary for their common defence. They are all, from the highest to the lowest, of more or less importance to one another. Their concord strengthens their necessary association – their discord always weakens, and might destroy it. . . .

In commercial countries, where the authority of law is always perfectly sufficient to protect the meanest man in the state, the descendents of the same family, having no such motive for keeping together, naturally separate and disperse, as interest or inclination

TABLE 6.4 *Mortality rates resulting from accidents and crimes*
(per 100 000 persons)

	Japan (1978)	USA (1977)	France (1976)	Italy (1975)	UK (England & Wales only) (1977)	West Germany (1978)
Motor-vehicle accidents (1 000 000 persons)	10.5	22.9	23.3	21.5	11.9	23.1
Accidents caused by fires	1.4	2.9	1.5	0.7	1.3	0.9
Suicides and self-inflicted injury	17.6	13.3	15.8	5.6	8.0	22.2
Homicides and injury purposely inflicted by others (legal interventions)	1.1	9.2	0.9	1.3	0.9	1.2
Total all types of accidents, etc.	46.4	72.2	93.0	53.8	41.3	74.5

SOURCE WHO (1979) *World Health Statistics,* WHO (1980) *World Health Statistics.*

TABLE 6.5 *Manufacturing output in India and Japan, 1948*

Items	India	Japan
Pig iron (million tons)	1.5	0.8
Steel (ingots or crude) (million tons)	1.2	1.7
Cement (million tons)	1.5	1.8
Cotton yarn and fabrics (million tons)	0.7	0.1
Cotton fabric (billion metres)	4.0	0.8
Paper and paper board (million tons)	0.1	0.5
Soda ash (thousand tons)	28.2	75.0
Caustic soda (thousand tons)	4.4	107.0
Super-phosphates (thousand tons)	21.4	955.0
Sulphuric acid (thousand tons)	80.0	1 950.0
Machine tools (nos)	1 690	8 050
Diesel engines (nos)	964	22 500
Bicycles (thousand units)	51.7	830.0

SOURCE UN (1949) *Economic Survey of Asia and the Far East,* pp. 70–85.

TABLE 6.6 *Income distribution in selected countries*

| Countries | Percentage share of household income | | |
	Lowest 20 per cent	*Highest 20 per cent*	*Highest 10 per cent*
India (1975–6)	7.0	49.4	33.6
Japan (1969)	7.9	41.0	27.2
USA (1972)	4.5	42.8	26.6
France (1975)	5.3	45.8	30.5
UK (1979)	7.3	39.2	23.8
West Germany (1974)	6.9	44.8	28.8

SOURCE   World Bank (1982) *World Development Report, 1982*

may direct. They soon cease to be of importance to one another; and, in a few generations, not only lose all care about one another, but all remembrance of their common origin, and of the connection which took place among their ancestors.[7]

With economic development, particularly the rapid pace of urbanisation which comes in the wake of large-scale industrialisation, disintegration of the extended family is further accelerated. In early stages of development, housing in urban areas is not only difficult to procure, but is extremely expensive. Parents cannot be easily accommodated in such houses. In cases where the parents possess some land in their original village homes they generally do not like to give up ancestral land and possibly the only source of income. Thus by necessity as well as by choice the separation between the parents and working children takes place. Not all the working children can easily obtain jobs in the same towns and cities therefore the brothers start living their separate lives, meeting only occasionally on festive occasions or family calamities such as serious illness or death. Sometimes link with the village is maintained merely to supplement the meagre income from the urban employment with food and other agricultural products from the village home. But in many cases the urban income is so low that it is not always possible to continue the link with the village and the parents except through some occasional remittances.

This natural tendency towards the disintegration of extended families has been further exacerbated both in India and Japan by the acceptance of the nuclear family as a better mode of life and individualism as the key to economic progress. (This can be evidenced in the fact that under the influence of Western advisers many African countries are converting communally owned land into private owner-ship).

The breakdown of tribal and/or family loyalty has had several unfortunate results in both India and Japan. With the extension of transport and communication, and particularly since the introduction of the 'Green Revolution' technology in India, the landlords have resumed land for personal cultivation by evicting their customary tenants. This has exacerbated the problem of rural unemployment. In many areas landlords have refused to pay the customary kind pay-ments to their local agricultural workers and have preferred to import cash wage-labour from other areas. Neglect by landlords or the community as a whole of traditional responsibilities for the construc-tion and maintenance of irrigation and local roads, etc., has also meant a considerable decline in such amenities.

This abdication of traditional social responsibility can be seen in the Japanese case as well. Traditionally the relationship between worker and employer in Japan is not so much a contractual as an emotional one. The workers' sense of identification, often reciprocated by the employer and reflected in the 'lifetime employment system'[8] has been one of the main reasons for the phenomenal success of the Japanese industrialisation. In recent years this harmony is being eroded by the unilateral actions of both the employees and the employers. Under the 'Western' influence younger employees, in search of quicker promo-tions, are changing their jobs at frequent intervals. On the other hand, large enterprises, under the pressure of increasing foreign competi-tion, are dismissing permanent employees on the grounds of recession and later employing the same people as temporary workers. This reduces their customary 'cradle-to-the-grave' responsibilities.

The worst sufferers of the premature decline of traditional mores (such as the disintegration of the extended family system before an official system of old-age pensions and social security is developed effectively) are the old people. This is reflected in a rocketing number of long-term older patients in Japanese hospitals as well as high rates of suicides, particularly among the Japanese old women. As would appear from the following statement of the director of an emergency hospital, families are extremely reluctant to take their elderly mem-bers back from hospitals once they are successfully hospitalised.

Ours is an emergency hospital, and as such, is open round the clock every day of the year. On New Year's Eve, we had a fleet of ambulances pulling up at our door, disgorging one old person after another. Apparently their families were going away for the holidays and wanted to leave grandpa and grandma under our care. Moreover, if the old folks were lucky enough to be assigned a bed fully covered by health insurance, their families would beg us to let them stay on even after the holiday season was over.[9]

This tendency of turning the hospitals into old people's homes has been one of the main reasons for the escalating cost of medical services in Japan.[10] While the family norms in Japan, as elsewhere, are changing rapidly, the official provision for the old-age pension is 'too small a sum for an old family to survive'.[11] Nevertheless, big business in Japan has been 'urging the government to cut down the already low pension levels still further' and substitute it by personal savings and other 'self-help' efforts.[12]

Since nearly three-quarters of the Indian population continues to live in rural environments, the problem of the old is still not as acute in India as it is in Japan, but urban experience clearly indicates that Indian old people will untimately suffer a similar fate. The situation may possibly be worse. Because of the scarcity of resources there is a tendency towards stressing 'productive' investment more than welfare expenditure and in an economic calculus of profit and loss, spending on the old, like spending on out-of-date machines, is the least productive.

Indiscriminate acceptance of the material possessions as the main measure of an individual's success or failure has another victim in children. Material possessions (televisions, videos and other household equipment) and 'keeping up with the Joneses' has forced many husbands in Japan to take second jobs and the wives to go out to work. Many young couples spend a lot of money on travels and on cars. Children do not fit into their plans. Many young wives in nuclear families living in small apartments describe their lives 'like serving a prison sentence, being chained down by a baby'.[13]

The disintegration of the extended family and the traditional value system has possibly brought some advantages to the younger women. They have been freed both in Japan and India to varying degrees from feudal disabilities. They have now greater opportunities for education and employment. The mechanical gadgets have come to their aid in domestic chores. With increased leisure time they have found opportunities of self-fulfilment in art, literature and other creative activities. As against these benefits one must allow for the inconveniences of the 'double burden of work inside and outside the home. Many working wives suffer from chronic fatigue. Of course, the strain is much worse for those with pre-school children.'[14] Such women often complain of 'fatigue, such as stiff shoulders, a general feeling of listlessness, drowsiness during work, and fatigue even on waking in the morning.'[15] The situation is gradually improving as the husbands of younger generations are giving up their traditional attitude to housework and rearing the children.

On the whole in both countries the number of people 'dropping out' of society is on the increase, as is vandalism, juvenile delinquency, the use of drugs and consumption of alcohol.[16] Reports of misbehaviour of students ranging from violence against their fellow students, smoking and drinking to acts of violence against teachers are quite common.[17] Nevertheless the crime rate and vandalism in Japan is roughly the same as in the Western European countries, although it is extremely low as compared with the USA (Table 6.4). The suicide rate in Japan is high: this partly reflects increasing social tension, but is also because traditionally Japanese society glorifies suicide. In recent years suicides seemed to have increased as a direct result of the process of modernisation and of changing social values. In thier effort to 'keep up with the Joneses' Japanese families have increasingly fallen into debt to 'loan sharks' whose activities until recently were not particularly regulated officially. They charged very high interest and the debtors in the event of failing to pay back their debts often committed suicide. Work-related suicides have increased as well. Recently it was reported that more than one-third of the school teachers' suicides in 1981 resulted from increasing work load of teachers and possibly their lack of contact with students causing a loss of confidence in themselves.[18] Some workers are reported to have committed suicide because of their inability to keep pace with the speed of automation.

Comparable statistics on mortality rates resulting from accidents and crimes are not readily available for India, but impressionistic surveys indicate that violence is on the increase. Emphasis on material possessions as the main symbol of success has led to an appreciable increase in bribery and corruption. The conspicuous consumption of the rich in the midst of extreme poverty has continued to divert scarce resources away from the needs of the poor to the luxuries of the handful of rich. This distortion in value system is clearly reflected in the conspicuous consumption of the state in terms of 'pop shows' like the India Festival in London or ASIAD in Delhi.

CONCLUSIONS

Both the Japanese and Indian experience over the last three decades suggest that economic betterment has been achieved, but at the cost of social harmony. The situation may not be explosive, but certainly is potentially risky. Does this mean that one has to reject modern technology and the material benefits it has bestowed upon us? Clearly the answer has to be negative. Without additional material benefits it will not be possible to eliminate hunger and deprivation from the world. On the other hand, the existence of considerable hunger and deprivation in the West itself is the testimony to the fact that ability to produce material goods does not in itself guarantee that their distribution will be appropriate enough to eliminate human deprivations within a country and between countries. Whether economic growth on Western standards can be sustained, given the finite availability of non-renewable resources, is a valid question to be asked. But a more important question relates to a fairer sharing of affluence between individuals and between countries. This requires a self-discipline (almost a self-negation after a certain level of affluence in order to enable the others to have similar affluence). Unless this happens social harmony is most likely to be threatened. This is not only likely to happen on the global level but within countries as well. With the growing pace of automation it is highly likely that the obsolescence of people and regions will increase even within countries. If robots can take over the physical chores society as a whole would be a gainer only so long as those who are displaced by robots have access to the resulting opportunities and affluence.

So far social scientists have not paid enough attention to this aspect of self-discipline.[10] As Hirsch rightly stresses:

the principle of self-interest is incomplete as a social organizing device. It operates effectively only in tandem with some supporting social principle. This fundamental characteristic of economic liberalism, which was largely taken for granted by Adam Smith and by John Stuart Mill in their different ways, has been lost sight of by its modern protagonists. While the need for modifications in laissez-faire in public policies has been increasingly accepted, the need for qualifications to self-interested behaviour by individuals has been increasingly neglected. Yet correctives to laissez-faire increase rather than decrease reliance on some degree of social orientation and social responsibility in individual behaviour. The attempt has been made to erect an increasingly explicit social organization without a supporting social morality. The result has been a structural strain on both the market mechanism and the political mechanism designed to regulate and supplement it.[20]

It is this search for a supporting social morality which can sustain our material affluence, requires increasing attention of social scientists both in the West and the East.

NOTES

1. Fred Hirsch, *Social Limits to Growth* (London, Routledge & Kegan Paul, 1977), pp. 4–5.
2. Ibid. p. 7.
3. *The Times*, 21 July 1980.
4. Radha Sinha, *Japan's Options for the 1980s* (London, Croom Helm, 1982), p. 4.
5. R. Sinha *et al. Income Distribution, Growth and Basic Needs in India* (London, Croom Helm, 1979), p. 27.
6. US–Japan Trade Council (1980) *Report No. 7*, p. 19.
7. Adam Smith, *The Theory of Moral Sentiments* (1759), (New York, Augustus Kelley, 1966), p. 327. It must, however, be noted that Adam Smith also emphasised that with economic progress a new social cohesion, in its widest sense is created. In fact, his concept of growing sympathy accompanying economic growth anticipates the modern welfare state. I am grateful to David Reisman for drawing my attention to this fact.
8. The 'lifetime employment system' does not have deep roots in the Japanese tradition – it developed around the turn of the last century.
9. Quoted in Akira Fujitake, 'Abuse of Egalitarianism', in *Japan Echo*, vol. VII (Special Issue, 1980) p. 14.
10. Other reasons, of course, increasing sophistication of the medical gadgetary and medicines. Ageing of the population itself is another cause.
11. *Sohyo News*, no. 375, 15 March 1983, p. 22.
12. Ibid.
13. Aki Goto, 'Where are Japanese Housewives Heading?', *Japan Echo*, vol. IX, no. 4 (1982) p. 107.
14. Takako Sodei, 'Family Stability in an Age of Working Women', *Japan Echo*, vol. IX, no. 4 (1982) pp. 96–7.
15. Ibid, p. 97.
16. Y. Yasuhiko, 'Analyzing Trends in Family Pathology: Trends in Family Pathology', *Japan Echo*, vol. VII, no. 3 (1980) p. 85.
17. *The Japan Times Weekly*, 11 June 1983, p. 7.
18. Ibid.
19. Social thinkers like Mahatma Gandhi clearly recognised the need for such a self-discipline. This was behind his idea of 'trusteeship'.
20. Hirsch, op. cit. p. 12.

7 Economic Development of Singapore since Self-government in 1959[1]

LIM CHONG-YAH

CONCEPTUAL FRAMEWORK

Economic development refers to the growth in economic welfare, measured though inadequately, by the growth in per capita national income, if not also by the distribution of national income.

National income refers only to the material aspects of life. It does not refer to the political, spiritual, cultural or social life of the nation, although in practice it is often difficult to separate the economic aspects of life from the other aspects, particularly in terms of cause and effect.

Human betterment, in my view, refers to an improvement in the totality of life of the country, not just the economic aspects, nor just the spiritual, cultural or political.

In other words, if human betterment consists of A, B, C, D and E as its constituents, economic development refers only to one of the component parts. However, things are not as simple as they may seem, in terms of separating the components and in terms of cause and effect among the components which are not independent parameters but interdependent variables. Moreover, to make matters more complicated, in order to be realistic in our abstraction from the matrix of a much more complicated actual world social forces, the interrelated component parts need not always move in the same direction, nor with the same speed, even if they were to move in the same direction. Put differently, economic development is helpful to human betterment involving cultural, social and political development, and vice-versa, but this relationship is not an 'iron law', a universal, perpetual truth.[2]

105

It is often stressed that economic development should take into consideration income distribution. However, income-distribution figures are often very inadequate and, if not carefully used, can be very deceptive and misleading.

Thus to measure economic development is tough enough. To measure human betterment is much tougher still. That is why there is no generally agreed quality-of-life index, as we have the GNP or GDP index to measure changes in the economic aspects of life. And without a single index, one's conclusion on human betterment or worsening can easily be misled by the statistics available or by the observations one sees. In other words, without a comprehensive quality-of-life index, one can be in danger of being like the fictional blind men and the elephant, thinking of the elephant only in terms of the part that they feel without having the gift of sight to see the elephant as a whole. The part is not the whole as the particular need not be the general, nor the general the particular.

There is more complication than that. Human betterment in many of its important aspects cannot be quantified, thus rendering objective measurement extremely difficult, if not impossible. If some people see mud and others see stars, that will be thus quite understandable. Even if all aspects of life and their changes are quantifiable, there are still the weightage problems associated with the construction of a representative index number to be solved.

Human betterment is a relative term. Thus, to be meaningful, inter-temporal comparison will have to be made, supplemented, if necessary, by inter-country comparisons.

With the above qualifications, in what follows, the paper examines the nature and courses of the economic development of Singapore and includes an appraisal of some other aspects of life in Singapore and the various economic policy options for the government since self-government in 1959.

ECONOMIC DEVELOPMENT OF SINGAPORE[3]

(I) GROWTH IN REAL GROSS DOMESTIC PRODUCT (GDP)

An assessment of the overall performance of the economy from 1960 to 1982, as measured by changes in real GDP, reveals several interesting features, as can be seen from Table 7.1 and Statistical Appendix 7.A.I.

TABLE 7.1   *Singaporean real gross domestic product growth rates, 1960–82*

Growth rates (%)	Years	Number of years
< 1	1964	1
0.1– 2		0
2.1– 4	1960, 75	2
4.1– 6		0
6.1– 8	1962, 65, 74, 76, 77, 82	6
8.1–10	1961, 78, 79, 81	4
> 10	1963, 66, 67, 68, 69, 70, 71, 72, 73, 80	10
TOTAL (–4.3% to 14.3%)	1960–82	23

SOURCE   Statistical Appendix 7.A.ı

Of note is that of the twenty-three years under review, only in one year was there negative growth or economic retrogression, namely, – 4.3 per cent in 1964. Singapore was then part of the bigger Malaysian Federation, and Indonesia, then under the late President Soekarno, was launching a policy of confrontation against Malaysia. The loss of the important entrepôt trade with Indonesia and the political uncertainties at home associated with the birth of the Federation were responsible for the retrogression. Two other years saw very slow growth rates by Singaporean standards, namely, 4.0 per cent in 1960 and also 4.0 per cent in 1975. Again, these two were abnormal years for Singapore. 1960 witnessed the first full year of self-government begun in June 1959. The extreme measures taken by the newly elected PAP government directed mainly against the entrepreneurial class, foreign and local, and the English-educated minority then, must have had their telling effects on GDP growth. The 1975 low growth was the impact of the serious global recession (stagflation, to be more correct) consequent on the quadrupling of global oil prices in late 1973, and the soaring of world food prices in the 1973–4 period.[4]

In other words, of the three negative and slow-growth years, one was the result of domestic political development (1960), the other, regional political development (1964) and the third, global economic adjustment (1975). The periods associated with these years have also been conveniently referred to respectively as periods of self-government, Indonesian confrontation and global oil crisis.

Another point of note is that, leaving aside the three abnormal years, the other twenty years all had a real growth rate exceeding 6 per cent. Indeed, in ten years, the real growth rate was double digit. For nine consecutive years since independence in 1965 Singapore had a double-digit real growth rate. This was slowed down only in the wake of the global oil crisis.

Obviously the overall performance of the economy was much more spectacular prior to the 1973–5 oil crisis period than after the period. However, if the 1960s and the 1970s were compared, the economy moved upward at roughly the same average cumulative rate for the 1960s (9.1 per cent per annum) as in the 1970s (9.0 per cent per annum). Obviously the self-government adjustment period of the 1960s and the confrontation and Malaysian formation period in the 1960s must have had a significant slowing-down effect on the economy so that both decades displayed roughly the same average growth rates, despite the slowing down of the economy during and after the oil crisis in the 1970s.

However, for comparative purposes, if we use World Bank figures, Singapore's real growth rate of 8.8 per cent in the 1960s significantly exceeded the 5.0 per cent rate for developing countries in the UN First Development Decade. Similarly, Singapore's 8.5 per cent per annum performance in the 1970s also significantly exceeded the UN Second Development Decade target of 6.0 per cent. The actual performance of middle income countries came to 5.9 per cent and 5.6 per cent for the 1960s and 1970s respectively. Similarly, the industrial market economies showed a real growth rate of only 5.2 per cent and 3.2 per cent respectively for the 1960s and 1970s. Countrywise comparison shows that Singapore's performance both in the 1960s and 1970s was among the highest in the world. Certainly, together with the other Asian NICs of South Korea, Taiwan and Hong Kong, and also with the other ASEAN countries of Indonesia, Malaysia, Philippines and Thailand, Singapore was able to significantly close the gap between her level of per capita income and those of the industrial market economies, as can be seen from the comparative real growth rates in Table 7.2

(II) GROWTH IN PER CAPITA INCOME

In 1959, at the time of self-government, Singapore had one of the highest rates of natural increase in population in the world. This rate of increase of 33.1 per 1000 population under the impact of government-

TABLE 7.2   *Comparative economic performance, 1960–82*

Country	Real GDP average annual growth (%)			
	1960–70	*1970–80*	*1981*	*1982ᵖ*
Low-income countries	4.4	4.6	n.a.	n.a.
Middle-income countries	5.9	5.6	n.a.	n.a.
Industrial market economies	5.2	3.2	1.5*	−0.5*
ASEAN				
Singapore	8.8	8.5	9.9	6.3
Indonesia	3.9	7.6	7.6	4.5
Malaysia	6.5	7.8	6.9	3.9
Philippines	5.1	6.3	3.7	2.6
Thailand	8.4	7.2	7.6	4.5
Other Asian NICs				
South Korea	8.6	9.5	6.4	6.0
Hong Kong	10.0	9.3	11.0	4.0
Taiwan	8.8	n.a.	5.5	4.0

SOURCES   World Bank, *World Development Report*, 1982 and *Economic Survey of Singapore*, 1982.

* Total OECD countries.
ᵖ preliminary.

pushed family planning policy and with rising per capita income and changing way of life, declined steadily to 11.9 per 1000 population by 1982. In terms of population growth rate the decline was from 4.1 per cent in 1959 to 1.2 per cent in 1982. This important progressive decline in population growth rate contributed to make the growth rate in real per capita income somewhat higher in the 1970s (7.4 per cent per annum), when compared with the 1960s (6.7 per cent per annum).

For the twenty-three-year period per capita income grew at a cumulative rate of 7.0 per cent per annum, compared with the corresponding growth in real GDP of 9.0 per cent per annum. Statistics on annual per capita income increase for the period are also given in Statistical Appendix 7.A.I. Compared with real per capita growth rates of other countries the Singaporean performance of 7.0 per cent per annum for the twenty-three-year period must be one of the highest in the world.[5]

(III) RESTRUCTURING OF THE ECONOMY

In Singapore economic restructuring is normally associated with the wage adjustment policy of the National Wages Council[6] for the period 1979–81. In fact, of course, restructuring is an on-going process in any dynamic economy experiencing a high rate of growth over a significantly long period. Certain low value-added economic activities are bound to give way to higher value-added economic pursuits. In terms of industrial structure, certain activities are bound to show a relative, if not absolute, decline.[7]

Over the twenty-three-year period the most important sectoral change lies in the rapid emergence of the manufacturing sector. As can be seen from the statistics in Table 7.3, whereas in 1960 that sector, in terms of current factor cost, constituted only 11.8 per cent of GDP, in 1982 it constituted 26.4 per cent, making it the largest sector in the economy. Notwithstanding the traditionally prominent position of trade, including entrepôt trade in the Singaporean economy, the trade sector as a whole in 1982 shared with the financial and business

TABLE 7.3   *Changing composition of Singaporean gross domestic product, 1960 and 1982*

Sector	Amount ($m) (at 1968 factor cost)		Percent of total (at current factor cost)	
	1960	1982	1960	1982
Agriculture and fishing	87.7	145.6	3.8	1.1
Quarrying	7.5	71.7	0.3	0.5
Manufacturing	279.7	3 013.5	11.8	26.4
Utilities	53.4	401.5	2.5	1.7
Construction	79.3	978.4	3.6	9.7
Trade	713.4	3 474.8	35.9	21.9
Transport and communication	297.6	2 942.4	14.2	13.4
Financial and business services	247.5	2 952.6	11.3	21.9
Other services	391.9	1 547.3	18.2	11.2
Less: imputed bank charges	35.7	1 309.9	1.6	7.8
TOTAL	2 122.3	14 217.9	100.0	100.0

SOURCE   Derived from statistics published in *Economic Survey of Singapore*, 1982.

services sector, the second place of 21.9 per cent in terms of contribution to current GDP.

In other words the Singaporean economy has been transformed, and this deliberately through government policy, from a largely trading economy to a manufacturing-trading economy.

Singapore also emerged as a tourist centre during this period. As late as 1971, the number of tourist arrivals was 0.6 million. In 1982 this increased to almost 3 million. The development of the tourist industry is partly reflected by the growth of new hotels in Singapore. Indeed, nearly all the well-known hotels in Singapore were built after independence in 1965.

Another important sector that has developed rapidly since independence is banking and finance. In 1968 there were only thirty-six commercial banks with a consolidated asset value of $3674 million. In 1982 the number of commercial banks increased to 118 with an asset value of $48 537 million. The total assets of the Asian Dollar Market in Singapore has now reached a value of US $103 296 million. The market came into existence in 1968.

Looking at the composition of GDP the main declining sector is trade, particularly entrepôt trade.[8] As a component of GDP trade declined from 35.9 per cent in 1960 to 21.9 per cent in 1982. The figures, of course, refer to relative composition of GDP, not to absolute figures or to external trading value. In terms of value added the absolute contribution of the trade sector indeed increased impressively, from $713 million in 1960 to $3475 million in 1982. Total external trade too expanded by leaps and bounds, from $7555 million in 1960 to $104 717 million in 1982.

Further growth of Singapore as a manufacturing centre, financial centre, tourist centre, centre of transport and communication and health-care centre can be expected. Strictly speaking the economic transformation of Singapore is not just from a largely trading economy to a manufacturing-trading economy, but, more correctly, it is from a largely trading economy to a manufacturing, trading and service economy. This is to take into account the development of Singapore as a centre of tourism, finance, insurance, transportation, communication and health-care.

The economic restructuring of Singapore in the manufacturing sector itself is worthy of further examination. The growth of the petroleum refinery industry has made Singapore the third largest refinery centre in the world, smaller only than Houston and Rotterdam.

The Singaporean manufacturing industry has without doubt under-

gone an internal structural change, from manufacturing simple products and products that require simple processes, to more sophisticated, more capital-intensive and higher-technology output (see Table
7.4). Among the expanding subsectors, in terms of labour utilisation in
manufacturing, labour intensive, low value-added activities have given
way to less labour-intensive and higher value-added activities. However, this can be said not just of the manufacturing sector, but of all the
other sectors as well.

TABLE 7.4 *Decline and expansion in manufacturing value added, 1960 and
1982*

Year Subsector	Percent of total	
	1960	*1982*
Contraction		
Food and beverages	31.0	6.3
Paper products and printing	18.6	4.6
Fabricated metal products	12.2	5.9
Wood products and furniture	8.0	2.6
Non-metallic minerals	3.9	3.2
SUBTOTAL	(73.7)	(22.6)
Expansion		
Machinery and appliances	5.6	30.9
Chemical products and petroleum	6.8	23.4
Transport equipment	5.8	11.4
Textiles and wearing apparel	3.1	4.8
Rubber and plastic products	2.3	2.5
Basic metals	1.3	1.8
Precision equipment	—	1.2
Other products	1.3	1.4
SUBTOTAL	(26.2)	(77.4)

SOURCE Derived from statistics published in *Report on the Census of Industrial Production, Singapore*, 1960, and *Economic Survey of Singapore*, 1982.

(IV) INFLATION

Global inflation today has abated somewhat. Until recently it was
rampant. The main cause is controversial. Milton Friedman would
attribute all inflation to an over-supply of money.[9] Others, such as

Wassily Leontief, would treat inflation as a social phenomenon.[10] The writer subscribes to the eclectic, many-causes theory of inflation. In other words inflation can have many causes, including an over-supply of money and a weakness in social structure. It can also be caused, *inter alia*, by rising import prices. More specifically, the galloping global inflation of the early 1970s was mainly caused by the oil crisis and the food crisis. The precipitous rise in the price of oil was due to a decision by OPEC and that of food was due to several serious food crop failures, particularly in Russia.

Not surprisingly, when the inflation statistics in Singapore are examined, only in two years out of twenty-two was the rate of inflation double-digit. Indeed, it was 19.6 per cent in 1973 and 22.3 per cent in 1974. The cause was simple: very much higher prices of imported fuel and food. Singapore, being a city-state with 618 square kilometres of land and 2.5 million people, has to import a large part of almost everything if she wants to maintain her present standard of living of having a per capita indigenous GNP of roughly $10 061.[11] She imports the bulk of her food supply and all her fuel supply. Since global fuel and food prices are given to her, inflation is easily imported. The policy in Singapore has been to allow global prices to be reflected in domestic prices. This is very much more so for fuel. For several essential foodstuffs, such as rice, the government has a rotating stockpiling programme which can act as a moderating buffer mechanism for short-term price changes.

Indeed a domestically generated cost-push inflation in Singapore can take place but, given a very high foreign leakage, will take largely the form of reducing the competitive edge of Singapore's exports and increasing the volume of her imports. So long as the balance-of-payments position continues to be in surplus, however, this deterioration in export competitiveness does not necessarily result in the external depreciation of the Singapore dollar. The Singapore dollar has remained very strong mainly because of long-term capital inflow. Its strength, however, also contributes to the lower inflation rates in Singapore due to lower import costs in domestic currency.

If the statistics in Table 7.1 and Table 7.5 are compared it will be found that the actual growth-rate figures skew heavily to the high side, whereas the inflation-rate figures concentrate heavily on the low side. The two sets of figures show that, for the period of twenty-three years under study, Singapore had, on the whole, very high growth rates with moderately low rates of inflation. Using World Bank figures, for the 1960s the average inflation rate in Singapore was 1.1 per cent com-

TABLE 7.5   *Singaporean inflation rates 1961–82*

CPI rates	Years	Number of years
<0	1969, 76	2
0.1– 2	1961, 62, 64, 65, 66, 68, 70, 71	8
2.1– 4	1963, 67, 72, 75, 77, 79, 82	7
4.1– 6	1978	1
6.1– 8		0
8.1–10	1980, 81	2
>10	1973, 74	2
TOTAL (−1.9 to 22.3)	1961–82	22

SOURCE   Statistical Appendix 7.A.I

pared with the 4.3 per cent rate for industrial market economies as a whole.[12] For the 1970s the average rate of inflation in Singapore was 5.1 per cent compared with the 9.7 per cent average for industrial market economies, 13.2 per cent for middle-income countries and 11.2 per cent for low-income countries.

Note that, in the discussion, neither government inflationary financing nor the growth of money supply has been discussed as causal factors of inflation rates in Singapore. The former cause is not applicable, as there has been no government inflationary financing. The latter is unimportant. Money supply in Singapore merely reacts to the demand for money by the private sector. The government has not created money to finance its expenditure.

(V) INCOME DISTRIBUTION

The growth of real income is important, particularly for a developing country. The equitable sharing of the fruits of growth is important too. Normally, when per capita real income rises, one can assume that the majority, if not all, of the population will benefit directly or indirectly, unless the rise in income is concentrated in the hands of a minority and not of a widespread nature. In Singapore all indications point definitely to the widespread generation of income. A single comprehensive and reliable index on income distribution for the twenty-three-year period from 1960 to 1982 is not available. An up-to-date income-distribution index is also not available. Evidence on the sharing of the fruits of growth will thus be discussed instead under three broad headings, namely, (a) unemployment, (b) housing and (c) wages. The inflation factor has really been taken care of when inflation adjusted per capita income figures are used. Real GDP per capita, it may be recalled, grew at a compound rate of 7.0 per cent per annum over the twenty-three-year period.

(a) *Unemployment*   The reduction of unemployment is one of the best ways of combating poverty, particularly in a society like Singapore, where there is no system of unemployment benefits, as a deliberate policy option. Unemployment means zero-wage income. The level of unemployment was very high in 1959, estimated at about 10 per cent. The unemployment level decreased particularly spectacularly after independence in 1965. Even as late as 1966, according to official statistics, the unemployment level was still at 8.7 per cent. This dropped to 2.6 per cent in 1982. This is contrary to the mounting unemployment levels in most industrial countries. For many years not only did Singapore not have an unemployment problem, it had the problem of labour shortage, particularly acute in some sectors, necessitating the import of thousands of guest workers not only from Malaysia, Indonesia, Philippines and Thailand, but also from India, Bangladesh, Sri Lanka and South Korea. Employment-creation each year has far exceeded the new domestic supply of labour, necessitating also the adoption of a deliberate policy to promote mechanisation and to introduce other incentives to increase the optimum rationalisation of labour usage.[13]

If stagflation means inflationary recession with mounting unemployment, then there is no such phenomenon in Singapore. Inflation rate is low and growth rate is still high by world standards. Most probably for 1983 Singapore would still be able to have a real growth of between 4 per cent and 6 per cent. In 1982 the growth rate was 6.3 per cent and in 1981 9.9 per cent.

(b) *Housing*   Housing is an important index of the quality of life in any society. In Singapore, by 1982, 75.0 per cent of the population were housed in government-built flats. Home ownership of such flats too has increased, as stated earlier, rising to the 1982 level of 66.1 per cent.

As can be seen in Table 7.6 the percentage of households living in public flats with four rooms or five rooms increased from 9.5 per cent in 1960 to 23.9 per cent in 1982. However, the percentage of households living in one-room flats has increased from 6.4 per cent in 1960 to 16.3 per cent in 1982, pointing to a deterioration in the quality of

TABLE 7.6 *Growth and nature of public housing*

Public flats	1960 Number of flats	1960 Per cent of total	1970 Number of flats	1970 Percent of total	1980 Number of flats	1980 Percent of total	1982* Number of flats	1982* Percent of total
1-room flats	1 397	6.4	40 781	34.4	66 910	19.2	65 257	16.3
2-room flats	6 911	31.5	28 983	24.4	47 237	13.5	48 634	12.1
3-room flats	11 571	52.7	45 992	38.8	162 483	46.6	191 063	47.7
4- or 5-room flats	2 089	9.5	2 788	2.4	72 285	20.7	95 702	23.9
TOTAL	21 968	100.0	118 544	100.0	348 915	100.0	400 656	100.0

SOURCE *Yearbook of Statistics, Singapore*, various issues.

* Prior to 1982, figures only include Housing and Development board flats. 1982 figures also include units managed by Jurong Town Corporation and Housing and Urban Development Company.

public housing. But if the 1970 statistics are used, instead of the 1960 figures, it will be found that in 1970 34.3 per cent of the occupants lived in one-room flats and this percentage decreased to 16.3 per cent by 1982. Obviously between 1960 and 1970, in a rush to clear slums and to provide public housing as quickly as possible, more smaller-sized flats were built, but the position has changed since then. As per capita income level rose the demand for better and bigger flats became more apparent and the government responded to this change in demand, as reflected in the housing statistics in the 1970s and in recent years.

(c) *Wages* This is a subject particularly close to the heart of the writer, as since 1972 when the National Wages Council (NWC) was formed, he has been chairman of this tripartite body. The NWC recommends a wage-increase guideline each year and the guideline is widely accepted and implemented in Singapore. However, as this paper is not on the NWC and to keep this subsection in proportion, only some wage statistics will be used, and only a limited discussion is deliberately resorted to.

Table 7.7 shows that wage rates in all sectors, as expected, have increased remarkably, the national wage average cumulative growth rate being 10.9 per cent per year for 1972–82. These wage rates, however, have not taken into consideration the compulsory contributions by employers to the individual accounts of their workers in the

TABLE 7.7 *Growth of average weekly earnings by industry, 1972–82*

Industry	Year 1972 $	1982 $	Growth rate (%) 1972–82
Agriculture and fishing	55.4	194.0	13.3
Quarrying	69.1	378.3	18.5
Manufacturing	63.2	172.6	10.6
Utilities	80.5	254.9	12.2
Construction	77.6	205.5	10.3
Trade	68.5	204.6	11.5
Transport and communication	84.7	232.8	10.7
Financial and business services	108.9	271.7	9.5
Other services	86.8	254.3	11.4
ALL INDUSTRIES	75.6	212.3	10.9

SOURCE *Yearbook of Statistics, Singapore*, 1980 and 1982.

TABLE 7.8 *Contributors to the Central Provident Fund by wage level 1965, 1975 and 1982 (at end of period)*

	1965		1975		1982	
Monthly wage level	Number ('000)	%	Number ('000)	%	Number ('000)	%
Below $100	44.0	17.2	24.0	3.7	7.9	0.9
$100 to under $200	117.2	45.7	117.5	18.1	60.8	6.6
$200 to under $300	45.8	17.9	162.1	25.0	81.7	8.8
$300 to under $400	17.6	6.9	93.1	14.4	108.2	11.7
$400 to under $500	10.7	4.2	62.2	9.6	119.1	12.8
$500 and over	20.8	8.1	188.5	27.8	549.8	59.3
$500 to $1000	(n.a.)	(n.a.)	(128.8)	(19.9)	(310.4)	(33.5)
$1000 and over	(n.a.)	(n.a.)	(59.7)	(7.9)	(239.4)	(25.8)
TOTAL	256.1	100.0	647.4	100.0	927.5	100.0

SOURCE *Yearbook of Statistics, Singapore*, various issues.

Central Provident Fund (CPF). Such contributions rose 12 per cent of each worker's monthly basic wage in 1972 to 23 per cent at present.

Also, as can be seen from Table 7.8, in 1965 (earlier figures are not readily available), only 8.1 per cent of the contributors to the CPF earned $500 or more per month. In 1982 59.3 per cent earned $500 or more per month. As late as 1975 only 7.9 per cent of the contributors earned $1000 or more per month. This figure increased to 25.8 per cent by 1982. Of note too is that, in 1965, 62.9 per cent of the CPF contributors earned $200 or less per month. In 1982 only 7.5 per cent earned $200 or less per month.

Theoretically, real wages can rise, the population can have a higher rate of savings and better housing, but the country can become poorer either through the depletion of irreplaceable natural resources or through the depletion of foreign reserves. Singapore has no irreplaceable natural resources, such as oil, tin or uranium to speak of. Her foreign exchange reserves are such that, in terms of both nominal and effective exchange rates,[14] her currency has appreciated against nearly all major currencies in the world, except the Swiss franc and the Netherlands guilder, when compared with the Smithsonian (cross) parity agreed in December 1971.

(VI) OTHER ASPECTS OF HUMAN BETTERMENT

Let us now turn to some other aspects of life in Singapore, to have a glance at changes in its quality. Discussion will be centred only on six broad facets of life under the headings of (a) health, (b) crimes, (c) education, (d) culture, (e) labour welfare, and (f) self-reliance (see Statistical Appendix 7.A.II). Shortness of time does not permit me to go into other areas. This is not because the omitted areas are not important or not interesting.

(a) *Health* First, let us look at the infant mortality rate. This has declined from 34.9 per 1000 live births in 1960 to 20.5 in 1970 and declined further to 10.8 in 1982 (see Statistical Appendix 7.A.II). Although we are a less-developed country, our infant mortality rate is lower than those of many developed countries, including England and Wales, Australia, New Zealand and the US.

Secondly, let us look at the longevity-of-life figures. These are referred to as mean expectations of life at birth. For 1957 it was 60.3 years for males and 65.2 years for females. For 1980 the latest figures available, the mean expectation of life increased to 68.7 and 74.0 respectively. In other words the males and females all live longer by an average of 5.3 years between 1957 and 1980. Male Singaporeans have a mean expectation of life at birth of 69 years. They are quite blessed though, considering most African males cannot even make it past 50. Male citizens in Upper Volta, for example, have a life-expectancy of only 39.

Third, let us look at the health of school children in Singapore, her dearest possession since she has no natural resources to boast about. According to yearly check-ups by the Ministry of Health, the incidence of dental caries, skin infection, eye infection, ear infection, respiratory infection, anaemia, worm infection and other common ailments bothering children have all shown very perceptible declines. This is true of both male and female school children. For the boys, for example, between 1966 and 1982, the incidence of dental caries declined from 30.7 per cent of total examined to 7.2 per cent, for skin infection, the corresponding decline was from 4.2 per cent to 2.8 per cent and for worm infection, it was from 5.7 per cent to 0.0 per cent. In other words our school children are certainly, on the whole, much healthier than they were before; however, one must quickly hasten to add that the only remarkable deterioration among our school children of both sexes is in eye vision. The incidence of defective eye vision for the boys, for example, increased from 9.1 per cent of the total examined in 1966 to 17.2 per cent in 1971 and 31.6 per cent in 1982.

(b) *Crimes*   The total number of offences against persons and property have shown an increasing trend from 75 per 10 000 population in 1967 to 114 in 1982. During this period an average of 54 persons per year were murdered. Rape cases are always there each year; in 1967 there were 4.9 cases per 100 000 females and this increased to 6.4 in 1982. Cases of outraging modesty too increased from 11.9 per 100 000 females in 1967 to a record high of 36.1 in 1982. So it appears that Singapore women are less safe now than they were before. Actual suicides nearly doubled from 5.1 per 100 000 population in 1969 to 9.7 in 1982. In other words, at present, about one suicide is committed every other day. On the other hand, the number of robberies per 100 000 population have fallen significantly from 68 in 1970 to 52 in 1982.

(c) *Education*   In Singapore primary school education commences at the age of six. Adult literacy rate reached 84.8 per cent in 1982, up from 72.2 per cent in 1970. Enrolment in university and colleges has increased threefold during the period 1960 to 1982. Important disciplines like Law, Engineering, Accountancy, Business Administration, Architecture, Estate Management and Computer Science, which were not available before are now established departments and faculties at the university. Indeed education in Singapore is very much tailored to the needs of our economic and social development. Emphasis is placed on acquisition of knowledge and development in science, technology and business. In order to foster greater communication and social cohesion in a multi-racial, multi-lingual and multi-religious society, students are required to be fluent in reading and writing at least two languages. Besides, all Singaporeans, irrespective of sex or family background, have an equal opportunity to be admitted to tertiary institutions of learning, selection being based on merit alone.

Equally important is that education goes beyond the formal years of schooling. School drop-outs have been trained in appropriate skills to equip them for more productive work in industry. Similarly, those in employment have also been given incentives to acquire better skills, particularly through the efforts of the Skills Development Fund. Singapore is singularly proud of the success of her family planning or population control programme which is very much accredited to a comprehensive social education programme.

(d) *Culture* The total private national expenditure on 'recreation, entertainment, education and cultural services' increased by 531 per cent between 1966 and 1982, much more than the average increase in total national private consumption expenditure of about 260 per cent. In other words, with increasing affluence there has also been a shift in the relative composition of private expenditure in favour of 'recreation, entertainment, education and cultural services', the so-called 'superior goods'. Radio and television licences shot up by more than ten times and the number of telephones increased by more than eight times from 1963 to 1982. The proportion of air-conditioned cinemas in the country increased from 42 per cent in 1966 to 88 per cent in 1982, again reflecting the change in the level of comfort which Singapore cinema-goers want, due no doubt again to the increase in material affluence.

(e) *Labour welfare* Unemployment, which is still a very serious problem in many societies, developing as well as developed societies, has steadily declined to the lowest level of 2.6 per cent in Singapore in 1982 from a recorded height of 8.7 per cent in 1966. How can one speak of improvement in the quality of life if one has mounting serious unemployment? Unemployment is not just the deprivation of wage income, but in its prolonged form, the deprivation of human dignity, and is especially serious in a society where there is no unemployment benefit.

If industrial stoppages or strikes are an extreme expression of dissatisfaction of working conditions including wage payment, then again Singapore has fared very well on this score. In 1966, for example, the number of man-days lost due to industrial stoppages was slightly less than 45 000 and this dropped to slightly above 18 000 in 1972 and dropped further to a negligible figure since 1978.

(f) *Self-reliance* As a society Singapore has become much more self-reliant. For better or for worse, after independence, she has learned to look after herself. The quality of life must also take into consideration to what extent she has been preparing herself against external aggression. Here, with her national service system, her young men have contributed so much of themselves to make this country much safer for Singaporeans.

If we look at the blood donation figures, we can be quite impressed too. The number of blood donors increased from about 13 000 in 1966 to 39 448 in 1982. Similarly, blood donations received increased from about 24 000 units in 1966 to 59 711 units in 1982.

(VII) ECONOMIC POLICY OPTIONS

(a) *National size and economic development* When Singapore became an independent political entity it was feared that Singapore would not be economically viable because she was small. Now that she has succeeded, it is at times said that she has succeeded because she is small.

In my view and in my study of economic development the size of a nation is not the crucial determinant whether that nation will develop economically or not. If small population size is a *sine qua non* to success then the forty-one nations that have a population size smaller than Singapore's population of 2.5 million would have a much higher level of per capita income than Singapore. This, however, is not the case. Of the forty-one countries, only six have a per capita income higher than that of Singapore, and of these six, four are oil-rich countries. The countries that are smaller in population size but have a much lower level of per capita income ranging from US $80 to US $800, as compared with Singapore's US $4430 (1980 figures), include Bhutan, Central African Republic, Yemen, Liberia, Togo, Mauritania, Equatorial Guinea, Western Samoa, Solomon Islands, Dominica, Guyana, Gambia, Grenada, Swaziland, Botswana and St Lucia. Most of these countries have a mean expectation of life at birth of below 50, compared with Singapore's 71.

If big population size is a *sine qua non* to economic success, then India and China, to name but two countries, would have a much higher level of per capita income than they have at present. The fact is that there are small nations that are rich and there are also small nations that are poor. Similarly there are big nations (the USA, for example) or middle-sized nations (West Germany, for example) that are rich, and there are also big or middle-sized nations that are poor. The fact is that there is simply no simple direct correlation between nation size and the level of economic development.

The purpose of this article is not, however, to provide a theory of economic development. That has its place elsewhere. Its purpose is to discuss the Singaporean development experience. Whether or not this experience provides any insight on the development experiences of other developing countries is completely a different matter. Every country is unique in its own way. No two countries are indeed exactly alike. Mere extrapolation of policy options or experiences thus can be very dangerous. Adaptation of ideas is different. One simple model doctrine for the world is the preserve of the fundamentalists as well as the neo-imperialists, both in the Communist and non-Communist world. The writer has no desire to advocate a holier-than-thou approach.

(b) *Priorities and economic development*   In Singapore the initial top economic priority following self-government was job-creation and slum-clearance. The serious Communist challenge then added to the urgency and importance of these twin-tasks ahead.

Industrialisation was the strategy adopted for job-creation. Not only did the traditional entrepôt trade not offer much scope for job-creation, there was also the fear that entrepôt trade would suffer a serious decline, with the understandably increasing desire to have direct trading between neighbouring countries and countries outside the region.

To have a successful industrialisation programme, various supportive and related programmes had to be adjusted accordingly. For one thing the economic environment conducive to industrial investment, both foreign and local, had to be created. Implied in this was a programme to build up the economic infrastructure of the country, including industrial estates, road networks, water and electricity supply, communication and port services and other facilities to permit the speedier flow of inputs of industrial raw materials and outputs of manufactured or semi-manufactured goods. Statistical facts show beyond a doubt that the government has succeeded in creating this environment conducive to not only rapid growth in the manufacturing sector, but also rapid growth in the other sectors.

(c) *Distribution and economic development*   On the social front there was the initial need to emphasise wage restraint in order to make Singapore an attractive place for investment, for it was with more investment that more jobs could be created. It was only after the successful programme of job-creation largely through industrialisation that the issue of sharing the growth in the wealth of the nation was seriously looked into. The National Wages Council, for example, was set up only in early 1972, when large-scale unemployment was no longer a problem. It was also after more than enough jobs had been created that there was the incessant talk about job-upgrading, higher skills acquisition, organisational improvement, mechanisation, computerisation and other ways and means of using less labour input to raise output. It was only after enough jobs had been created that the industrialisation strategy switched from any job to better jobs, from labour-intensive, low value-added pursuits to higher value-added, higher-technology and more skill-intensive economic activities.

(d) *Comparative advantage and economic development*   To remain competitive, products and services should meet the challenge of open international competition through imports and exports. The adoption of this policy ensures only strong economic plants find their roots in Singapore, not plants that have to be supported by state crutches.

The pursuance of this export-orientated policy ensures that only economic activities in which Singapore has a comparative advantage would be located in Singapore. A deliberate policy of autarchy or self-sufficiency or that of protectionism would have meant a less-competitive, less-viable economy. That Singapore continues to import from the cheapest world markets also ensures cheaper inputs, besides keeping the rate of inflation of consumer goods low. This policy also ensures that besides competitive prices, more options are available to producers and consumers in terms of the range, the quantity and the quality of goods.

(e) *Private interests and economic development*   Throughout, too, there has been the realisation that both private and public enterprises can play a very useful role in economic development. And more often than not, the state acts as a supporter, promoter and catalyst in this quest for economic upgrading.

Where private enterprise is slow to deliver the goods, such as in housing particularly in the early stages, the government stepped in to supplement the effort. International trade, however, has almost completely been operated by private enterprise, and so have retail trading and manufacturing activities. Government has not, however, opted itself out by ideology to participate in any line of economic pursuits, if in its calculation, it considers it in the interest of the country to do so.

It must be added that since public and private enterprises draw from the same catchment of manpower resource and since both operate under the same politico-socio-economic environment, by and large, the performance of both sectors do not differ that much. The thesis that the public sector must of necessity be less efficient has no validity in Singapore. This is due to the existence of a clean and efficient government at the helm. Its task, however, has no doubt been facilitated by the small size of Singapore. The economically weaker brethren in both sectors have to disappear and have disappeared without undue fuss.

(f) *Ideologies and economic development*   Singapore is not shackled by any particular ideology or dogma. This to me is one of Singapore's greatest assets. She is free to choose the best from political-economic doctrines that can help to bring about a better life for Singaporeans. Thus, she does not have to follow only Keynesian or monetarist dogmas. Neither must she follow Marxist class conflicts. She is free to draw the best from Keynes, Schumpeter, Adam Smith, Thomas Malthus, Milton Friedman, John Hicks, Wassily Leontief, Gunnar Myrdal and from others, and from practices that have no convenient name tags.

The main policy guideline is rationality, not ideology. It is pragmatism. The acid test is whether or not the policy can work in the special context of Singapore. Will it stifle individual initiative, imagination, enterprise and innovation? Will it increase the level and quality of exports? Will it increase the level of efficiency of the Singaporean society and improve the quality of life of the people? The economic policy is non-denominational and ecumenical. The policy options are not automatically circumscribed by ideology.

(g) *Comprehensive planning and economic development*   If Singapore had resorted to a comprehensive planning system and the inevitable rigidities and bureaucratic controls that went with it, this chapter would undoubtedly be a study of mass poverty and deprivation instead of a study of successful economic development. This does not imply that there is no planning in Singapore. There is always project planning, whether in the private or public sector. There is planning by institutions. There is planning by individuals and companies. There is also budgetary planning by the Ministry of Finance. There are also frequent government statements on objectives and aims. There are also more frequent government exhortations, if not lectures, on how to achieve such objectives and aims. There is, however, no comprehensive Plan, no Ministry of Planning and no Planning Commission. There is no supreme body that lays down detailed iron-rules and activities that must be carried out covering every facet of human life for the next five or ten years. Such rigidities and the need for a gargantuan bureaucracy would have, without doubt, brought the Singapore economy to a standstill and Singapore's international trade, which stands at US $43 384 million, exceeding, by way of comparison of magnitude only, that of India, Pakistan, Bangladesh, Sri Lanka and Burma combined (US $34 466 million), to a complete insignificance.

Similarly, if Singapore had followed slavishly the monetarist approach Singapore today would be characterised by self-created large-scale unemployment, bankruptcies and falling output instead of still widespread labour shortage and an unprecedented construction boom. Faced with global recession the rational approach obviously is more investment, not further contraction, as is unfortunately done in some countries. Monetarism is only good for a country that has long practised a permissive monetary policy. It is good for a country that has serious inflation caused by an over-supply of money. Singapore is not one of such countries.

(h) *Government and economic development* Singapore has been singularly fortunate in that throughout the twenty-three years she has been ruled by one government (the PAP government) and this government had to seek and obtained the general mandate from the people in 1959, 1963, 1968, 1972, 1976 and 1980. A strong and stable government, ruling with general consent, has thus been in existence throughout the period. Political stability has allowed attention to be concentrated on solving problems. It has allowed a co-operative syndrome to develop in Singapore in place of the antagonisms and strifes of the pre-independence period, particularly the pre-self-government era.

Society is built by man, not by natural resources. Ultimately it is the quality of the people, particularly the quality of its leaders, that decides the tone and texture of that society. Singapore too has been singularly fortunate in that it has its quota of able and dedicated men at the helm, without which the spectacular achievemments described earlier would not have been possible. In addition, it must be added that the attitude and priority of the leaders also played a decisive role in steering the main course of action of the country. In short, if one has Hitler as one's Prime Minister, one must not expect love for peace or for the Jews. If one has Ayatollah Khomeini as one's Prime Minister, one must not expect emphasis on material achievements, certainly not for this life. If one has the Gang of Four at the apex of power, then one has to expect the advocacy of pure Communist romanticism, not economic development. But if one has pragmatic leaders all out to promote the welfare of the people for this life and blessed with the ability to do so, not just the determination, then one should not be that surprised if a high quality of life, including material affluence, is achieved. Nations, like men, normally reap what they sow. The only difference between nations and individual men is that one can trace the results of individual efforts or misdoings much more easily than their individual contribution or lack of contribution to the nature and policy of a nation. Everybody's business, it is well said, is nobody's business. If state business is nobody's business and state finance is nobody's finance, then the country is on the road to ruin.

In short, Singapore has been able to develop most impressively for the period, because of the existence of a good and able, although not faultless, government that has been providing the leadership and choosing the right basic policy options and priorities for the country. The existence of a responsive, hard-working, achievement-orientated people, the strategic location of Singapore and the existence of a good trading tradition and institutional base are, of course, also important factors, but ultimately it is the cook that determines the quality of the cooking, not the ingredients. If one crucial determinant is to be singled out on which the quality of the future Singaporean society depends, in my view, for Singapore it will continue to be, without doubt, the quality of the government.

NOTES

1. The writer wishes to thank Miss Tan Lin-Yeok, Senior Tutor of the Department of Economics and Statistics, National University of Singapore, for her assistance in the preparation of this paper.
2. See Morris David Harris, *Measuring the Condition of the World's Poor*, p. 3: 'While there is some general correlation between levels of per capita income and longevity, health, literacy etc., the relationships in specific countries are not obvious. However, there are striking exceptions'. (Oxford: Pergamon Press, 1979.)
3. All '$' in the text and Appendices denote Singapore dollars, unless otherwise specified. At the time of writing, the Singapore dollar is equivalent to US $0.47.
4. For a more detailed discussion by the writer on global stagflation during this period and its impact on Singapore, see 'Singapore and the World Economic Crisis', in Lim Chong-Yah, *Economic Development in Singapore* (Singapore: Federal Publications, 1980).
5. For comparative statistics by country, see World Bank, *World Development Report*, 1982, pp. 110–11.
6. See Lim Chong-Yah, 'The NWC as I See It', in NTUC, *Our Heritage and Beyond* (Singapore, 1982) pp. 52–9.

7. For more discussion on economic restructuring in Singapore in more recent years, see 'Restructuring the Singapore Economy' and 'Economic Restructuring in Singapore', in Lim Chong-Yah, op. cit. pp. 134–47.

8. In 1960, exports of primary commodities, excluding fuels, minerals and metals, constituted 73 per cent of total merchandise exports. In 1982 this declined to about 14 per cent.

9. See Milton Friedman and Rose Friedman, *Free to Choose* (London: Secker & Warburg, 1980), particularly chap. 9.

10. Based on discussion with Professor Leontief, who visited Singapore in 1982 at the invitation of the Economic Society of Singapore.

11. This is equivalent to about US $4729.

12. World Bank, op. cit. table 1.

13. The writer had the privilege of serving as the first Chairman of the Singapore Skills Development Fund Advisory Council, in short, SDF. The main functions of the SDF are to promote skills training, mechanisation, computerisation and rationalisation in the use of labour.

14. This is true whether the effective exchange rate is trade-weighted, export-weighted or import-weighted.

STATISTICAL APPENDIX 7.A.I Economic indicators, Singapore, 1959–82

(1)	(2)	(3)	(4)	(5) Population					(6)	(7)	(8)	(9)	(10)
Year	Gross Domestic Product (at current factor cost)	Gross Domestic Product (at constant 1968 factor cost) annual growth rate	Per Capita Gross Domestic Product (at constant 1968 factor cost) annual growth rate	(a) Mid-year estimates	(b) Annual growth rate	(c) Crude birth-rate	(d) Crude death-rate	(e) Rate of natural increase	CPI Annual growth rate	Unemployment	Official foreign reserves	Total merchandise trade 1	Total value of manufacturing output 2
	$ million	%	%	'000	%	per 1000 population			%	% of labour force	$ million	$ million	$ million
1959	1910e	n.a.	n.a.	1590	4.1	39.5	6.4	33.1	n.a.	10e	n.a.	7348.7	n.a.
1960	1985	4.0	0.5	1646	3.5	37.8	6.2	31.6	n.a.	n.a.	n.a.	7554.8	1667.1
1961	2153	8.5	4.9	1703	3.4	35.5	5.9	29.6	0.2	n.a.	n.a.	7271.5	1415.0
1962	2328	7.1	4.1	1752	2.8	34.0	5.9	28.2	0.7	n.a.	n.a.	7452.6	1740.7
1963	2594	10.5	7.8	1795	2.4	33.5	5.7	27.8	2.2	n.a.	n.a.	7753.6	1591.9
1964	2504	-4.3	-6.8	1842	2.6	32.0	5.7	26.3	1.4	n.a.	n.a.	6250.6	1544.9
1965	2707	6.6	4.1	1887	2.5	29.9	5.5	24.1	0.3	n.a.	1068.6	6811.3	1686.0
1966	3037	10.6	7.9	1934	2.5	28.3	5.4	22.9	1.9	8.7	1207.3	7439.3	1979.9
1967	3445	13.0	10.5	1978	2.2	25.6	5.3	20.2	3.3	8.1	1517.2	7896.9	2254.0
1968	3971	14.3	12.4	2012	1.7	23.5	5.5	18.0	0.7	7.3	2180.7	8974.5	2806.2
1969	4610	13.4	11.7	2043	1.5	21.8	5.0	16.8	-0.3	6.7	2530.5	10984.3	4290.8
1970	5320	13.4	11.7	2075	1.7	22.1	5.2	17.0	0.4	6.0	3097.9	12289.6	4627.2
1971	6279	12.5	10.5	2113	1.8	22.3	5.4	16.9	1.9	4.8	4094.8	14035.3	5288.8
1972	7254	13.3	11.3	2152	1.9	23.1	5.4	17.7	2.1	4.7	4929.9	15687.3	6126.7
1973	9438	11.1	9.2	2193	1.8	22.0	5.4	16.6	19.6	4.5	5800.1	21419.6	8705.6
1974	11738	6.8	5.0	2230	1.6	19.4	5.2	14.2	22.3	4.0	6502.9	34559.4	14237.0
1975	12507	4.0	2.4	2263	1.4	17.7	5.1	12.6	2.6	4.5	7486.0	32028.3	13197.4
1976	13586	7.2	5.8	2293	1.4	18.7	5.1	13.6	-1.9	4.5	8261.5	38670.4	16175.0
1977	14847	7.8	6.3	2325	1.3	16.5	5.1	11.4	3.2	3.9	9022.9	45612.2	18293.5
1978	16382	8.6	7.3	2354	1.2	16.8	5.1	11.6	4.8	3.6	11473.8	52586.8	20492.3

continued overleaf

130

STATISTICAL APPENDIX 7.A.1 Economic indicators, Singapore, 1959–82

(1)	(2)	(3)	(4)	(5) Population					(6)	(7)	(8)	(9)	(10)
	Gross Domestic Product (at current factor cost)	Gross Domestic Product (at constant 1968 factor cost) annual growth rate	Per Capita Gross Domestic Product (at constant 1968 factor cost) annual growth rate	(a) Mid-year estimates	(b) Annual growth rate	(c) Crude birth rate	(d) Crude death rate	(e) Rate of natural increase	CPI Annual growth rate	Unemployment	Official foreign reserves	Total merchandise trade 1	Total value of manufacturing output 2
Year	$ million	%	%	'000	%			per 1000 population	%	% of labour force	$ million	$ million	$ million
1979	18905	9.3	8.0	2384	1.3	17.1	5.2	11.9	4.0	3.4	12562.4	69274.5	26331.0
1980	22382	10.2	8.9	2414	1.2	17.1	5.2	11.9	8.5	3.5	13757.7	92797.1	32805.8
1981	26196	9.9	8.6	2443	1.2	17.3	5.3	12.0	8.2	2.9	15491.1	102538.8	37559.7
1982p	28907	6.3	5.1	2472	1.2	17.1	5.2	11.9	3.9	2.6	17917.9	104717.4	36087.9
1960–70		9.1	6.7		2.3				1.0				
1970–80		9.0	7.4		1.5				6.4				
1980–82		9.0	7.0		1.9				4.0				

SOURCES Compiled from Economic Survey of Singapore and Yearbook of Statistics, Singapore, various issues.

1 Since 1963 trade figures do not include trade with Indonesia.
2 Establishment engaging ten or more workers. Data include rubber processing and granite quarrying.
e estimated.
p preliminary.

STATISTICAL APPENDIX 7.A.II Social indicators of development, Singapore, 1960–82

	Health		Education		Communication		Public housing*			Crimes
	Infant mortality rate (per 1000 live births)	Persons per doctor (no.)	Literacy rate (per cent)	Enrolment in universities and colleges (per 1000 population)	Radio and TV licences (per 1000 population)	Telephones (per 1000 population)	Total no. public flats	% population living in public flats	% population living in owner-occupied public flats	Offences against persons and property (per 10 000 population)
1960	34.9	2553	–	–	–	–	21 968	9.1	..	–
1961	32.2	2530	–	–	–	–	26 168	11.4	..	–
1962	31.2	2400	–	5.8	–	–	37 374	15.3	..	–
1963	28.1	2225	–	6.7	17	42	43 889	18.3	..	–
1964	29.9	2047	–	7.0	30	43	54 312	21.1	..	–
1965	26.3	2029	–	7.4	33	46	69 660	23.2	..	–
1966	25.8	1956	–	6.9	43	49	80 915	24.4	..	–
1967	24.8	1799	–	6.7	49	54	84 683	25.9	1.7	75
1968	23.4	1736	–	6.3	56	59	95 573	29.0	4.4	71
1969	20.9	1536	–	6.2	64	66	108 823	32.0	7.1	66
1970	20.5	1522	72.2	6.6	76	78	118 544	34.6	9.1	68
1971	20.1	1390	73.3	6.8	85	90	126 710	37.4	11.0	79
1972	19.2	1457	74.4	7.1	95	102	138 027	41.6	13.6	67
1973	20.3	1401	75.6	7.7	105	114	161 312	42.7	16.2	70
1974	16.8	1406	76.7	8.0	113	126	185 581	45.6	18.5	74
1975	13.9	1395	77.9	8.2	124	141	211 079	50.0	21.4	67
1976	11.6	1345	79.1	9.0	135	163	236 966	55.0	25.7	63
1977	12.4	1259	80.3	8.9	142	196	274 048	59.0	31.3	71
1978	12.6	1265	81.5	8.7	150	229	305 540	64.0	35.2	71
1979	13.2	1287	82.8	8.7	156	262	328 562	66.0	38.4	80
1980	11.7	1222	84.0	9.3	165	291	346 371	68.0	42.0	91
1981	10.7	1168	84.2	9.9	170	317	356 291	69.0	43.7	107
1982	10.8	1111	84.8	10.8	172	345	399 935	75.0	49.4	114

SOURCE Department of Statistics, *Yearbook of Statistics Singapore*, various years.

*Prior to 1982 figures only include Housing and Development Board flats. In 1982 figures also include flats managed by Jurong Town Corporation and Housing and Urban Development Company.

.. = not available.   – = negligible or nil.

8 The Concept of Human Betterment

ANTONY FLEW

1. A STRATEGY OF INDIRECT APPROACH

Dugald Stewart, in his *Account of the Life and Writings of Adam Smith, LL.D.*, is led 'to remark a very striking contrast between the spirit of ancient and modern policy in respect to the wealth of nations. The great object of the former was to counteract the love of money and a taste for luxury, by positive institutions; and to maintain in the great body of the people, habits of frugality, and a severity of manners. The decline of states is uniformly ascribed by the philosophers and historians, both of Greece and Rome, to the influence of riches on national character. . . .' But now, Stewart exclaims: 'How opposite to this is the doctrine of modern politicians! Far from considering poverty as an advantage to a state, their great aim is to open new sources of national opulence, and to animate the activity of all classes of the people, by a taste for the comforts and accommodations of life.'[1]

Having sketched his historic contrast Stewart proceeds to offer an explanation; an explanation which, in the traditions of the Scottish Enlightenment, is in terms of what later came to be labelled not *A* but *The* Materialist Conception of History: 'One principal cause of this difference between the spirit of ancient and of modern policy, may be found in the difference between the sources of national wealth in ancient and in modern times. In ages when commerce and manufactures were yet in their infancy, and among states constituted like most of the ancient republics, a sudden influx of riches from abroad was justly dreaded as an evil, alarming to the morals, to the industry, and to the freedom of a people.'[2]

But our concern today is not with the interesting yet unpractical question whether the later Roman Republic might fairly be character-

132

ised as – to revive one mischievous historian's *ad hoc* verbal miscegenation – a lootocracy. Instead we are supposed to consider whether it would be better, or perhaps only what it would mean to say that it would be better, if everyone, or almost everyone, became, or becomes, better off. Most of the classical economists would, I suppose, have taken as obvious: both what it means; and that it would be, or will be.

Of course, they were as aware as any of us of various grounds upon which reservations might be entered. Certainly there are many sorts of goods and services which will never be entered into any indices of national production or national income. Again, when other people become richer they may not always expend their extra funds in ways which we should ourselves approve. Everyone here, surely, will share George Stigler's dissatisfaction 'with the tastes of nine-tenths of the population . . .'? I consider it, he continues, and we cannot but concur, 'shocking that more Americans have read *The Affluent Society* than *The Wealth of Nations.*'[3] Once again, and less lightheartedly, the comparatively poor will often be by any standards better people than the comparatively well-to-do.

Nevertheless, here and today, I shall not be labouring such traditional, hackneyed, yet improving points. In any case, along with all those great men of old, I myself remain quite unrepentantly persuaded that, in general and in the end, as my St John's, Oxford contemporary Kingsley Amis might have said, better off is better. So, instead of embarking on a direct examination of the concept of human betterment, I propose to attend first to the ever more formidable advances of those who hold equality to be a good in itself, if not the supreme or sole good in itself. What I have to say about the topic officially prescribed will emerge indirectly as I try to show how very far removed is the pursuit of that other now most fashionable ideal, both in intention and in effect, from a generous – and, I might add, classical – concern for human betterment.

2. EQUALITY AS A GOOD IN ITSELF

'A growing number of economists', the same George Stigler was remarking back in 1948, 'implicitly argue that no other injustice equals in enormity that of large differences in income.'[4] In the years between, the assertions, if not the supporting arguments, have become more explicit; while a great many others, besides professional economists, have joined the chorus. During the 1974 British Association meeting the most respected of Fleet Street's corps of Economics Correspondents contended that this demand for equality of income or, more generally, equality of outcome has become a major national and international menace: 'The ultimate sin of the politicians, academics and the media has been their obsession with interpersonal and intergroup comparisons. Liberal democracy . . . could yet be saved if contemporary egalitarianism were to lose its hold over the intelligentsia.'[5]

(a) The first point to be seized about cherishing equality as a good in itself, a value, is how different this is from pursuing equality only as the perceived means to some other end. If you are a classical Utilitarian, maintaining the greatest happiness of the greatest number to be the Supreme Good, and if you notice that an extra few pounds will typically mean more the fewer the recipient happens to have already, then you will have reason to see equality of distribution as a means to what is for you the sole and supreme proper end – the maximisation of the sum total of satisfactions, regardless of their distribution. Thus, in his *Leading Principles of a Constitutional Code*, Jeremy Bentham himself said: 'The more remote from equality are the shares . . . the less is the sum of felicity produced by those shares.'[6]

It was perhaps in part with this consideration in mind that – flat contrary to all the popular Marxist slanders against 'paid lackeys of the capitalists' – Adam Smith and his successors were so concerned to promote, in Stewart's phrase, the 'diffusion of wealth among the lower orders';[7] which, being translated into a contemporary political idiom, is 'raising the living standards of the working people and their families'. A second likely source of this concern, and one equally far removed from any commitment to equality as a value, is that they, like almost everyone else, were more disposed to what Sir Karl Popper has distinguished as a negative utilitarianism than to the classical positive kind.[8] They felt, that is to say, obligations to relieve, as far as they might, severe suffering; but little or none to go out of their ways to promote positive happiness.

(b) The second crucial distinction is between two entirely different possible objectives for policy within the field of political economy. With one of these kinds the intention is to make all those subject to the policy in some respect more, or even perfectly, equal; in income perhaps, or happiness, or welfare, or whatever else.[9] With the other the aim is to hang up a sort of safety-net, to establish a metaphorical floor; a level below which none of those for whom those for whom this provision is made needs to fall. I suggest that we label policies of the first kind Procrustean, and those of the second sort Good Samaritan.[10]

If we were dealing with people who had set a sacrificial example by first imposing their ideal of equality upon themselves, and were now trying to persuade others freely and individually to follow that challenging model, then this reference to the violent practices of that legendary Greek innkeeper would be altogether unfair. Yet it is, as things are, entirely apt and fully warranted. For our contemporary political Procrusteans propose to realise their iron ideal only and precisely through social engineering, backed up by the whole power of the state.

The second label, on the other hand, will on many occasions of its application be too kind. We should never forget that the Good Samaritan of *The Gospel according to St Luke* performed famously excellent deeds himself, at his own expense. Many supporters of what I nevertheless want to call Good Samaritan policies hope, and perhaps even have good reason to expect, that the taxes required to finance their policies will fall mainly if not entirely upon other people. In these cases we have further tokens of a familiar but unlovely type of spectacle – a 'concerned and relevant discussion', one in which A and B join together to decide what C should be compelled to do for D.

Now, surely, it is not too impossibly difficult to master this essential distinction between the quite different objectives of Good Samaritan and Procrustean policies? How can it be anything but obvious, for instance, that the Procrustean has as such a reason for taking away from the better-off even if the worse-off are as a result advantaged only relatively, and not made in any way absolutely better-off? Is it not equally obvious that, whereas the Procrustean must want both floors and ceilings, and those ceilings screwed down as close as may be to the floors,[11] the Good Samaritan as such will not demand any ceiling in addition to his welfare floor? He will call for seizure from the better-off only in so far as that is seen as the least unsatisfactory way of financing the erection and maintenance, at whatever absolute height it is desired that it should hang, of the safety-net.

Nevertheless, and notwithstanding that all this is or ought to be manifest, many prominent Procrustean intellectuals appear to find the making and maintaining of the present distinction a task wholly beyond their conceptual powers. I have, for example, long treasured a letter received from one of them, one who was later to be picked out by *New Society* as a uniquely authoritative spokesperson. The most revealing sentence reads: 'It *is* arguable that bad housing, squalor, pollution, ignorance etc. are "good". But unless you are prepared to argue that case you must be an egalitarian . . .' (italics and punctuation original). The difficulty which such highly intelligent people meet here in recognising an elementary yet correspondingly fundamental distinction spring in the main, I believe, from their partisan resolution to represent their own side as possessed of a monopoly on all virtue, and especially a monopoly on compassion. But this seeming obtuseness is certainly reinforced by what must in their eyes appear a very reasonable reluctance to attend to argument adduced by those who, in part on account of precisely that initial self-righteous obtuseness, they themselves cannot but see as heartless scoundrels.

3. PROCRUSTEANISM AS THE SUPPOSED IMPERATIVE OF JUSTICE

In Section 1 I explained that I intended to approach our prescribed topic only indirectly, by way of considering the main contemporary alternative to any ideal of human betterment. Then in Section 2 I distinguished that main alternative – the imposition of equality as a good in itself – both from a concern with equality as a means only and from the furtherance of a quite different policy objective, an objective with which this Procrustean ideal is in fact constantly confounded. Now in Section 3 I proceed to bring out that, when argument is offered for accepting equality as a value, it is taken to be an imperative of justice – almost always and without explanation qualified as *social* justice. Then, after indicating certain important presuppositions and implications of thus identifying Procrusteanism as a kind of justice, I intend in Section 4 to show that this levelling ideal can be realised only at what must be, in terms of any wider and more generous understanding of human betterment, heavy costs. Finally, in Section 5 I shall by way of illustration present fragments of evidence indicating that Procrustean public educational policy is today for many both diminishing opportunity and reducing achievement.

In 1975, defying the appeals Samuel Brittan made to it in the previous year, Section F devoted itself to *Economics and Equality*. In his Presidential Address Aubrey Jones noticed: 'Inequality of all sorts has lost its legitimacy.'[12] But he refrained from asking whether this should be, or why. Every contributor eventually choosing to write on the title subject assumed that (more) equality in wealth and income must be the main though never the only element in social justice; or, in one case, economic justice. No one, it appears, felt any call to explain that and how all the various good things with which in their ideal world of social justice everyone would be supplied – presumably by Providential and omnipotent government – are exactly the things which, as a matter of *justice*, those several persons deserve, or to which they are in some other way, morally if not yet legally, entitled.

C. D. Harbury, for instance, opens with what is to him a glimpse of the obvious: 'Economic equality . . . is one aspect of a wider theme of social justice.'[13] T. W. Hutchison speaks of 'the social injustice of unemployment', while Tim Tutton thinks that 'There can be little doubt about the relevance of a high level of employment to the achievement of economic justice'.[14] Certainly there can be no doubt at all but that a very high level of employment is essential to the welfare of all concerned. Yet it is at least not equally self-evident that this is a matter of any sort of justice. Throughout, only Hutchison, when he excoriates the monstrous (social) injustice of inflation,[15] and Harbury, when he condemns 'the social injustice of taxing what are, in reality, negative investment incomes in an inflationary age',[16] attack anything which is in terms of the traditional meaning of that word indisputably and unequivocally an injustice. Even they do not spell out just why these things are in truth unjust: that it is because people are being robbed and cheated out of what is properly their own; and because the law here is not treating all relevantly like cases alike.

Before making the mandatory references to John Rawls, it is salutary to cite a statement from the *Institutes* of Justinian: the mark of a just man, we read, is 'a constant and perpetual will to assign to each their own, their due'. The crucial phrase of this statement is itself borrowed from a stock maxim made famous by the still earlier Roman jurist, Ulpian: to do justice, Ulpian used to say, 'is to live honourably, to harm nobody, and to allow to each their own'.[17] Some account on these lines must, surely, have been provided in every treatise on justice from the very earliest until 1971, Then in that year Rawls – most unphilosophically impatient to 'leave questions of meaning and definition aside, and to get on with the task of developing a substantive theory of justice'[18] – was able to find no room in the over 600 pages of his monster book either to quote these traditional phrases or to offer and to defend any preferred alternative definition. The result, whatever the merits or demerits of the political and economic vision developed therein, is that Rawls has not in fact contributed, as his title pretends, *A Theory of Justice*.[19]

The truth is that what Rawls actually does there is precisely what, in his famous first article, he undertook not to do. For at that time he was at pains to insist: that justice is 'but *one* of the many virtues of social institutions'; and that he was not providing 'an all-embracing vision of a good society'.[20]

In the book, by contrast, he begins: 'During much of modern moral philosophy the predominant systematic theory has been some form of utilitarianism.' What previous anti-utilitarians have, he alleges, all failed to do is 'to construct a workable and systematic moral conception to oppose it'.[21] Nevertheless, given the title of the book of Rawls, and given too the innumerable employments of the word 'justice' and its semantic associates in that book, it is no wonder that, in *Economics and Equality*, Paul Grout, and so many more elsewhere, have been misled to read Rawls as developing an alternative: not to the Utilitarian account of the nature of the Supreme Good; but to a Utilitarian conception of justice. Thus Grout proposes to compare 'the economic implications of Rawls's approach ... to the most historically entrenched of all the concepts of justice – utilitarianism'.[22] Where, however, Grout was dead right was in recognising the intractable and fundamental clash between Utilitarian directives to a maximisation of the collective good and the claims of particular individuals; claims which, we have to add, include but are not exhausted by the claims of justice.

At this point, if not much sooner, someone will want to object that all this fuss about the word 'justice' is so much frivolous and onanistic verbal trifling; perhaps adding something equally and generally offensive about 'Oxford linguistic philosophy'. Such an objection, though understandable, would be wholly misconceived. For the question whether to say that the enforcement of equality is or is not a matter of justice is no more and no less merely verbal than the question whether any other proposition can be properly accounted true or false. The point is that the application of any significant word is bound to carry implications. Just what those implications are is determined by the established meaning of that word.[23] Three of the implications of maintaining that the enforcement of equality is indeed a matter of justice must on no account be overlooked.

(a) In the first place Procrusteans want both to be seen and to see themselves – and who would not? – as vigorous and dedicated followers in the footsteps of the *Shane* figures of old-fashioned Westerns, or of the *Four Just Men* of Edgar Wallace. Even Denis Healey, who promised a wildly cheering Labour Party conference in 1973 that he was going to impose confiscatory new taxes 'to make the rich howl in agony', does not wish always to see himself or to be seen by everyone else as a sadistic boor. So when a few months later, in the first of his thirteen budgets, he was to his delight able to raise the top rates of extraction to 83 per cent on earned and 98 per cent on investment income, and to impose additional heavy levies on capital transfers, what he said to the House of Commons was: 'I believe that this type of redistribution through the tax system makes a major contribution to the health of the community, and I intend to go a great deal further before I have finished.' It is not perhaps manifest what precisely, or even what vaguely, the cash value of this is in terms of the betterment of individuals. Yet there is no doubt but that the health of the community is a more admirable objective than that revealed earlier to and by Healey's party comrades.

In order to maintain any halfway respectable self-image the Procrusteans need to present themselves as pursuing something possessed of a much wider appeal than any purely personal and private ideal. Still more important, to insist that you are obeying the imperatives of justice is to equip yourself with a sufficient response to what might otherwise prove an embarrassing challenge: 'By what right do you propose to seize by force from some in order to give to others; and also in other ways so to coerce recalcitrants that everyone shall live in accordance with your chosen ideal?'

All, however, are agreed that the claims of justice may be – indeed ought to be – enforced by the public power. The great Smith himself wrote in his other masterpiece: 'Mere justice is, upon most occasions, but a negative virtue. . . . The man who barely abstains from violating either the person, or the estate, or the reputation of his neighbours, has surely little positive merit. He fulfils, however, all the rules of what is peculiarly called justice, and does everything which his equals can with propriety force him to do, or which they can punish him for not doing.'[24] J. S. Mill substantially agrees: 'When we think that a person is bound in justice to do a thing, it is an ordinary form of language to say that he ought to be compelled to do it.'[25]

(b) So far the Procrustean protagonist of 'equality and social justice' is sitting pretty. There is nevertheless a savage sting in the tail, waiting to strike those who are, as so many of the articulate spokespersons are, underdeprived. 'Take what you like', says God in the Spanish proverb, 'take it; and pay for it.' The price of proclaiming, with Rawls, that 'the first principle of justice' calls for 'an equal distribution', must be the acceptance of the entailment that no one has any right to anything above the average.[26] Yet this clearly carries the additional, most uncomfortable consequence that all such underdeprived Procrusteans are holding on to what must be, on their own account, stolen property; and that, necessarily, property stolen from people worse off than themselves.

Although I am, suspiciously, reluctant to concede that all these well-televised Procrusteans are quite so singlemindedly and disinterestedly devoted to the public weal as they and their promoters would have us believe; and even though I flatly refuse to approve their constantly reiterated and politically profitable abuse against opponents as being, for that single yet sufficient reason, heartless and uncompassionate; nevertheless I cannot persuade myself that many or even any of them are so inexcusably odious as the argument of the previous paragraph suggests.

The at least partially excusing secret is, surely, that they do not in their hearts believe the conclusion that everyone is already – under the moral if not the positive law – entitled to an equal share, no more and no less? They are well content to describe their Procrustean policies as measures to enforce 'equality and social justice', and they themselves very much want to benefit from certain of the overtones and implications carried by the good word 'justice'. Yet they have no scruples about reneging on other elements in the package deal involved in that description. They do not really, that is, believe that ideally equal shares of everything, no less and no more, already are the justly acquired and rightful property of everyone; and hence that anything which they themselves hold above that austere minimum/maximum is so much stolen property. Their constant appeals to (social) justice should – in charity – be seen as disingenuous propaganda designed to blackguard their hated political opponents.

(c) The third point is a development of the second. It is implicit in the definitions already quoted. What it is just for anyone to have is precisely and only whatever that person either deserves or is entitled to. There may be, and no doubt are, many other and perhaps sometimes quite different things which it may or might be good for people to have, which in a more ideal world they would have, and even which some others maybe have some obligation to provide. Suppose, for example, that through your own incontinent folly you yourself are in danger of drowning. Then it may be that I am in duty bound to try to save you. Certainly it would be good for you if I were to try, and succeed. But you have, I believe, done nothing to deserve, and are, surely, in no other way entitled to, my rescue services?

One consequence of this third point about the meaning of the term 'justice', and hence about the implications of its application, is that there can be no question of putting forward 'The Entitlement Theory' as only one of several possible, rival conceptions of justice.[27] There is, of course, room for many contesting conceptions, both of what various people's several deserts and entitlements actually are, and of what it is which determines true deserts and legitimate entitlements. But a conception which makes no reference to either, which is not concerned 'to render to each their due', simply is not a conception of justice. If it is now objected that this is where social justice is different, then the correct conclusion to draw is that social justice so conceived is no more a species of justice than Bombay Duck is a sort of duck or Soviet democracy is a kind of democracy.[28] By first rejecting the very idea of individual desert, and then failing to recognise the possibility of undeserved entitlement, Rawls completely disqualifies his work as *A Theory of Justice*.[29]

A second consequence of the present third point is that anyone setting out to vindicate the contention that an equal distribution of all goods is indeed an imperative of justice faces an uphill task. The very words of our definition suggest, although they do not strictly require, that there will be differences in what is due to different individuals. Since deserts and entitlements necessarily must be grounded on what their subjects have done or failed to do, or what in the broadest conceivable sense they are or are not, it would be surprising if all differences in all these respects were in the present context simply to cancel out.

Rawls achieves this in his eyes happy result by blankly denying such differences to be anything but 'arbitrary from a moral point of view'; and then quite failing to appreciate that, if this were true, the concept of justice could find no application.[30] Many begin their attempts by taking it for granted that everything which they might wish to redistribute is available for such reassignment, totally free of any prior claims. Rawls, for instance, has been fairly charged by Nozick with assuming, altogether without warrant, that, within the to them still unknown territories of his initial contracting parties, all goods and services, whether already produced or in the future to be produced, are, as it were, Manna-from-Heaven falling on collectively owned ground. Others have talked of the fair and equal slicing up and dishing out of gratuitously provided cakes, cakes presumably baked by the givers from materials available in their own larders, and all to be distributed to eaters having no or no differentiating claims upon the generosity of those benevolent givers. Really, they do need to do better than that!

4. THE CONFLICTS WITH BETTERMENT

Most Procrusteans recognise that their ideal would be realised only at some cost in human betterment, at least where betterment is measured by the usual indices of economic performance. Most are prepared, therefore, to permit some modicum of trading off.[31] David Donnison, for instance, once picked by *New Society* (20/11/75) as the perfect spokesman, in *The Observer* three years later (12/11/78) expressed both his devotion to all 'equalizing policies', and his revulsion against all 'inequalities in earnings'. These are, we were assured, tolerable to him only in so far as they may be 'required to keep the economy moving'.[32]

Again, the man whom, despite his own protests, so many took as the very model of the modern (non-socialist) social democrat wrote in his final publication, aptly nicknamed *The Epistle to the Costa Ricans*: 'The standard of living of working class people, it is (rightly) said, can be improved much faster by economic growth than by any conceivable redistribution of existing income. .... But this is not the point. For, ... the argument for more equality is not based on any direct material gain to the poor but on the claims of natural and social justice. And the question is: do these claims conflict with the need for incentives?'[33]

It is indeed. For, in the words of the author of what was in its day and maybe remains a standard treatise on *Welfare Economics*, 'personal gain is surely the only possible effective motive force for a free economy, whatever some idealists may think'.[34] The task in the present Section 4 is to develop this first point a little, and then to go on to notice other ways in which the requirements of the Procrustean ideal conflict with the claims of human betterment.

(a) It would be merely frivolous to deny that, in order to induce people to acquire useful skills or to work at all, to say nothing of going to work where their efforts and their skills are most needed, we cannot do without either a sort of sticks or a kind of carrots. Yet the compulsory direction of labour must be admitted to constitute in itself, apart from all consequent inefficiencies and administrative costs, a worsening of the human condition. So it has to be carrots. But then it must be not so much frivolous as perverse or just plumb stupid to deny that, to the extent that successive slices of income are taxed away progressively, financial incentives are for the people concerned either diminished or even altogether removed.

At the upper end of the scale this increases the attractions both of leisure and of staying put (or of emigration to freer countries, so long as that is possible and permitted) – to say nothing of the attractions of tax evasion and of barter. At the bottom end of the scale it creates or extends a poverty trap; although here it is fair to add that Britain's today extemely populous poverty trap has in fact been brought into existence more by Good Samaritan than by peculiarly Procrustean policies. It is, by the way, enormously to the credit of those concerned that so many of the victims are still, despite the lack of significant financial incentives, eager to work for their livings. But we cannot and we should not rely on that proud and self-reliant spirit surviving an indefinite postponement of action to dismantle this degrading institution.

All this is pretty well undeniable, notwithstanding that prominent Procrusteans are sometimes heard proclaiming their ignorance of any evidence to show that even the highest of marginal tax rates actually are disincentive, while usually refusing to entertain the suggestion that the Healey imposts may have been not only economically but also fiscally damaging.[36] It is, however, easier to overlook the importance both of non-tax disincentives to productive employment and of tax disincentives to productive investment. An example of the former is our sprawling and ramshackle structure of rent-controls and housing subsidies. This is the major obstacle discouraging 'working people and their families' from moving to places where their labour and skills can usefully be employed. As for the latter it should be obvious that any taxation of investment income reduces the attractions of wealth-creating investment; and, of course, the more Healey-confiscatory the rates the greater the disincentive. Consider too a statement made by a supposedly socialist Finance Minister in the dynamic city-state of Singapore. I copied it down in 1969 from a plaque in the central market-place: 'A society which wishes for economic growth should nurse the creative talent which its enterprising members possess, and should encourage the development of such talent to its full stature.'

(b) The previous subsection consisted in reminders of issues fairly frequently discussed. Procrusteanism is less often seen as threatening economic betterment through support given to the maintenance and extension of all forms of state monopoly supply of goods and services. Yet it is reasonable for a Procrustean to be a socialist also. Which gives all the more reason why the rest of us should be aware: both that many Procrusteans have an independent and perhaps prior Clause IV commitment to the 'public ownership of all the means of production, distribution and exchange'; and that in these days a socialist interest group, such as a public employees trades union, will sometimes seek to commend itself as disinterestedly egalitarian.

The case has two sides. On the one hand nationalisation is seen as a means of equalising the ownership of capital. On the other hand, monopoly, and in particular state monopoly, is seen as a necessary albeit by no means sufficient condition for the equalisation of the output; mainly, of course, so far the output of services rather than of goods. As for the trades union interests here, you would have to be quite as innocent as all too many members of the general public in fact appear to be if you were not to recognise the trades union interests involved in the 'total support' offered by NUPE and COHSE to state monopoly in medicine, and by the NUT and the AUT to state monopoly in education.

(i) The first of these two reasons is often put, yet rarely argued through. For instance: in an inordinately obese and admittedly mis-titled book Peter Townsend tells us of his lifelong longing for a 'wider distribution of land, property, and other assets'; something which, he insists, can be achieved by (among other things) 'extending public ownership'.[37] If 'extending public ownership' really did produce a 'wider distribution of land, property, and other assets', then Townsend and his fellows would become in academic honour bound never again to flourish any of those familiar Radical statistics purporting to show that many of us possess no wealth at all. For on this assumption, that we all have as it were shares in all the nationalised industries and in all other state assets, every citizen must in a country with so large a public sector be endowed with a by no means derisory nest-egg.

But, of course, no one really believes that ordinary citizens are in any genuine sense owners of shares in such public holdings. Nor does Townsend, diehard socialist that he is, really want any 'wider distribution of land, property, and other assets'. If he did, then he would favour many measures which are in truth altogether abhorrent both to him and to his party: selling or even giving council houses to sitting tenants; an Accessions Tax to encourage a breakup of large into smaller estates; selling or giving shares in the existing nationalised industries to those employed therein; and so on.

The truth, surely, must be that to Townsend and his fellows the appeal of nationalisation – the appeal to them, that is, *qua* Procrus-teans – is that it is seen as tending directly to equalise by cutting down some unequally, and therefore to them offensively, tall poppies.

(ii) The second reason for favouring state monopoly applies, or so far is applied, primarily to the provision of health and education services; although the more extreme the Procrusteans the wider, presumably, will be their applications. Nor is there any reason to believe that familiar considerations about the benefits to the public of competition between alternative suppliers of goods and services do not apply here. If anyone doubts this, then their doubts can most conve-niently be put to rest by contemplating the vociferous and often militant opposition of all the NHS and local government unions to suggestions that the provision of many of the services at present manned by their members might be put out to competitive tender.

The leaders of these unions are in a far better position than most of the rest of us to know how economical or otherwise are the operations in which their members are engaged. One of the most articulate and sober of these leaders, the General Secretary of NALGO, explained in a recent letter to the *Daily Telegraph* (25/5/81): 'Private contractors tender for local authority services in order to make money. Because they do not need to cream off a profit, local authorities can always be more cost effective.' So, if they not merely could be but actually are, then Geoffrey Drain and his colleagues – to a man, it would seem, card-carrying socialists – are by those who want to put operations out to tender being given the chance of a lifetime to demonstrate the superior efficiency of public provision.

These union leaders however, who are in so good a position to know, are aware of what must be the fact – that there are plenty of places where a competitor both could and would provide, while still turning an honest profit, a better and/or a cheaper service. It is, surely, precisely and only because they do know this that the unions are so stubbornly opposed to putting the issue to the test? In the Wandsworth campaign one of the local manual workers' leaders protested that if they were defeated there it would be 'the hole in the dyke'. His give-away words have since been echoed on other socialist and trades-union platforms. Yet whyever should anyone expect a torrential breakthrough of privatisation, unless there really is something substantial and worthwhile in it for the taxpayers?

Again, a few months later, a Councillor from a District in Buckinghamshire reported to *The Economist* (11/9/82) that their officers – presumably, I fear, NALGO members – had been lying in defence of their empires, falsely maintaining that there are no firms in the home counties offering a private refuse-collection service. There was there, for the public, a happy ending: '. . . the contract for our refuse collection has now been awarded to a private-sector company which gives us savings of £160,000 – approximately 20 per cent – in the coming financial year'.

5. PROCRUSTEANISM: THE PRICE IN EDUCATION

In Britain today the area offering perhaps the most scandalous illustrations of the costs in terms of human betterment of principled Procrustean politics is that of public primary and secondary education. It seems, incidentally, also to be the area in which we have least reason to feel confident that ever-rising public expenditures have been cost-effective; as well as that in which we possess the least adequate battery of indices for determining whether or not they have been. Once again the most powerful reason for suspecting that things are indeed awry is the ferocity of opposition to anyone having the impertinence to ask such questions, or to publish what little evidence they may succeed in obtaining; opposition, I may say, not only from the trades union and bureaucratic establishment but also from most of the educational press and from many of the Education Correspondents of the national dailies.

Here and now there is time and space for but two short, snapshot glimpses of a picture which is in large part obscured. Both supply strong hints of the cruel price being paid, both generally by the nation and in particular by many able children from less fortunate homes, for the paradigmatically Procrustean policy of universal, compulsory com-prehensivisation.

(a) Until, against the 'total opposition' of the NUT and most of the rest of the state educational establishment, Mark Carlisle as Minister of Education insisted on including a public information clause in the 1980 Education Act, local authorities were permitted to conceal the results achieved in independently assessed public examinations by individual maintained schools. But, in that period, the 1978 A-level results from ninety of the comprehensive schools run by the ILEA fell into the hands of two actives of the (unofficial and *Black Paperite*) National Council for Educational Standards. After being refused the scores of the ILEA's other schools, and against much protest from the ILEA and elsewhere, they proceeded to publish all they had. It was bad enough. Indeed for anyone genuinely concerned, as they are, for the education of all our children it was appalling.

Of those ninety ILEA comprehensive schools thirty-six had no A-level French or Geography, twenty-eight no Physics, twenty-five no Chemistry, twenty-two no Mathematics and twenty no Biology. Just how wastefully the available teachers are employed is seen from the further fact that 46.5 per cent of the subject groups in eight major subjects produced no more than two A-level entries; and, hence, even fewer passes.[38] So these precious teachers were teaching tiny classes, while in the other neighbourhood comprehensive schools to which they are doctrinally confined able and willing children must have had no chance of A-level teaching in these major subjects.

(b) The second snapshot glimpse has to be even more brief, and it refers to what must surely be another consequence of the dissolution of maintained selective schools. In the late 1960s as a junior minister in the Department of Education and Science Mrs Shirley Williams was able to tell a conference of European Ministers of Education that over 26 per cent of our university students and as many as 35 per cent of all students in all tertiary institutions came from working-class homes. It was left to others to make comparisons with other countries, and to draw out the morals: that the achievement of our supposedly class-divided and socially static society was in this respect superior to that of every other country in Western Europe; and that that achievement could not but have been the glory of the grammar schools.

In 1982 Dr Rhodes Boyson, at that time the successor of Mrs Williams, asked his civil servants to update those figures. Be warned that the information which follows covers only university students. From the 1920s to the early 1960s the proportion from working-class homes hovered around 26 per cent. It reached its peak of 31 per cent in 1968, thereafter beginning a slow and steady decline. From 31 per cent in 1968 we go to 28 per cent in 1973, 23 per cent in 1978, 22 per cent in 1979, and – a provisional figure still – 19.4 per cent in 1981.[39]

This lamentable decline was a foreseen consequence of the comprehensive revolution. Successive *Black Papers* were full of it.[40] And, furthermore, I can myself vouch personally for the fact that warnings of this consequence were given to several of the leaders of that revolution – people who I knew could not be expected to attend to any printed material coming from unofficial or non-socialist sources. They did not care. Or, if they did care at all, that many young people should thus be deprived of opportunity to better themselves seemed to them nothing more than one maybe mildly unfortunate cost of enforcing their Procrustean and levelling ideal. They call it 'social justice'.

NOTES

1. See, in the Glasgow Bicentenary Edition, W. P. D. Wightman (ed.), *Essays on Philosophical Subjects* (Oxford and Indianapolis: Clarendon Press, and Liberty Press, 1980, and 1982) pp. 312–13.
2. Ibid. p. 313. Compare William Robertson's *History of America* first published in 1777, one year after *The Wealth of Nations*: 'In every enquiry concerning the operations of men when united together in society, the first object of attention should be their mode of subsistence. Accordingly, as that varies, their laws and policy must be different.' See his *Works* (Edinburgh: Edinburgh University Press, 1980) vol. II, p. 204.

3. *The Intellectual and the Market Place* (New York: Free Press of Glencoe, 1963) p. 89.

4. *Five Lectures on Economics* (London: Longmans, Green, 1948) p. 1.

5. Samuel Brittan, 'The Economic Contradictions of Democracy', in K. J. W. Alexander (ed.), *The Political Economy of Change* (Oxford: Blackwell, 1975) pp. 27 and 29.

6. See the *Works*, ed. J. Bowring (London, 1843) vol. II, p. 27; and compare I. M. D. Little, *Welfare Economics* (Oxford: Clarendon Press, 2nd ed., 1957) p. 259 and passim.

7. Dugald Stewart, loc. cit. p. 313.

8. *The Open Society and its Enemies*, 5th ed. (London: Routledge & Kegan Paul, 1966) vol. I, pp. 284–5: note 2 to chap. 9.

9. Little, loc. cit. p. 76, remarks that the phrase 'increase of welfare' possesses far greater emotive force than the expression 'increase of happiness'. The present preference for the former, like that greater commendatory force itself, is surely based upon something more solid. For if we speak of someone's welfare, rather than of their pleasures or of the satisfaction of their actual wants, we are taking it that such reservations as were indicated in the penultimate paragraph of Section 1, p. 133, have been removed. Persons whose true welfare has been thus maximised will not be revelling in the enjoyment of all those squalid pleasures which they themselves in their still unenlightened condition may actually favour. They will instead be worthy characters who, if poetry is indeed to be rated higher than pushpin, will be attending to the one rather than indulging in the other; and so on.

10. For a fuller discussion of this distinction, and for further evidence and argument in support of charges laid hereafter, above, see my 'Good Samaritans become Procrusteans', in June Stevenson and Catherine Jones (eds) *The Yearbook of Social Policy: 1982* (Henley: Routledge & Kegan Paul, 1983).

11. It is well to remind both actual or potential high earners, as well as those who appreciate the economic importance of the possibility of both high earnings and high profits, that during (what one must hope will be) the last Labour administration the most powerful of union bosses argued strongly, both for a legal maximum income and against percentage as opposed to flat-rate wage increases. See Jack Jones, 'The Case against Percentages', in the *New Statesman and Nation* (5/9/75).

12. Aubrey Jones (ed.), *Economics and Equality* (Doddington, Oxon.: Philip Allan, 1976) p. 2.

13. Ibid. p. 87. I draw several illustrations from the proceedings of a previous year: partly because this is a source on which I have not drawn elsewhere; and partly because, unless we do attend to our predecessors, we cannot expect our successors to attend to us.

14. Ibid. pp. 59 and 154.

15. Ibid. pp. 48 and 59.

16. p. 97.

17. The Latin goes: 'constans et perpetua voluntas ius suum cuique tribuere'; and 'honeste vivere, neminem laedere, suum cuique tribuere'.

18. *A Theory of Justice* (Harvard and Oxford: Harvard University Press and Oxford University Press, 1971 and 1972) p. 579.

19. For a thorough defence of this contention, see *The Politics of Procrustes* (London and Buffalo: Temple Smith, and Prometheus Bound, 1981) chap. III: 'Social Justice or Justice?'; also 'Justice: Real or Social?', in *Social Philosophy and Policy* for 1983–journal of the Social Philosophy and Policy Center (Bowling Green, Ohio).

20. 'Justice as Fairness', in The *Philosophical Review* for 1958, p. 165 (italics original). I have in the article mentioned in note 19 listed other counts on which the first-published draft was superior to the final product.

21. Pp. vi and viii.

22. Aubrey Jones, loc. cit. p. 136.

23. For a witty and subtle development of this point, see the discussion at the beginning of J. L. Austin, *Sense and Sensibilia* (Oxford: Clarendon Press, 1962) of Ayer's insouciance about what we may legitimately say.

24. *The Theory of the Moral Sentiments* (II (ii) 1: p. 191 of volume I in the 11th edition of 1808).

25. *Utilitarianism* (chap. V: p. 44 in the Everyman Edition of 1910).

26. *A Theory of Justice*, pp. 150–1. Rawls does not himself draw this conclusion; and in any case proceeds to try to justify, if not to demonstrate the justice of, his different Difference Principle.

27. As, at p. 150 of his most excellent and exciting book *Anarchy, State and Utopia* (New York and Oxford: Basic Books and Blackwell, 1974), Robert Nozick much too modestly does.

28. I recommend here Wallace Matson's 'What Rawls Calls Justice', in *The Occasional Review*, no. 8/9 (San Diego: World Research, 1978). This contains, among other good things, a witty comparison with someone presenting as a conception of chastity, or perhaps of social chastity, only notions of poverty and obedience; while all the time eschewing any mention of sex.

29. Compare *The Politics of Procrustes*, chap. IV, sec. 1.

30. Ibid. sec. 2.

31. After all that he says about how 'Justice is the first virtue of social institutions...', and; how it ought on that account to be 'uncompromising', Rawls has no business to be flexible. So he is, though sensible, inconsistent in permitting through the Difference Principle a tradeoff against his own 'first principle of justice'. See *A Theory of Justice*, pp. 3–4, 151, and passim.

32. Having in that earlier article confessed that the egalitarianism for which he was speaking is 'muddled', he proceeded in *The Observer* to a public demonstration. Listing 'Britain's longer term aims' as three, of which none was in fact any more Procrustean than this third – 'the expectation that work will bring its reward' – Donnison still insisted on describing them all as 'egalitarian aspirations'. To no one's surprise he neither asked nor answered the question: 'How, under universal equalization, is often unequal work "to bring its reward"?'

33. C. A. R. Crosland, *Social Democracy in Europe* (London: Fabian Society, 1975) p. 6.

34. Little, loc. cit. p. 262.

35. See Hermione Parker, *The Moral Hazards of Social Benefits* (London: Institute of Economic Affairs, 1982).

36. They are also, oddly yet none the less outrageously, inclined to discount the equalising impact of these and other favoured measures; citing high incomes before tax as if these were what was eventually received by the abominated rich, and so on. See, for quoted specimens of this academic outrage: both the article mentioned in note 10, above; and Melville Ulmer, 'Our Egalitarian Economists', in *Commentary* for Sep. 1982 (pp. 51–4).

    It is altogether typical of such socialist, supposed social scientists that in *Encounter* for April 1983, amidst various snarls against 'the present regime', Donnison complains that even its immediate predecessor was 'Unwilling or unable to impose any effective discipline on the rich ...'; and that without so much as mentioning any of the extra taxation, of which he was himself so enthusiatic an advocate and supporter, designed to make them howl in agony!

37. *Poverty in the United Kingdom* (Harmondsworth: Penguin, 1979) p. 925.

38. See Caroline Cox and John Marks, *Sixth-Forms in ILEA Comprehensives: A Cruel Confidence Trick?* (London: National Council for Educational Standards, 1981).

39. The figures given in the text come from a speech by Dr Rhodes Boyson to an NCES meeting on 25/10/82, and were confirmed by him in a private letter dated 28/10/82. They were, of course, compiled by the successors of the DES officials who provided Mrs Williams with the earlier figures. Those can be got most conveniently from Tibor Szamuely, 'Comprehensive Inequality', in C. B. Cox and A. E. Dyson (eds) *Black Paper Two* (London: Critical Quarterly, 1970). The fact that I cannot for the more recent figures provide a reference to either a major national daily or a specialist periodical says much about the present condition of British educational journalism.

40. See, for instance, C. B. Cox and A. E. Dyson (eds), *Fight for Education: A Black Paper* (London: Critical Quarterly, 1969). There R. R. Pedley's 'Comprehensive Disaster' begins: 'It is one of the more grotesque ironies of our times that a Labour Government claiming a particular interest in the needs of the poor and the lowly... should have determined a policy for secondary education which will beyond doubt lead to... a reduction in the opportunities open to able children....' The theme is taken up in other articles in this and in all later volumes. It should therefore be surprising that Mr Callaghan as Prime Minister of a later Labour Government found it convenient in his famous Ruskin speech to see in all this only '*Black Paper* prejudices'. He added: 'We all know those who claim to defend standards but are simply seeking to defend old privileges and inequalities.' We may perhaps hope that he was misinformed by speech-writers, and had never himself read any *Black Papers*. We cannot and must not be so charitable to the many who wrote such speeches and all the many furious and mendacious reviews.

9 T. H. Marshall on the Middle Ground

DAVID REISMAN

T. H. Marshall was a highly intelligent and original thinker who first taught history at Trinity College, Cambridge, then immersed himself in the study of social theory and social institutions for three decades at the London School of Economics, and ultimately made, almost entirely between his retirement from the School in 1956 at the age of 62 and his death on 29 November 1981 in his 88th year, a unique and important contribution to the theory of the middle ground. Every student knows his influential text *Social Policy in the Twentieth Century* (first published in 1965 and now in its fourth edition), an exemplary attempt to explain welfare not only in terms of the wider society that surrounds the dependent, but in terms of the historical evolution of that society as well. Every theorist has studied the two Alfred Marshall lectures which he gave in Cambridge in February 1949 (and which were published as *Citizenship and Social Class* a year later) in which he enthusiastically associated himself with Alfred Marshall's objective of substituting for the divisiveness of the Two Nations a common culture in which 'every man is a gentleman'. Every literate person interested in the mixed economy, social policy, social philosophy or the political economy of social democracy must read *The Right to Welfare*. These books demonstrate how much the British approach to the theory of the middle ground owes, as to Tawney, Titmuss and Crosland, to the intellectual stimulus of T. H. Marshall.

*   *   *

The social thought of T. H. Marshall is about many things, but most of all it is about 'democratic-welfare-capitalism',[1] about that hyphenated society which exists 'when a country with a *capitalist* market

151

economy develops *democratic* political and civil institutions and practices out of which emerge a mixed economy including both private and
public capitalism similarly organised and using the same calculus,
together with that complex of public social services, insurances and
assistances which is the eponymous element in what all the world
knows as the *welfare state*'.[2] The hyphenated society is thus nothing
less than the compromise of the middle ground, involving as it does
elements derived from each of three independent subsystems. Those
three subsystems have 'separate identities' and 'equal contributory
status'[3] and are the following:

(a) THE CAPITALIST MARKET ECONOMY

The most important thing to remember about the market mode of
allocation is that it is itself a part of freedom precisely because
command is by definition unfreedom: 'Socialists have maintained that
capitalism treats labour as a *commodity*. Of course it does, and that is
its contribution to freedom, for the alternative was to go on treating the
labourer as a commodity, and that meant slavery and serfdom.'[4] His
answer is historically correct but still not logically satisfying – partly
because he tends to confuse capitalism with markets (and yet the
worker's perceptions of freedom may vary even in a world of non-
planned allocation by price as between firms where labour hires capital
and firms where capital hires labour), partly because he seems to have
an exaggeratedly optimistic view of the flexibility and self-directedness
of the employee in a world of corporate structures, oligopolistic
competition, bureaucratic hierarchies and non-transferable pensions.
To this Marshall would probably reply simply that everything is
relative; and that – the main point – the civil rights which evolved in
Europe in the eighteenth century (and which involve the freedoms of
speech, movement, assembly, religion, petition) include some rights
(to own property, to make voluntary contracts subject to the rule of
law) which are better exercised under market capitalism than under
any other system we know.

Marshall supported market capitalism because of its close association (in British history and in pure logic) with civil rights, and because
he believed that, for the greater part of men, 'the essence of freedom
consists in the right and power to choose and to act according to one's
choice'[5]. Yet he also made a further four points about market capitalism which are of little or no interest to the student of the economy in

isolation and of tremendous interest to the student of the multidisciplinary hyphenated society of the middle ground.

First, the market is the friend, not the enemy, of welfare. Both
market and welfare, after all, set themselves the same task, 'that of
satisfying the needs and wants of the population'[6]. Besides that, 'the
superstructure of welfare can be firmly built only on the foundation of
a viable economy',[7] where welfare is here to be defined narrowly as the
welfare state. Speaking of Germany he notes that it was the 'economic
miracle' which enabled her 'to take in her stride the high costs of
top-grade social services and social security'.[8] Speaking of Britain he
comments that it was the slow growth of recent years perhaps even
more than the revival of libertarian ideologies which led to the
challenge to universalism: 'Capitalism is most dangerous when it is
weak and frightened, not when it is strong and confident.'[9] Speaking of
the human family in general he makes clear that even the staunchest
opponent of the baubles and trinkets of affluence ought to defend
growth if he wishes also to defend welfare. Growth, after all, does not
merely generate resources which could be utilised for collective consumption. It also generates the will to utilise them in this way: 'If new
resources are created, the pressure to spread the benefits is likely, in
the long run, to be irresistible',[10] for welfare in truth 'represents the
natural reaction of the majority to a rising standard of living' and
'receives the powerful support of collective action in favour of common enjoyment and general welfare'[11]. It is, however, never made
clear why growth should generate the sufficient (altruism) as well as
the necessary (funds) condition for welfare (Marshall hints at poverty
in the midst of plenty and the new perception of contrasts that
characterises our own times – 'The men and women of the twentieth
century came to feel that where there was wealth there should be no
poverty'[12] – but an aside concerning relief of poverty is by no means a
full explanation of popular attitudes in periods of growth towards
grants to students or improved meals for long-stay mental patients in
preference to colour televisions, video recorders or expensive holidays
in exotic places). It is interesting too, that Marshall himself seems to
have had occasional doubts about the high-income elasticity of
generosity, and one cannot help but recall his rather pessimistic
account in 1961 (only three and four years respectively before he
penned the more optimistic passages cited above) – in 'The Welfare
State – A Comparative Study' – of the rebarbarisation of the 1950s. In
the 1950s, he argued there, people more and more took the view that
'in times of prosperity increased productivity should enable nearly all

the people to meet all their needs out of their own pockets and through the mechanism of the market, thus reducing free or subsidised welfare provisions once more to the level of a peripheral affair'.[13] In such a case, of course, the market becomes the enemy and not the friend of welfare.

Whether generosity and fellowship represent 'the natural reaction of the majority to a rising standard of living', or whether, alternatively, people in prosperous societies are keen to reduce the institutionalised gift-relationship 'once more to the level of a peripheral affair', there is none the less one constant which runs throughout the discussion – the tacit assumption that the market mechanism (accompanied, needless to say, by the usual Keynesian-type measures that made the era of the Butskellite Compromise one of confidence bordering on complacency) will ensure sustained growth and full or near-full employment. What Marshall does not discuss is the impact on sociability and the caring society of stagnation and large-scale unemployment. Yet where paid employment acquires the status of a 'positional good', where welfare to an unprecedented extent takes the form of income-maintenance to those genuinely unable to find work, it is particularly important to know whether fraternity and concern will expand, contract or remain constant; and it must be confessed that Marshall, genuinely unable to envisage such a sad state of affairs recurring in a Britain where we had 'never had it so good', does not give us much assistance in trying to predict how the community will react to the downs as well as to the ups. Nor is he tempted to make altruism self-interested in the case of unemployment benefits by pointing out that what used to be called 'outdoor relief' is now known as a 'built-in stabiliser'. In this latter case a social duty (to spend) would be wedded to an individual right (to receive cash benefits) and generosity – this is an argument which, as we shall see, even the kindly Marshall was himself capable of employing – can thus prove cost-effective. But Marshall has no need of such a solution for the simple reason that he does not believe there is a problem to solve: there is one constant which runs throughout his work, and that is that the stagnation and large-scale unemployment of the 1930s are dodo phenomena with which the historian of the future need not concern himself. For this the efficacy and dynamism of (managed) market capitalism are largely responsible; and this returns us to our point of departure, that the market is the friend, not the enemy, of welfare.

Second, normative pluralism is possible without normative confusion setting in. The ethos of the market sector is an individualistic, competitive, acquisitive and self-regarding one, and there is evidence to suggest that this mentality is seeping into the welfare sector – as in the case of the winter of 1978–9 when even welfare professionals went on strike for more money,[14] or where middle-class students seek to squeeze out of the tax-payers (the great bulk of whose children fail to get into university) 'the last legitimate penny with complete disregard of the general community interest'[15]. Marshall stressed, however, that pluralism need not lead to absorption – 'This kind of ethical relativity has been a feature of very nearly every society since civilisation began'[16] – and gave an example of peaceful coexistence: 'A hyphenated relationship between Church and State is a much commoner historical occurrence than either a theocracy or a totally secular social order'.[17] His retreat into history is perhaps unfortunate in so far as it does not solve the problem of the welfare professionals and the middle-class students (a problem with which he became increasingly concerned as he grew older in an England progressively less Merrie). His plea to them to show a sense of social responsibility in eschewing what he obviously regarded as legalised scrounging (the benefits analogue of tax avoidance[18]) – scrounging of the non-legal type, as in the case of fraudulent claims, he regarded as 'relatively rare'[19] – has an air of desperation about it and seems to suggest that Marshall was unable to envisage the possible demise of the moral double-think on which his hyphenated society so much depends for its normative viability. The following lines, written not long before his death, illustrate the extent to which his model had difficulty in incorporating the professionals and the students without falling back on the circular argument and the tautological statement: 'The hyphenated society can survive – by which I mean survive without drifting towards a state of *anomie* – only if it is recognised that both the welfare sector and the mixed economy are contributing to the creation of welfare in the broad, non-technical sense of the word and if the way in which the task is shared between the two spheres receives that measure of acceptance or approbation which is normally accorded to decisions reached through the processes of democratic government.'[20]

Third, market-determined pay differentials have an important allocative function to perform: 'The incentives provided by and expressed in competitive markets make a contribution to efficiency and to progress in the production and distribution of wealth which cannot, in a large and complex society, be derived from any other source.'[21] Such inequalities in pay are in no sense incompatible with 'full membership of a community'[22] and indeed contribute to perceived membership in so far as they are the precondition for economic growth and thereby for welfare. Yet Marshall's argument does not stop there and seeks to introduce a conception of legitimation that is in his work increasingly independent of the market. The general rule is given in the following passage from *Social Policy*: '"Fair shares" does not mean equal pay; it implies that some inequalities are fair and acceptable, and others are not.'[23] Certainly in his earlier work Marshall seems to have related such equity to an equal start in life and the career open to the talents, as where in *Citizenship and Social Class* the thrust of his argument is that first civil and then political and social rights 'provided the foundation of equality on which the structure of inequality could be built'.[24] In *The Right to Welfare*, however, the condition has been narrowed: 'Equality of persons is compatible with inequality of incomes *provided the inequality is not too great.*'[25] Note he is not here questioning the legitimacy of the inequality in the sense of being the product of supply and demand. What he is saying is that even the economically legitimate can be an undesirable social distance factor – a stricter condition than he would have imposed in the 1940s, when his view seems to have been simply that 'equality of status'[26] and 'equal social worth'[27] are 'not inconsistent with the inequalities which distinguish the various economic levels in the society.'[28] The T. H. Marshall of the 1970s was a somewhat less confident observer. He confesses that after all 'the capitalist market economy can be, and generally has been, a cause of much social injustice';[29] he decides that the vital question of whether it is possible to obtain more justice without sacrificing some efficiency 'has not yet been answered';[31] and he then hints that the alternative to the clash of values might have to be some state intervention in the labour market. Thus he comments: 'It is clear that, although unequal incomes and differential earnings are accepted as legitimate, there is no general agreement about the principles by which the inequalities and the differences should be regulated. Both the major political parties in Britain today talk about the need for an incomes policy.'[31] Even this, however, is not fully developed, neither by the parties nor by Marshall, into a workable blueprint for restructuring differentials in accordance with some undefined but presumably widespread perception of social justice that transcends (without, obviously, annihilating) mere allocative efficiency.

And there is the problem of the unions. In *Citizenship and Social Class* Marshall had accepted the union view that traditional differentials have the character of a social right independent of supply and demand: 'The claims of status are to a hierarchical wage structure, each level of which represents a social right and not merely a market value.'[32] By the time of *The Right to Welfare*, however, Marshall had become somewhat anxious about the bullying tactics of strong unions which increase pushfulness in preference to productivity,[33] elbow the weak out of their rightful place in the queue,[34] and refuse to obey the mandate of the sovereign Parliament because they have a mandate of their own from their own members.[35] Speaking of unions, Marshall said 'freedom, if it is not to be anarchy, must be built upon a foundation of law';[36] and it is almost certainly because of what he clearly regarded as the irresponsible exercise of concentrated power on the labour side of collective bargaining that Marshall began to think in terms of an incomes policy. Be that as it may, his views on incomes policy were never fully developed into theories and recommendations, and his fundamental position on income derived from work can only be taken as being a guarded admiration for market-determined pay differentials precisely because of their important, indeed indispensable, allocative function.

Fourth, 'social insurance is . . . a hybrid of welfare and capitalism and a bridge between them',[37] and is likely to remain such. On the one hand it bears witness to the 'fundamental principle of the welfare state that the market value of an individual cannot be the measure of his right to welfare'.[38] On the other hand, being earnings-related (albeit only up to a ceiling limit), it is responsible inevitably for 'subordinating welfare to some extent to market value'.[39] Marshall was prepared, in other words, to accept one evaluatory standard for entitlement and another for amount. Even those readers, however, who are willing to countenance inequalities with respect to income-maintenance in old age and similar states of pecuniary dependency which they would unhesitatingly have rejected if arising in the fields of health or education, will still have some difficulty in swallowing what follows: 'Social insurance has become a part of incomes policy. It is no longer a bearer of the welfare message.'[40] Here again we encounter Marshall's reliance on the tautologous statement – since it is hard to imagine an earnings-related measure which is totally insensitive to national policies on incomes – and perhaps even Marshall's ambiguous attitude to the tailoring of 'primary income'[41] – since the only way to narrow differentials in old age is to tamper with incentive-bearing differentials of men and women still at work. Such tampering would be authoritarian and paternalistic and probably incompatible with civil rights, quite apart from allocative efficiency; and there is clearly a conflict of principles here.

(b) THE DEMOCRATIC POLITY

The democratic polity is buttressed by the political rights which evolved in the nineteenth century and reposes on the principles of one man/one vote and majority rule. It is intimately linked to the market economy in a relationship which seems to be one of reciprocal causality: 'I am one of those who believe that it is hardly possible to maintain democratic freedoms in a society which does not contain a large area of economic freedom.'[42] Indeed it is, more generally, the very civil rights which legitimate economic freedom and are in turn strengthened by it which also render political despotism unlikely. Civil rights refer to people as actors, not takers, and are so embedded in the *psyche*, so internalised in the consciousness of the individual, that they 'spell power',[43] dispersed and diffuse: 'Nothing is more remarkable in the world of today than the impotence of the powerful.'[44] In general, events 'seem to testify more to the resilience of democracy than to its vulnerability.'[45] Disagreeing with Tocqueville on the need for a corporate state of intermediate groups so as to keep the ruling élite in check – he was particulary unhappy with the idea of utilising stratification via ascribed status as a means of warding off what would otherwise be an amorphous mass society: 'What social classes are particularly good at defending is privilege.'[46] – he argued that it is civil rights and democratic expectations which in truth constitute the best bulwark against totalitarianism. In such a culture, 'if the dictator chops one head off, a new one is likely to grow in its place,'[47] as the example of Czechoslovakia in recent years reminds us.

Marshall welcomed the democratic polity buttressed by political rights and drew attention to at least four ways in which it interacted with the other subsystems of his hyphenated society.

First, regarding the social interest, he found it perfectly legitimate that we as a social group should from time to time, via our democratically elected representatives, choose to introduce an element of coercion so as to ensure that all agree to serve the wider interests of the community: 'Though we may boggle at Rousseau's idea that citizens in a democracy "will be forced to be free", we can accept more easily the view that they may be induced to be healthy'.[48] Again, society has a need for educated citizens and may thus compel children to attend school; it only encourages families to keep a tidy home.[49] Marshall did not believe that a genuinely false social interest was likely to be propagated by a small number of democratically selected political leaders (or by their faithful instruments in the civil service), and this is perhaps why he did not fear to support centralisation of power: 'Political rights in a representative democracy can function at full strength only at one point, and through one institution, the national sovereign parliament. It is true that they function also, in a subordinate way, at the level of the local community, and more significantly at the level of the state in a federal system. But the ultimate power resides at the centre. The body politic, in short, has a single head.'[50] Nor did Marshall fear a perhaps more common form of tyranny in a regime of equal political rights, that of the majority over the minority. Yet in a needs-based welfare state which also enjoys political democracy, such a danger is ever-present. Marshall shows a high degree of optimism in a world of accountability via election when he makes statements such as the following: 'The welfare principle cannot be derived from the principle of majority rule; its duty is to provide not what the majority want but what minorities need.'[51]

Second, regarding separability, he argued that it is preferable for civil and political rights to evolve before social rights, but recognised that the order could be reversed, as in some developing countries where 'planned economic development and social welfare are put before effective democracy and personal freedom.'[52] This was also the German experience: 'Bismarck had made the first experiment in national social insurance in order, as he said, by satisfying the legitimate claims of the working classes, to discourage them from pressing their illegitimate ones.'[53] Development and welfare given from above, however, 'may stunt the growth of liberty'[54] or even encourage selfishly consumerist attitudes and vested interests; and in that sense 'social rights are no danger to totalitarian regimes, and indeed flourish in them.'[55] No one would deny, Marshall argued, that state action carried to excess can destroy individual liberty,[56] but he reminded the reader that the proposition is reversible and that 'individual liberty in a developed or developing society is possible only under the cover of state action.'[57] The problem with the second part of this statement is that it is profoundly ambiguous. If state action is here taken to refer to civil rights, then it is tautologous (since law and order are the preconditions for market capitalism), while if it is taken to refer to social rights then it is controversial (since perceived citizenship rights do not in all circumstances include social rights). All in all, Marshall does not convince the reader that the hyphenated society is inevitable (as opposed to desirable); and one wishes he had said more about the reasons (ranging from cultural attitudes to conflicts of vested interests of both the dysfunctional and the functional kind) which explain the differences in the evolutionary experience of different countries at approximately the same stage in their development. The separability thesis is undeniably a cause for concern to all those who believe in the right to welfare.

Third, regarding participation, he noted that men accustomed to active involvement in the democratic political system will experience a regrettable frustration of expections in the social welfare system if treated as objects rather than subjects. Thus, to provide what people need without asking them what they want 'is what I call welfare without citizenship.'[58] Apparently, however, the act of asking is, in the welfare sector at least, not automatically accompanied by the act of obtaining ('Although it must take careful note of expressed desires, it does not simply react to or obey them. Its responsibility is to satisfy needs, which is a different undertaking'[59]), and this may be the reason why Marshall has so little to say about formal consumer consultation schemes ranging from Parent Teacher Associations to neighbourhood pressure groups on council estates. Some frustration of expectations with respect to involvement is clearly inevitable in the hyphenated society (particularly since Marshall in 1949 opted for the strong definition of political participation – 'the right to participate in the exercise of political power, as a member of a body invested with political authority or as an elector of the members of such a body'[60] – and thus came close to equating the power of the politician and the power of the voter). One reason is the elementary truism that 'the right to choose, if it is to have real substance, must include the right to choose wrongly and to take the consequences'[61] (although Marshall in practice played down the contentious nature of the qualitative distinction between mistakes made out of income and mistakes made out of welfare transfers). A second reason is the resources constraint and the resultant need for the administrators to weigh efficiency against initiative so as to arrive, as usual, at 'balance and proportion': 'You cannot make the optimum use of scarce skills and resources in a nation-wide service open to all if you allow every applicant for its help to pick and choose as he pleases.'[62] A third reason is the existence and efficacy of professional standards – and discretion, albeit within a framework of formal laws and administrative rules.

Discretion must, of course, be 'sustained by publicity, accountability, supervision and, finally, the right of appeal'[63]; but if it is, the outcome is not just administrative flexibility, but a certain sense of participation as well. As Marshall puts it, 'the right to appeal implies that the claimant is the subject of welfare, not merely the object of it'.[64]

The right to appeal thus returns civil rights (even if only in a rather limited manner) to the stage; helps make the client believe he is an actor in (as opposed to being a spectator of) his own welfare drama; and reduces the extent to which democratic practices and attitudes fostered by one subsystem might be discouraged by another. It must be noted, however, that the need for a border solution is only mentioned in connection with the polity/welfare interface; and that Marshall makes no recommendation for utilising the capitalist market economy as a school for democrats through the extension in industrial and commercial organisations of formal schemes for consultation and participation. In some areas of activity the frustration of democratic expectations is therefore evidently to survive.

Fourth, regarding the residual supplier argument, Marshall made some concession to the structural (as opposed to the rights-based) explanation of the evolution of welfare states by adopting the view that as poor countries industrialise so their governments are compelled to take over more and more of the welfare functions previously performed within the family. After all, family ties will inevitably loosen with the geographical mobility so important for economic growth: 'This process of emancipation from familial power, like the other freedoms, can only take place if the society, through its government, provides for the individual outside his group the security and the opportunities he previously enjoyed within it.'[65] As a historian he noted that the frequent failure of private pension schemes in Europe in the nineteenth century undermined confidence in the efficacy of market insurance as a substitute for the security born of consanguinity and encouraged governmental intervention in this field.[66]

(c) THE WELFARE STATE

It is not easy to say what T. H. Marshall understood by the welfare state, and his discussions of the terminological problem in *Social Policy* is by no means entirely satisfying. There he explains that social policy 'does not lend itself to precise definition'; that its meaning in a particular context 'is largely a matter of convenience or convention'; that in trying to pinpoint its nature we should look 'not simply at the measures adopted, since these are but means to an end, but at the nature of the end itself';[67] and that it seeks 'to achieve results which the economic system would not achieve on its own, and . . . in doing so . . . is guided by values other than those determined by open market forces'[68]. The clearest statement of the scope of the welfare state to be found in *Social Policy* is probably this one: 'A "needs test" ... in the broadest sense of the term, is the foundation of every benevolent welfare service.'[69] When, however, he sought to apply this condition, as in *The Right to Welfare*, Marshall rapidly discovered just how much he was a Sorcerer's Apprentice seeking to quantify the qualitative with the aid of a rubber yardstick. Thus he states: 'In my estimation, welfare must be envisaged as an integral part of the whole apparatus that includes social security, education, public health, the medical services, factory legislation, the right to strike, and all the other rights and legitimate expectations which are attached to modern democratic citizenship.'[70] He then extends his list by situating subsidisation of the arts and even of exports under the rubric of states of dependency[71] and also throws in 'community services for the preservation and development of the physical, social and cultural environment'.[72] Ultimately he finds himself obliged to ask an economic question of great interest – 'why ... should housing and school meals be run as quasi-social services and not gas and electricity?'[73] – but does not provide an answer. So what emerges from his discussion of definition and scope is really only that some kinds of social interaction are needs-based while other kinds presuppose a *quid pro quo*; and that it is difficult to say precisely which kinds go in which pigeon-hole. That there should be a welfare pigeon-hole at all, however, is not in question, for it (like the capitalist market economy and the democratic polity) has the firmest possible foundations – in citizenship rights, and specifically in social rights. These Marshall described – in *Citizenship and Social Class* – as 'the whole range from the right to a modicum of economic welfare and security to the right to share to the full in the social heritage and to live the life of a civilised being according to the standards prevailing in the society.'[74] Because I in the twentieth century acquired social rights, therefore we in the twentieth century developed social policies.

Marshall advocated social policy for the fundamental reason that a social being has a social right – a right 'social in origin',[75] incidentally, as well as in function – to draw support 'from membership of the family, the neighbourhood, and the community';[76] and he made four points about the social policies which he so much wanted to see.

First, the welfare sector should be regarded as a mutual aid society, and analogous in that respect to the family and the local community. The model, in other words, is not philanthropy but 'mutual aid on the basis of common citizenship'.[77] Perceived citizenship, after all, 'permeates the whole life of the society and penetrates the consciousness of its members'[78] and reflects in addition an instinct, a 'natural reaction', namely 'the urge to sociability within the group': 'So when modern welfare policy set itself to breach the barrier of shame and replace it by the bridge of sympathy, it did not have to plant new instincts in the human psyche, but primarily to enlarge the human group.'[79] Even charitable contributions to the Church in a bygone era reflected more than simply a self-regarding desire to purchase an entry-ticket to Paradise in so far as they indicated as well a 'genuine concern for the sufferings of the poor and . . . personal devotion to their service'.[80] It would appear to be the existence of sincere sociability of this kind – sociability firmly rooted in what Marshall in 1949 described as 'a direct sense of community membership based on loyalty to a civilization which is a common possession'[81] – that explains why, although 'democratic voting is egoistic', electors none the less opt for taxes and transfers not in their own immediate self-interest: 'Welfare decisions depend on altruism – both concern for others and mutual concern for one another.'[82]

Such sociability is essential, for many an aspect of the mutual benefit system (national social insurance, for example) at least to some extent 'favours the weaker at the expense of the stronger'[83] and thus can only be regarded as 'help given by the privileged to the under-privileged'[84]. We are evidently concerned here not merely with a mutual aid society which shares burdens (the weak condition), but with one which consistently redistributes responsibilities (the strong condition), and the precondition for the survival of such a club is inevitably a high degree of agreement among the members as to the charter and statutes of the organisation: 'Without a foundation of near-consensus, no general social welfare policy would be possible.'[85] Without such a foundation, 'there could be no welfare state'; but fortunately, in modern Britain, 'a very high degree of consensus exists about the aims of the welfare services'.[86] Why consensus exists is, as it happens, not entirely clear, but Marshall does hint at the importance of autonomous and antecedent ethical norms. Alas, 'it is impossible to say exactly how these ethical standards arise in a society or are recognised by its members',[87] so we cannot know whether they are likely to be put at risk by the values of the acquisitive society, whether they are buttressed by the teachings of revealed religion, or whether the movement from *Gemeinschaft* to *Gemeinschaft* involves any further moral commitments to the community beyond an eagerness to pay monetary subscriptions (the duty to donate blood, for example, or to give employment to a released prisoner, or to abstain from litter and from acts of discourtesy). It would be fair to say that Marshall is not at his best when explaining the independent contribution of the ethical constraint to society's decision that it has a 'collective responsibility to seek to achieve welfare'.[88]

Second, consensus produces welfare and welfare in some measure returns the compliment: 'Medical care and education ... are areas in which differences of opportunity and experience, and particularly an institutionalised standard (which would inevitably follow), do more to create and sustain class distinctions than any other.'[89] And that is why, although the state sector now exists side by side with the public schools, 'the two cannot coexist indefinitely in their present form'[90] any more than two nations can coexist within the bosom of a common citizenship. The integrative function of welfare arises precisely because welfare focuses on need alone whereas market focuses in addition on ability to pay: 'I imagine ... that when you are weighing a naked baby on a pair of scales, the idea of social class does not obtrude itself unduly.'[91] More generally, welfare, because it is committed to optimal rather than minimal standards (not 'the lowest that is tolerable, but ... the highest that is possible'[92]) is by its very nature a levelling force in that it applies a common standard: 'A common standard cannot, of course, be an absolute one, but it is relative, not to the individual concerned, but to the level of civilisation of the society.'[93] Witness the 'class fusion' produced by 'a new common experience'[94] – the introduction of the National Health Service – to which he had drawn attention in *Citizenship and Social Class*. One might wish to extend this concept of class fusion to embrace racial fusion and thus to the integration of new immigrants and non-citizens in a common culture that was here before they were; but, having noted that, it must immediately be added that Marshall has little to say about racial tensions, ethnic diversity and radical cultural pluralism associated with the multinational nation that Britain has increasingly become.

Welfare not only integrates but individuates, and Marshall offers along these lines yet another argument for welfare in the form of one which is to some extent the obverse of the first. The argument is as follows: as the segmental structure of society broke down, as the spread of mass production made work less differentiated and less personalised, as the forces of mass consumption and mass communication made us all, 'more or less, members of the same crowd',[95] so mass welfare became both more acceptable and more threatening. Noting the danger that state education, for example, can easily degenerate into mass-produced education – education operating 'in the same way, at the same time, and with the same content on the minds of all those within reach'[96] – Marshall none the less insists that state welfare can if it so wishes distribute a 'highly individualized product'[97] and thus encourage the 'free development of personality':[98] 'Welfare, like peace, is indivisible. However specialised the services it offers, it must always keep in view, and pay respect to, the integrity of the whole person. And it is only this kind of individualism of the whole person that can resist the assault of the mass society against the individual personality.'[99] This insight is not fully developed, but is clearly an intriguing one – that *laissez-faire* liberalism today means massive economies of large scale, and that planned diversity is the (more acceptable) means by which collectivism ensures individualism. What is not clear is how the quest for variety relates to the need for adequate overlap in life-experiences; or to what extent differentiated welfare (given that equality of opportunity is undeniably a 'great architect of inequality'[100] with respect to outcome) might create a differentiated (and perhaps therefore not an integrated) society. And there remains the problem of the private sector; for Marshall, a man of compromise with a strong respect for persons, could not when it came to the crunch opt for the suppression of the dual system. The public schools, he decided, cannot legitimately be abolished. At the same time, however, the state system must remain 'potentially comprehensive'[101] and able to provide for anyone who returns ('for financial or other reasons'[102]) from provision via civil to provision via social rights; which suggests in turn that even those who opt for the benefits of independent education should not be allowed to opt out of the costs of the state alternative, lest those services shrink in consequence. Otherwise, simple considerations of freedom of choice speak in defence of 'a private sector of acceptable size and scope'.[103]

Third, duties are associated in some way with rights – as in the simple declaration that 'every right to receive implies an obligation to give'[104] – but the precise specification of the association is by no means an unambiguous one. On the one hand Marshall seems to be talking of ascribed absolutes, of 'rights created by the community itself and attached to the status of its citizenship'[105] regardless of the *quid pro quo*: 'The old morality stressed obligations more than rights; in the new it is the opposite. It is in the nature of the polity and of the economy to foster this change; can the third component resist it?'[106] On the other hand, speaking elsewhere about the 'third component', he seems to suggest that status after all implies contract: 'If you concede to a poor person an absolute unconditional right to relief, the question then arises how to deny him the right to become poor if he so wishes. The obligation of the community to relieve destitution must somehow be matched by a duty of the individual not to become destitute, if he can help it.'[107] Even the absolute is thus in some measure conditional on the performance of socially contingent duties, as indeed Marshall himself had made clear in *Citizenship and Social Class*: 'Social rights imply an absolute right to a certain standard of civilization which is conditional only on the discharge of the general duties of citizenship.'[108] The concluding words of this passage remind us that Marshall is really only telling us a part of the story when he declares, as he so frequently does, that social rights reflect 'the strong individualist element in mass society' and refer to 'individuals as consumers, not as actors'.[109] For the whole story we must go to Marshall's lecture on 'Social Selection in the Welfare State' (delivered in 1953), where he carefully distinguishes two separate dimensions in social welfare. There is, first of all, the 'intense individualism' with which so much of rights-talk has become identified: 'The claim of the individual to welfare is sacred and irrefutable and partakes of the character of a natural right.'[110] There is also, however, a stratum of 'collectivism'' which is quite separate from 'intense individualism' and helps to explain what Marshall meant when he wrote, almost two decades later in the very first issue of the *Journal of Social Policy*, that 'it would be dishonest to pretend that there is not about welfare policy decisions something intrinsically authoritarian or ... paternalistic':[111] 'The Welfare State is the responsible promoter and guardian of the welfare of the whole community, which is something more complex than the sum total of the welfare of all its individual members arrived at by simple addition.'[112]

What Marshall is saying is that we acquire duties at the same time as we acquire rights, and in some places – notably where speaking of health or education – he actually treats a right as equivalent to a duty. Health, because it 'is in large measure a form of public discipline': 'Your body is part of the national capital, and must be looked after, and sickness causes a loss of national income, in addition to being liable to spread.'[113] Education, because it 'is a process by which citizens are made': 'Education is of such vital importance for the health and prosperity of a nation, that it is regarded as something of which the individual has a duty to avail himself, to the extent that his natural abilities warrant.'[114] But if welfare is to be regarded as social investment – if society has a right to educated adults, just as children have a right to learning – then some alternative legitimation must be found for that welfare which is allocated to the mentally handicapped, the unemployable or the aged: 'It cannot be said that society needs happy old people in the same way that it needs a healthy and educated population'[115] and in such a case the motive for the stranger-gift once more becomes 'your duty to your neighbour',[116] 'compassion rather than interest'.[117] Marshall than reaches the following conclusion: 'Though compassion (or "the impulses of common humanity") may create a right, having almost the force of law, to minimal subsistence, it cannot establish the same kind of right to the benefit of services which are continuously striving to extend the limits of the possible.'[118] Marshall believed, in other words, that there was a hierarchy of social rights, and was prepared, showing a surprisingly healthy interest in the *quid pro quo*, to look the proverbial cherub in the mouth. It is this curious mixture of individualism and functionalism which constitutes his unique contribution to the conceptualisation of social rights.

Fourth, poverty means poverty ('The common factor in the state of the poor is the urgency of their need.'[119]) and the concept of relative deprivation is therefore to be handled with care: 'If it means that poverty is relative to the standard of civilisation of the country concerned, it is beyond dispute. If it means that I may not say that A is poor, but only that he is poorer than B, I cannot accept it.'[120] What is today called relative deprivation, Marshall notes, was once classed among the seven deadly sins, and is in any case a problem of perceptions which cannot be solved simply by scaling down differentials ('however necessary this may be'): 'It can be done only by changing the attitude towards them. The problem is structural in origin, but there is no purely structural solution to it.'[121] It is not clear what cultural change he has in mind to restore perceived legitimacy to the distribution of income (a distribution which reflects income derived from capital as well as income derived from labour, a point which reminds us in turn how little he had to say about the existence and/or breaking down of agglomerations of – perhaps inherited – wealth through government policy in the social democratic future). What is clear is simply that, in the hyphenated society, inequality of incomes is here to stay: 'In such a society poverty is a disease, but inequality is an essential structural feature.'[122] We are not, of course, told precisely who the people are who are most likely to be afflicted by the disease; and it is frustrating that some of Marshall's more controversial remarks – his reference to 'low wages and irregular employment';[123] to the 'wounds inflicted by the social system';[124] to society's 'conspicuous failure to substitute prevention of poverty for relief of poverty'[125] for example – are neither fully explained nor followed up. But what we are told is certainly worth hearing – that the task of eliminating deprivation relative to the cultural norm 'must be undertaken jointly by welfare and capitalism; there is no other way'[126] – and his general conclusion is cause for a moderate amount of complacency: 'Our particular type of social system has got nearer to achieving this objective than any that has gone before or now exists.'[127]

Poverty, where it does exist, should be no grounds for exclusion from universal welfare services, and it is a tribute to the universality of 'welfare-consciousness'[128] that it is not: the 'utter rejection' of the two-tier system (involving as it would a 'second-class service for second-class people'[129]) is something 'I regard . . . as an intrinsic quality of twentieth-century civilisation.'[130] A classless welfare system need not be a free-on-demand system, however, and Marshall saw no reason why those who could afford to pay for services received should be exempted from doing so. Those whose means are insufficient relative to their needs will be identified by the means-test (which is no more inquisitorial or stigmatising than the other selective standards that must be applied in the field of welfare – the test to determine if unemployment is genuinely involuntary, for example);[131] and the final result is that rich and poor alike share in the same kinds of benefits in a manner determined exclusively by need and not at all by ability to pay. Here again, however, once he strayed from the fields of health and education, Marshall appears not always to have been absolutely clear in his own mind as to what he really understood by allocation based on need and need alone. The following passage is a case in point: 'All dwellings, however different in size, should be equally convertible by the families that occupy them into homes.'[132]

*   *   *

T. H. Marshall was a man of considerable learning who seems to have spent a great deal of his time scouting in dictionaries for authoritative meanings and who was never afraid to leaven the stew of his own social theory with more than a few 'slices of good nourishing history',[133] such food for thought being essential preparation – Tawney makes the same point – 'for an attack on the problems of today'.[134] His approach is multidisciplinary and synthetic, concerned with *why* questions rather than with *how* questions, orientated more towards concepts and insights than towards measurement and evidence, characterised at all times by a sincere belief that the theoretical and moral emphasis should be placed firmly 'on persons rather than on things'.[135]

It is also rather provincial – surprisingly so since Marshall had spent long periods abroad (including two in Germany – one as a civilian prisoner of war, the other on the staff of the British High Commission) and also served for four years as Director of the Social Science Department of UNESCO. Yet, although he does speak of the different perceptions of class inequality which obtain in Sweden as compared with Britain,[136] and although he convincingly explains the lesser tolerance of poverty in America in terms of features particularly characteristic of that country (notably a super-normal belief in equality of opportunity, a widespread propensity to take competitive performance as an indicator of will to succeed, a valuation of hard work),[137] the fact remains that these are mere footnotes to his general account of citizenship rights – an account which seems to repose almost entirely on British historical experience, British sources and British values, and may for that reason be open to the criticism that it indulges in the dubious methodological practice of inducing social theory from the unique, the one-off and perhaps even the once-for-all.

To be fair, however, T. H. Marshall was a man of considerable commonsense as well as of considerable learning; and he himself drew attention in *The Right to Welfare* to the many 'loose threads'[138] in his system, just as he had thirty years earlier drawn attention to the loose threads in the human condition itself. Then he had declared 'Social behaviour is not governed by logic',[139] but had immediately added a moving defence of moderation and muddle-through: 'A human society can make a square meal out of a stew of paradox without getting indigestion.'[140] We must, in other words, remain cautious and tolerant precisely because of the great difficulties involved in any form of dogmatism. Thus in his inaugural address on 'Sociology at the Crossroads' Marshall came out in 1946 for the 'middle way which runs over firm ground' in preference to the 'way to the stars' of the abstract-theoretical speculator or the 'way into the sands'[141] of the fact-gatherer and the number-cruncher. Similarly, in his discussions of economic issues he makes a practice of searching for the middle way – a road evidently lying somewhere to the left of the monetarist option (since 'a trend towards the greater protection of the individual against the fluctuations of the market' is 'a trend which many would argue is an expression of the spirit of the welfare state',[142] and this even where lowering expectations, many others would argue, is precisely the duty-counterpart of the right to employment), but somewhere to the right of the nationalisers and the planners (since despite his frequent references to the 'mixed economy',[143] the mix to which he most often refers is that of welfare with capitalism, as opposed to that of public-owned industry with private). His approach to social welfare, finally, yet again demonstrates his obsession with the need to 'strike an acceptable balance'[144] and his tendency wherever possible to seize the average and split the difference. Solomon, whose favourite colour was not tartan and who believed that half a child was not necessarily preferable to none at all, would certainly have asked for more explanation than is provided of passages such as the following: 'All human situations are psycho-social. . . . In the matter of welfare, I contend, the emphasis should be bang in the middle, on the hyphen.'[145] Solomon would, one imagines, then certainly have reminded us that there exists not one middle way but two. On the one hand there is the precarious path atop the icy razor's edge. That middle way is neither optimal nor stable. On the other hand there is the golden road which is wisely constructed in the lush valley, not on the barren ridges which border it, Left and Right. That middle way is both optimal and stable. T. H. Marshall never entirely clarifies the nature of the middle ground to which his hyphenated society belongs. It is the right and duty of the concerned citizen to find out.

NOTES AND REFERENCES

All works cited are by T. H. Marshall.

1. T. H. Marshall, *The Right to Welfare and Other Essays* (London: Heinemann Educational Books, 1981) p. 104. The seven papers, in five cases accompanied by an extended 'Afterthought', are 'Changing Ideas About Poverty' (no date) (pp. 29–52), 'Welfare in the Context of Social Development' and 'Welfare in the Context of Social Policy' (both 1964) (pp. 53–66 and 67–82 respectively), 'The Right to Welfare' and 'Freedom as a Factor in Social Development' (both 1965) (pp. 83–103 and 157–75 respectively), 'Reflections on Power' (1969) (pp. 137–56), and 'Value Problems of Welfare-Capitalism' (1972) (pp. 104–36).
2. *RW*, p. 107.
3. *RW*, p. 124.
4. *RW*, p. 163.
5. *RW*, p. 157.
6. *RW*, p. 133.
7. *RW*, p. 169.
8. *RW*, p. 106.
9. *RW*, p. 120.
10. *RW*, p. 93.
11. *RW*, p. 61.

12. *RW*, p. 39.
13. 'The Welfare State – A Comparative Study', in *Sociology at the Cross-roads and Other Essays* (London: Heinemann, 1963) p. 307.
14. *RW*, p. 132.
15. *RW*, p. 115.
16. *RW*, p. 129.
17. *RW*, p. 129.
18. *RW*, p. 115.
19. *RW*, p. 115. See also p. 90.
20. *RW*, p. 131.
21. *RW*, p. 135.
22. 'Citizenship and Social Class', in *SC*, p. 72. These lectures were originally published in *Citizenship and Social Class and Other Essays* (Cambridge: the University Press, 1950) and later reprinted as the very long Chapter Four of *Sociology at the Crossroads*, to which our notes refer.
23. *Social Policy in the Twentieth Century* 4th ed. (London: Hutchinson, 1975) p. 111.
24. 'Citizenship and Social Class', in *SC*, p. 91.
25. *RW*, p. 65. Emphasis is mine.
26. 'Citizenship and Social Class', in *SC*, p. 107.
27. 'Citizenship and Social Class', *SC*, p. 95.
28. 'Citizenship and Social Class', in *SC*, p. 72.
29. *RW*, p. 135.
30. *RW*, p. 135.
31. *RW*, p. 64.
32. 'Citizenship and Social Class', in *SC*, p. 118.
33. *RW*, p. 164.
34. *RW*, p. 109.
35. *RW*, pp. 155–6.
36. *RW*, p. 172.
37. *RW*, p. 113.
38. *RW*, p. 107.
39. *RW*, p. 113.
40. *RW*, p. 132.
41. *RW*, p. 135.
42. *RW*, p. 135.
43. *RW*, p. 142.
44. *RW*, p. 144.
45. *RW*, p. 154.
46. *RW*, p. 139.
47. *RW*, p. 142.
48. *RW*, p. 91.
49. *RW*, p. 68.
50. *RW*, p. 141.
51. *RW*, p. 126.
52. *RW*, p. 169.
53. *RW*, p. 59.
54. *RW*, p. 169.
55. *RW*, p. 141.

56. *RW*, p. 158.
57. *RW*, p. 158.
58. *RW*, p. 170.
59. *RW*, p. 107.
60. 'Citizenship and Social Class', in *SC*, p. 74.
61. *RW*, pp. 157–8.
62. *RW*, p. 114.
63. *RW*, p. 89.
64. *RW*, p. 96.
65. *RW*, p. 165.
66. *RW*, p. 111.
67. *SPTC*, p. 11.
68. *SPTC*, p. 15.
69. *SPTC*, p. 88.
70. *RW*, p. 81.
71. *RW*, p. 52.
72. *RW*, p. 135.
73. *RW*, p. 134.
74. 'Citizenship and Social Class', in *SC*, p. 74.
75. *RW*, p. 91.
76. *RW*, p. 82.
77. *RW*, p. 71.
78. *RW*, p. 71.
79. *RW*, p. 73.
80. *RW*, p. 73.
81. 'Citizenship and Social Class', in *SC*, p. 96.
82. *RW*, p. 108.
83. *RW*, p. 88.
84. *RW*, p. 71.
85. *RW*, p. 109.
86. *RW*, p. 113.
87. *RW*, p. 109.
88. *RW*, p. 88.
89. *RW*, p. 112.
90. *RW*, p. 112.
91. *RW*, p. 78.
92. *RW*, p. 59.
93. *RW*, p. 78.
94. 'Citizenship and Social Class', in *SC*, p. 107.
95. *RW*, p. 61.
96. *RW*, p. 62.
97. *SPTC*, p. 14.
98. *RW*, p. 63.
99. *RW*, p. 62.
100. *RW*, p. 119.
101. *RW*, p. 112.
102. *RW*, p. 112.
103. *RW*, p. 113.
104. *RW*, p. 92.

105. *RW*, p. 88.
106. *RW*, p. 175.
107. *RW*, p. 90. See also p. 92.
108. 'Citizenship and Social Class', in *SC*, p. 98.
109. *RW*, p. 141.
110. 'Social Selection in the Welfare State', in *SC*, p. 246.
111. *RW*, p. 109.
112. 'Social Selection in the Welfare State', in *SC*, p. 247.
113. *RW*, p. 91.
114. *RW*, pp. 90–1.
115. *RW*, p. 91.
116. *RW*, p. 67.
117. *RW*, p. 92.
118. *RW*, p. 92.
119. *RW*, p. 117.
120. *RW*, pp. 116–17.
121. *RW*, p. 119.
122. *RW*, p. 117.
123. *RW*, p. 40.
124. *RW*, p. 133.
125. *RW*, p. 132.
126. *RW*, p. 117.
127. *RW*, pp. 117–18.
128. *RW*, p. 89.
129. *RW*, p. 79.
130. *RW*, p. 79.
131. *RW*, pp. 99–100.
132. *RW*, p. 66.
133. 'Sociology at the Crossroad', in *SC*, p. 5.
134. 'Citizenship and Social Class', in *SC*, p. 73.
135. *RW*, p. 57.
136. *RW*, p. 119.
137. *RW*, pp. 35, 46.
138. *RW*, p. 123.
139. 'Citizenship and Social Class', in *SC*, p. 127.
140. 'Citizenship and Social Class', in *SC*, p. 127.
141. 'Sociology at the Crossroads', in *SC*, p. 21.
142. *RW*, p. 52.
143. See *RW*, pp. 52, 107, 123–4, 127, 135.
144. *RW*, p. 102.
145. *RW*, p. 81.

10 The Welfare State, Economics and Morality

DAVID COLLARD

1. HUMAN BETTERMENT, ECONOMIC WELFARE AND MORAL DEVELOPMENT

Human betterment is a grand theme, rather too grand for mere economists who are most likely to have encountered the word 'betterment' in tomes on the improvement of property or land. By direct analogy human betterment has to do with 'human capital', with improvements in health, skill and education. Economists will also have come upon the semi-technical term 'Pareto-better' to describe arrangements whereby all parties gain. The primary dictionary definition does indeed refer to the state or condition of being better (*Shorter Oxford English Dictionary, New English*). Yet it gives priority to the process of making or *becoming* better. The crucial concern of this paper is the welfare state as a link between economic and moral development.

The discussion which follows is organised roughly along the lines of Figure 10.1, though it eventually becomes clear that relationships are much more complex than those indicated there. Once we have defined economic welfare and moral development we shall want to be able to

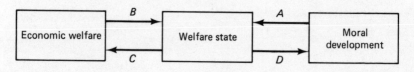

FIGURE 10.1

174

refer to positive changes in each of them. It will not be necessary to talk much about human betterment as a whole, but it would be useful to be able to say that positive changes in economic welfare *and* in moral development represent an unambiguous improvement. Beyond that, one has to resort to intuitionism.

The remainder of this first section gives working definitions of economic welfare and moral development and also presents two slightly extravagant scenarios to emphasise the sorts of point that need to be made. Of the relationships indicated in Figure 10.1, *C* is by far the most written about, but it is, of course, only one element in the picture.

Economic welfare may be said to have increased when there has been an increase in real income, appropriately adjusted for changes in the income distribution. The easiest case to take is the 'Pareto-better' one, where everyone has become better-off. For other, more usual, cases economists have devised compensation tests to show whether or not real income has increased. The more hard-headed economists are content to take increases in real income as themselves indicating increases in economic welfare. The standard modern treatment, however, is to have some inequality index (e.g. the Gini coefficient) *and* real income as arguments in a social welfare function. An important thing to note about this modern definition is that increases in real income are only *certain* to increase economic (social) welfare, if not accompanied by a worsening income distribution. (It is unfortunate that we have got into the habit of calling what is very obviously an *economic* welfare function a *social* welfare function.)

Associated with this is an ethical (as opposed to a descriptive) approach to inequality which has caused some writers considerable anxiety. Thus, Sen (1978) has condemned it as fundamentally flawed. The ethical element is potentially embarrassing here, as it has already been introduced before any discussion of morality. A suggested resolution is that the welfare function implied by the state of moral development is the appropriate one when society is making its own judgements about its own inequality but not otherwise. In this case there would be an equality, as it were, between those ethical judgements employed in policy-making and those used in measurement. But already there is a breakdown in the tidy boxes of Figure 10.1.

In spite of what I said earlier there is, of course, no necessary link between increases in real income and increases in happiness, let alone human betterment. The weakness of the relationship, both in cross-section and over time is a commonplace. The link between real income and human betterment is even weaker. Are people 'better' if they become richer or healthier but less loyal or less honest or less loving? One could even assert that human betterment had nothing whatever to do with real income: a much less dangerous position than an uncritical association of one with the other.

Moral development has to be broken down into its component parts. One part is to do with preferences, affections, tastes, sympathy and the other is to do with reason: both are discussed in more detail in Section 2. The distinction is an ancient one. For example, Smith based his whole schema on a reasoned generalisation of sentiment (1759). In contrast Kant's system (1930) was built upon 'practical reason' and sentiment played no part at all. This faculty of moral reasoning is indeed a general one, not tied at all to any particular sentiment: it may be applied just as readily to liberty as to sympathy. I wish to concentrate in what follows less on altruism than on moral reasoning. But while altruism is not the only, or even the most important, aspect of moral development, it is the aspect which most concerns us here.

Whether sympathy, or empathy, or fellow feeling increases over time is not at all certain. If it does, as I should like to think it does, so much the better. (In *Altruism and Economy* I outlined a possible dynamics of the development of altruism over time.) But whatever these feelings the really difficult step (or series of steps) is their translation into some kind of social action. I shall concentrate, in the next section, on a particular kind of moral development, the emergence of what I call *economic rights*.

A *welfare state* is one in which citizens have rights or entitlements to goods or services independently of rights based on property or income.

Finally in this section, I consider two strong cases, one of positive association and one of negative association. In the negative case the welfare state is badly designed so that not all those in need receive benefits. People are unwilling to work at the high marginal tax rates and replacement ratios prevailing (see below) so economic welfare falls. The built-in inadequacies cause resentment and suspicion of 'scroungers' so that sympathy is blunted and moral reasoning deteriorates into stereotyping. The welfare state has had damaging effects on both economic and moral development – it has resulted in worsenment rather than betterment.

In the positive case the welfare state is well designed so that all those in need receive benefits. It imposes tax rates which are generally felt to be fair and have no discernible effects on output or the willingness to work. Indeed the high quality of education and health care have favourable output effects. Little or no resentment is caused and the public is proud of what it is doing to help the less fortunate. Earnest debate takes place about the next extensions of the welfare state which has fostered both economic and moral development and resulted in human betterment.

2. MORAL DEVELOPMENT AND THE WELFARE STATE (A)

Suppose, for the sake of analysis, that real income is given. I wish to argue that moral development of an altruistic kind tends to increase the welfare state. However, there are several steps in the argument, which is not quite as simple as one might expect. It is certainly not the case that an index of altruism amounts to more or less the same thing as an index of welfare provision, at least at the level of society as a whole. At the individual level it is relatively straightforward.

Consider some contingency, like illness, unemployment or old age, that may be 'insured' against by buying cover at some known premium (the cover could, of course, take the form of saving). Amounts of cover bought will depend upon incomes. With constant tastes across income groups and logarithmic demand functions, relative provision will depend solely upon income elasticity: relative provision is easily shown to be y^η where η is the income elasticity and y is the income of a higher income group. So if $\eta = 2$ and $y = 5$ the higher income group will buy for itself twenty-five times as much as the poorer income group. Someone with sympathetic or altruistic feelings might wish to improve provision for the less well-off and there are several things that he or she might do.

The obvious and immediate action is to provide financial or other help at the moment of need: but reflection will often suggest a generalisation of both sentiment and action. Indeed action is an essential part of altruism: which is defined as concern for others as a principle for action. If no generalisation at all is made from the first stage of altruistic feelings, giving will be the outcome of chance encounters. The generalisations I refer to are of *sympathy* and of *action*. The generalisation of sympathy requires imagination and reason. Most people have the greatest regard for themselves and then their family and friends. Generalised sympathy requires similar feelings towards distant and unknown others in similar situations: a generalisation to children in general from my child. To persuade people to generalise in this way has always been a major task of social reformers – that is why publicity about particular hard cases is so effective; it converts a general and elusive problem into a personal and comprehensible one. This act of sympathetic generalisation is an important part of moral development.

The inadequacy of random and spontaneous giving will be evident to the donor in another way. Once he has made the first sort of generalisation it will be rational to wish to help others in similar circumstances and perhaps the same individual on other occasions. Donations will then need to be systematised and organised and the individual might very well feel that some sort of discipline is required. Otherwise, although rational reflection dictates regular contributions he will sometimes forget or sometimes feel that he can't afford it that week. If he is very efficient he will covenant money regularly to a charity: but even then he might forget to increase it for inflation.

At this stage the 'free-rider' problem has to be introduced. The act of giving to unknown others may usefully be modelled as a prisoners' dilemma problem (see Collard, 1978). The details of the model need not concern us here. The important thing is that once the number of donors becomes large – even if each donor is altruistically motivated – it will, apparently, be rational for each to free-ride on the backs of other donors. Hence charitable giving breaks down. But charitable giving does not *in fact* break down. Why is this?

The answer lies in a form of Kant's moral imperative: that it is one's duty to carry out an action which, if universalised, would lead to a good outcome. This accords with a common moral argument made in everyday speech: 'it wouldn't do if everyone behaved like that'. In the case of giving, the universalisation would need only to be among like-minded others, not among the whole of society. If we could rely totally on what I have elsewhere called 'Kantian altruism' (1978, 1983) there would be no further difficulty. There would be no need for compulsory insurance, taxation and public provision: the welfare state could wither away.

It is at this stage of the argument that we must cross over into compulsion and political decision-taking, for it is almost inconceivable that private charities could provide the major items in the modern welfare state package. Each level of provision will carry with it tax implications and, in principle, voters may choose the levels of provision they prefer. Under any voting system, except the veto, there will be some individuals paying more than they want and some less. The system is 'voluntary', however, in that it is the one chosen under the democratic decision rule in operation and there will be a broad basis of consent for it.

So far the argument has been taking us away from a sole reliance on spontaneous individual giving (for efficiency reasons) and upon charities (for free-rider reasons), but it has not yet taken us to direct provision by the state. Two of the principal alternatives to state provision are (i) income subsidies by the state to enable the less well-off to buy the desired quantities and (ii) price subsidies. The first would do only if 'altruistic' sympathy had no paternalism in it – which is rarely the case – for recipients would be able to buy more of goods other than the target good. The second is much more attractive, especially if the subsidy can be varied from individual to individual.

If 'cover' is good the subsidised insurance solution might be an attractive one. But it must be remembered that we are dealing with institutionalised altruism which implies that certain economic rights have been established – to ensure this the cover must be easily and automatically available. Further, the cover itself will have to be reliable so if produced privately the state will need to underwrite it. In the case of health and sickness some extremely large subsidies would have to be paid to those individuals likely to require prolonged and expensive hospital care. In short, direct public provision might be the simplest way of *implementing* an economic right. To set against this, public provision could be costly, cumbersome and bureaucratic. The nub of the issue here is uncertainty and related search and information costs. In other words, the advantage of a national health service over an insurance based private service is that no questions whatsoever are raised at the moment of need about income, status or contributions.

Some of the foregoing argument is captured in Figure 10.2. 'Cover',

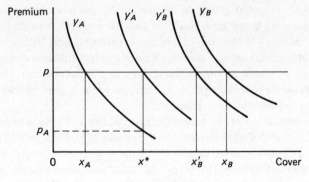

FIGURE 10.2

on the x-axis is available at a premium p. In the free market individuals of income y_B purchase x_B of cover and of income y_A purchase x_A. As we saw above, these levels of provision will be more unequal than incomes whenever the income elasticity is greater than one. Now suppose that (by a democratic decision rule) the As and the Bs together decide that x^* will be publicly available to everyone. Various methods of finance are possible, but all will imply a reduction in Bs incomes to, say, y'_B. Hence x^* is public provision (available to both) and $(x'_B - x^*)$ is private provision for the Bs. If the As are politically powerful or the Bs very altruistic (or both) x^* could be greater until x^* and x'_B coincided. There would then be no private provision whatever. Of the alternative methods mentioned above, an income subsidy would require an income of y'_A (so that y'_B would contract further to y''_B, not shown) and a price subsidy, ignoring income effects, would require a price of p_A.

3. THE ECONOMY AND THE WELFARE STATE (B)

In the previous section I took the general level of real income to be constant and we found a rough positive relationship, though admittedly a complex one, between altruistic feelings and welfare provision. In this section I wish first to concentrate upon real income instead and then to look at the two together.

Being richer does not make us better but it certainly makes it much easier to have a welfare state. There is a rough relationship between the economic prosperity of a country and its level of welfare-type provision. Figure 10.3 gives expenditures on education, health and social security and welfare together with per capita income for a fairly arbitrarily selected group of countries. At this aggregated level it is impossible to know how much of this expenditure was downwardly redistributive – in the case of education probably very little.

No one would suggest that the British are five times as caring or five times as altruistic as the Indians: they are, however, thirty times as prosperous. Prosperity plays at least as great a part as morality *in making welfare provision possible*.

How would we predict the effects on welfare provision of increases in real income? Policy debates on the nature of poverty should provide a clue. Discussion often concentrates upon whether poverty should be measured absolutely (in terms of calorific requirements, etc.) or relatively (as a proportion of average income). This not merely a

	Education %	Health %	Social security and welfare[†] %	Per capita GDP index
India	1.1	0.6	0.2	100
Ghana	2.9	1.0	1.6	488
Venezuela	4.4	1.9	1.0	1623
UK	5.0	5.2	1.5	3007
West Germany	4.0	5.9	1.7	5585

SOURCE: *UN Yearbook of National Accounts,* 1980.
[†] presumably excluding transfers themselves.
FIGURE 10.3 *Welfare expenditures in selected countries*

technical discussion, for poverty is regarded as a 'bad thing', on the agenda for elimination, so definitions are tied up with preferences for action. With the 'absolute' definition and the preferences implied by it, one would expect transfers to decrease as average real incomes increase and, as real incomes 'trickle-down', transfers would eventually disappear altogether. In so far as they do not do so it is because the absolute poverty-line is taken to be a conventional one and is permitted to move up over time. If it moves up proportionately with income it merges into the 'relative' definition. In that case the alleviation of poverty requires increasing absolute transfers but constant relative transfers. Sen (1983), developing Townsend's analysis of relative deprivation (1979), has recently suggested that 'relative poverty' may be given an 'absolute' justification, i.e. the goods and services required in order to be able to carry out basic functions in terms of work, community, movement, etc. Equal capabilities require different goods in different communities and, of course, within communities. This is closely related to long-standing debate about the place of 'needs' in economic analysis.

At the other end of the scale we must not neglect those apparently extreme writers who have argued – almost utopianly – that increasing relative transfers will be appropriate as one approaches satiation at very high levels of income (Keynes, 1930; collected ed. 1972). In this distant scenario the rich would be prepared to pay high taxes until everyone else had caught up: *richesse oblige.* But the constant flow of new gadgets suggests that the marginal utility of income will not readily reduce to zero.

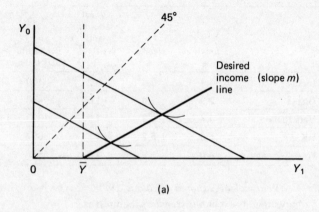

(a)

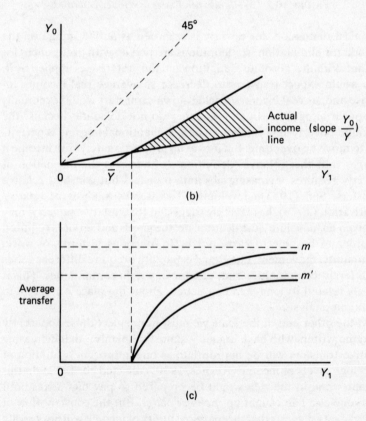

(b)

(c)

FIGURE 10.4   *Transfers and income*

The relative-poverty approach is not entirely plausible at low levels of taxpayer income. It is not reasonable, neither does it accord with casual empirical evidence, that taxpayers in very poor countries should be expected to transfer the same proportion of income as taxpayers in much richer countries. For the rest of the discussion I shall be assuming that people are concerned only with their own goods up to subsistence income, but that their preferences are homothetic on their own and others' goods thereafter. It is also convenient to assume that relative incomes (in the absence of redistribution) are given. In Figure 10.4(a) the desired distribution line is given where the homothetic indifference curves are tangential to the income lines – $\bar{y}$ is 'subsistence' income for class I (the richer group). To obtain actual transfers we need to subtract the actual income line from the desired income line so the hatched lines in Figure 10.4(b) indicate the amounts of redistribution actually undertaken.

The analysis is similar in spirit to the assumptions used in some of modern demand analysis (see Deaton and Muellbauer, 1980). Desired transfers will be given by:

$$y_i = m_{iT}(Y_I - \Sigma Y_j) - m_i Y_o \qquad (1)$$

Here y_i is the desired transfer of good i, Y_j is necessary expenditure of good j, Y_I and Y_o are pre-tax incomes of the two groups, m_i is the private marginal propensity to spend on good i and m_{iT} is the marginal propensity to transfer good i through the tax system. Clearly m_{iT} is equivalent to a constant marginal earmarked tax. This formulation makes it particularly easy to distinguish between paternalistic and non-paternalistic transfers: if m_{iT} bears the same relation to private m_i for all goods a general redistribution will be in order. It is very likely that many commodities, or even broad groups of commodities, carry zero m_{iT} and that a few commodities (like health care) will carry relatively high m_{iT}s.

Figure 10.4(c) shows the proportion of income transferred as income rises and is derived by dividing equation (1) by Y and eliminating subscripts. This gives

$$\frac{y}{Y} = m\frac{(1-y)}{Y} - \frac{m_o}{Y} \qquad (2)$$

which may be taken to relate to a specific good or service or to income in general. The average transfer tax rises with income but at a decreasing rate and, as income becomes high, it approaches m. The dotted line shows the same relationship with a lower value of m, m'. It is very likely that the same rough relationship holds both across countries and over time within a country. For example, it seems likely that social security transfer payments in the UK will balance out at around 25 per cent: for relatively new services (e.g. the early years of a health service) the analysis *predicts* a fairly rapidly rising transfer tax before it begins to flatten out.

Using this analysis there are three grounds for anxiety about the welfare state in the UK:

(i) Though there is no reason to believe that people have become more or less altruistic it is the case that politically those groups preferring lower values of m have become more decisive.

(ii) Income has ceased to rise much so average transfers cannot increase as fast as they might have been expected to on the basis of past performance.

(iii) The changing population structure (a higher ratio of beneficiaries) reduces the slope of the income line so that (with given preferences) desired transfers reduce.

4. THE WELFARE STATE AND THE ECONOMY (C)

There is an almost universal assumption that the welfare state is harmful to economic welfare. Presumably this is meant to apply to rather advanced and developed welfare states, as public investment in improving the physical and mental health of the people – by eliminating contagious and infectious diseases and illiteracy – can hardly fail to increase real income at the same time as it reduces inequality. These basic functions of a welfare state contain very large externality elements; very few economists would, I imagine, quarrel with the view that improvements in child health in India increase economic welfare.

The problem is often discussed in terms of a 'trade-off' between efficiency and equality. The principal disincentive effects of high levels of taxation and of welfare benefits are associated with

(i) an unwillingness to work extra hours, take on extra responsibilities or move to a more highly paid job;

(ii) an unwillingness to work rather than not to work.

The size and indeed direction of these effects is still controversial. Economic theory teaches us that the effect of an increase in the marginal tax rate on working hours may be split into income effects (which imply less leisure and therefore more work) and substitution effects (which imply a switch away from work into leisure). The practical outcome depends on the net balance of these two effects so cannot be determined *a priori*. Some of the most detailed studies (e. g. Brown, 1980) show the net effect to be probably quite small. It is, however, relatively large in the case of second earners (where the income effect is relatively unimportant) and it may very well be that the methods of measurement that we have are not yet sufficiently sophisticated to pick up the more subtle or longer term effects.

The second sort of disincentive effect, the question of whether or not to work, is now highly controversial in the UK because some economists have argued that the replacement ratio is too high. (This is the ratio of what an individual could receive out of work compared with what he or she, working normal hours, could earn in work.) The controversy surrounds the size of the replacement ratio itself and the elasticity of unemployment to the replacement ratio. The size of the ratio will depend upon the abilities and personal circumstances of the individuals concerned, upon benefit rates, tax rates and work expenses, and on average is of the order of 70 per cent (*Fiscal Studies*, March 1983). The elasticity presumably lies somewhere in the range 0.5 to 1.5. If it is unity a 10 per cent cut in benefits will bring (roughly) a 10 per cent reduction in unemployment: so if unemployment is 10 per cent a 10 per cent reduction in benefits might lead to a once-and-for-all increase in employment of 1.1 per cent and an increase in output of, say, 0.8 per cent. But to this would need to be added the direct incentive effects of the tax reduction accompanying the benefit reduction. If transfers of all kinds amount to 20 per cent of Gross Domestic Product (GDP), a 10 per cent cut is equivalent to a 2.5 per cent increase in non-transfer-incomes. It is unlikely that tax elasticity of output is numerically greater than about 0.1. So this additional output effect would be of the order of 0.25 per cent. Altogether, therefore, the effects of a 10 per cent reduction in unemployment and other benefits would be a once-and-for-all output increase of about 1.05 per cent, a tax reduction equivalent to 2.5 per cent of income and a 10 per cent cut in the incomes of the remaining unemployed. It is not obvious that this is a recipe for increasing economic welfare.

A particularly strong form of the benefit-reduction argument was put by ministers in the first Thatcher administration. It was argued that savings in public expenditure (including benefits) would (by reducing taxation and/or interest rates) increase output. The poor, although getting a reduced share of output, would therefore eventually be better-off (see Budget Resolutions, March 1980; Social Services Committee, May 1980). As we have just seen, the poor cannot possibly be better-off in the short-term as a result of cuts: so the argument must rely on growth effects. Again it is useful to do some arithmetic to get at the order of magnitude of the result. It is possible that a small redistribution from beneficiaries to taxpayers would increase the marginal propensity to save and hence (with fixed incremental capital-output ratios) increase the rate of economic growth. But the difference in savings propensities is probably not more than 0.2, so, of the 2 per cent of Gross National Product (GNP) transferred, extra savings would not be much above 0.4 per cent of GNP and with an incremental capital output ratio of four the growth rate might be expected to rise by about 0.1 per cent. This is very small. It means that a 10 per cent cut in benefits could generate enough growth to get recipients back to their pre-cut position in a mere forty-six years.* Jam quondam et jam futurus sed numquam jam jam!

On the whole the efficiency effects are probably significant though extremely difficult to disentangle and to quantify. The hard evidence that we have points so far to small quantitative effects. Whether these quantitative effects would be greater if only we could penetrate the mysteries of economic psychology and the black economy remains an open question. But the existence of larger effects would not, in itself, settle any policy issues, for, as we noted in Section 1, economic welfare cannot usually be measured independently of distribution. As in the example of unemployment benefits which we have just discussed, one has to trade-off output gains (or losses) against distributive losses (or gains).

5. THE WELFARE STATE AND ECONOMIC MORALITY (D)

It is quite possible to argue that the welfare state actually damages certain moral values, the values of self-reliance, hard work and thrift. These are sometimes referred to as 'Victorian' values. But the view I shall take here is that a positive relationship exists, not a negative one.

Some human rights, like the right to liberty, are absolute in the sense of being in no way contingent upon the level of economic welfare. They stand outside of issues such as distributive justice and may, as in Rawls (1972), be given priority. But an important class of right is *goods-*

contingent. There can be little doubt that some goods are more important than others, not in the technical sense of having low-income (and price) elasticities of demand but in the sense of being 'primary' or more essential to the process of life. These are the goods that carry high values of m (Section 3). Provision of basic means of subsistence is an obvious example. Health and education (though not the cumbersome apparatus that seems to go with them) are also examples. Thus an unconditional right to some specified level of health care is a goods-contingent right. As societies become richer so the quality of goods-contingent rights may be increased.

Goods-contingent rights may, it is true, be acquired simply by democratic *force majeure*: the economic rights and the redistribution that normally accompanies them may be entirely a matter of self-interest. But the rights of weak minorities, the physically and mentally handicapped, the chronically ill, can hardly be thus acquired (indeed not, says the cynic, that is why they are so inadequate). Other members of society have perceived a duty to grant certain goods-contingent rights. The welfare state may be seen as an institutionalisation of goods-contingent rights.

Once goods-contingent rights have become institutionalised in this way it becomes rather difficult to slip back into the pre-rights situation. Consolidation has, as it were, a ratchet effect. The development of economic morality is a fumbling process during which 'sympathy', at our better moments, suggests generalised duties which in turn lead to collective action. Once consolidated, new goods-contingent rights are mentally 'ticked-off' – it is no longer necessary to fill collecting-tins or to run campaigns – and we can move on to something else. The agenda for action has changed.

Finally, we need to say a little about the *decision-rule* whereby voters' preference about goods-contingent rights are translated into legislative action. There is no unique way of making this transition: only in one case, that of single-issue majority voting, is the outcome unique; otherwise there are many possible mappings of one into the other. Economic rights are never the only (or even the most important) issue in an election so that it would be quite possible for the decision rule to produce outcomes at variance with the wishes of the majority on particular issues. All we need for this part of the discussion is that some decision rule exists. A convenient shorthand (see Collard, 1978) is to suppose an effectively decisive preference group. In simple majority voting this is the median preference group: in representative democracies a higher than median preference group will often be decisive. Perhaps the decision rule is tied to median preference by an elastic string, for public preferences have a variety of expression apart from the ballot box so that the ruling party finds it politic to take heed of pressures from the press, the establishment, parliamentary opposition and protest movements. The elastic string ensures that the legislature cannot for long remain too far ahead of or too far behind public opinion. But the power of consolidation and of altering the agenda does give one the means of nudging things in an upward direction. Pinnacles of achievement are not normally torn down in the less glorious days that follow.

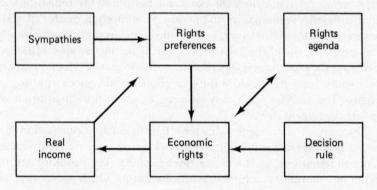

FIGURES 10.5   *The ratchet effect and economic rights*

The process I have in mind is outlined in Figure 10.5. As we saw in Sections 2 and 3, the level of real income and symathetic preferences between them determine rights preferences. But these preferences are only translated into economic rights (underwritten by taxation) once the current agenda and the decision rule are known. Once economic rights are determined there will be effects upon real income and also upon the rights agenda. Thus the proces continues, a constant revision and correction being superimposed upon a generally upward process.

6. CONCLUSIONS

To summarise what I have said in the preceding sections:

(A) The development of sympathy and of moral reasoning carries with it a duty to grant certain 'economic rights'.

(B) The ability and willingness to grant them increase with income.
(C) The granting of economic rights in the form of a welfare state probably has efficiency effects, but these are not numerically large and in any case have to be 'traded-off' against equity.
(D) The institutionalisation of economic rights has a ratchet effect: it enables one to move further down the agenda.

Rather than draw out a formal conclusion I would like to finish by examining one very well-known proposal for reform against the background of the analysis offered – that is to say the social dividend (or what I prefer to call 'universal flat benefit') proposal. This is not the place for reviewing the proposal in detail (see Collard, 1980): it was first advocated by Rhys-Williams (1952) and has been exhaustively discussed in the Meade Report (1978). Its main attractions are:

(i) As an efficient device for implementing economic rights it is vastly superior to any more selective system. All such systems provide hurdles which impose costs on potential beneficiaries (see Collard, 1978).
(ii) It makes absolutely certain that the replacement ratio is less than one.
(iii) It is a good long-term device for dealing with the problem of labour-saving technical progress. The universal flat benefit would simply be allowed to grow so as to provide very adequate living standards for everyone (see Meade, 1964).

However, reformers discuss the universal flat benefit only to reject it as being too expensive. Figure 10.4(b) and (c) suggest that such a benefit may be an acceptable solution in the longer term but not yet – the higher the (proportionate) benefit the higher the level of income needed to sustain it. In the meantime the ratchet effect suggests that granting high levels of particular flat (non-means-tested) benefits might be useful interim steps in the process of the consolidation of economic rights.

Finally, it is often remarked that 'duties' are neglected in discussion of economic rights. This is true. Economic rights are not natural rights and to grant them, through the institution of the welfare state, is a duty. It is part of the process of human betterment.

NOTE

* The formula for working out 'jam day' is

$$j = \frac{1}{\Delta g} \log \left(\frac{1}{(1-r)(1+y)} \right),$$

where Δg is the increase in the growth rate (in percentage points),
     y is the proportionate output effect, and
     r is the percentage reduction in benefits.

REFERENCES

C. V. Brown, *Taxation and the Incentive to Work* (Milton Keynes; Open University Press, 1980).
D. A. Collard, 'The Case for Universal Benefits', in D. Bull (ed.), *Family Poverty* (London: Duckworth, 1971).
D. A. Collard, *Altruism and Economy* (Martin Robertson, 1978).
D. A. Collard, 'Social Dividend and Negative Income Tax', in C. Sandford, C. Pond, *et al.* (eds), *Taxation and Social Policy* (London: Heinemann, 1980).
D. A. Collard, 'The Economics of Philanthropy', *Economic Journal* (September 1983).
A. Deaton and J. Muellbauer, *Economics and Consumer Behaviour* (Cambridge: Cambridge University Press, 1980).
I. Kant, *Lectures on Ethics* (Methuen, 1930).
J. M. Keynes, *Economic Possibilities for our Grandchildren*, 1930, collected works vol. 9 (London: Macmillan, 1972).
J. E. Meade, *Efficiency, Equality and the Ownership of Property* (London: Allen & Unwin, 1964).
J. E. Meade, *The Structure and Reform of Direct Taxation* (London: Allen & Unwin, 1978).
J. Rawls, *A Theory of Justice* (Oxford: Oxford University Press, 1972).
J. Rhys-Williams, *Something to Look Forward to* (London: Macdonald, 1942).
A. K. Sen, 'Ethical Measurement of Inequality: Some Difficulties', in W. Krelle and A. A. Shorrocks (eds), *Personal Income Distribution* (Amsterdam: North-Holland, 1978).
A. K. Sen, 'Poor, Relatively Speaking', *Oxford Economic Papers* (July 1983).
A. Smith, *The Theory of Moral Sentiments*, 1759 (London: Bohn, 1853).
P. Townsend, *Poverty in the United Kingdom* (Harmondsworth: Penguin Books, 1979).

11 The Crisis of the Welfare State – the Dutch Experience

MICHAEL ELLMAN

1 THE CRISIS OF THE WELFARE STATE

Recently much has been written about the crisis of the welfare state (O'Connor, 1973; Veldkamp, 1976; Gough, 1979; Hirschman, 1980; OECD 1981; Preadviezen, 1981; Glennerster, 1983). The crisis as generally conceived has the following aspects. First, a fiscal aspect arising from increasing budgetary problems in financing welfare state expenditures. Second, a taxpayers' revolt arising from reluctance by taxpayers to pay for the welfare state. This can take the form of open opposition, either political or industrial, or passive resistance. Politically the taxpayers may organise to elect tax-cutting governments (as in California, the USA and the UK). Industrially either firms or employees may seek to pass on tax increases in the form of price or pay increases. Passive resistance manifests itself when instead of obeying the law and observing the regulations of the welfare state, the citizens organise economic activity outside the confines of these regulations (the 'black economy'). Third, a decline in support for the welfare state as traditional supporters die or lose confidence and new citizens enter the adult population without acquiring confidence. Fourth, a failure by many social programmes to achieve their objectives. Fifth, increasing awareness that the personnel employed on social programmes are often not the selfless servants of the clients. Sixth, an ideological struggle resulting from the revival of the liberal idea that the price mechanisms is inherently preferable to the budget mechanism because it provides a better means for the expression of individual preferences.

Whereas at one time, at any rate in Western Europe, the desirability of the welfare state was generally accepted, this is no longer so. The ability to finance it has declined, the opposition to it has grown, support for it has shrunk, its failure to achieve its objectives has become more noticeable, the conflict between the needs of the clients and the self-interest of the personnel has become more obvious, and the ideology of the welfare state has lost its hegemonic position.

The crisis of the welfare state is particularly deep in the Netherlands. This is because of the high level of development it achieved there, combined with the seriousness of the economic problems with which the country is now confronted.

2. THE EMERGENCE OF THE WELFARE STATE IN THE NETHERLANDS

The first Dutch social insurance law was the 1901 law regulating financial consequences of industrial injuries. In 1930 a law came into operation making provision for income maintenance during illness and in 1941 a child benefit scheme for employees was introduced. Nevertheless it is basically true to say that the Dutch welfare state is a post-Second World War phenomenon. An important role in developing it was played by the confessional parties, in particular by the Roman Catholic KVP. This reflected Catholic social teaching as set out in encyclicals such as *Rerum Novarum* (1891) and *Quadragissimo Anno* (1931). The main laws regulating the current transfer payments came into force between the mid-1950s and the mid-1970s. Major landmarks were the adoption of an unemployment insurance scheme (1952), old-age pensions (1956), child benefits (1962), supplementary benefit (1963), long-term unemployment benefit (1965), inability to work pensions (1966) and the minimum wage (1969). A detailed history can be found in Veldkamp (1978) pp. 49–182. The Dutch welfare state developed during a secular boom marked by high rates of economic growth, full employment, social peace and general expectations of continued prosperity.

Although the rapid expansion of the income transfer programmes was opposed by the employers and the VVD (a liberal political party ideologically close to the Institute of Economic Affairs and the Thatcher wing of the Conservative Party) opposition in society as a whole remained muted. Both Christian Democracy and the Labour Movement were strongly in favour. Quite suddenly, however, in the mid-1970s, attention began to switch from the benefits of the system to the costs. The first official body seeking economies in the system reported in 1976 and a widespread mood developed from 1976 onwards that the system as it stood was too dear and having undesirable side effects.

3. THE WELFARE STATE IN ITS HEYDAY

The main features of the Dutch welfare state in its heyday were as follows:

(1) All large firms were required to establish works councils which had extensive rights of information and also veto power over certain key decisions. For example, whereas in the UK shareholders alone can transfer a company from one management to another, in the Netherlands the consent of a works council is required.

(2) Security of employment. In general, dismissal was impossible without the approval of the local Employment Exchange. This approval was only given in special circumstances. The grounds on which anyone could be dismissed were narrowly limited by law. So were the procedures. For example, dismissal of someone who was ill or pregnant was illegal. So, in general, was dismissal without an earlier reprimand.

(3) Cheap and secure housing. This was ensured by rent control, allocation of privately rented accommodation by local authorities, rent allowances to those for whom rent would otherwise have formed too high a proportion of their income and laws guaranteeing security from eviction. In addition there were income-related subsidies for the purchase of cheap housing for owner occupation.

(4) A high-quality education system paid for out of general taxation and not by the users or their parents. There is no élite private education system.

(5) High-quality medical care for the whole population paid for by compulsory or voluntary insurance, with the bulk of the population covered by a compulsory 'insurance' scheme which cross-subsidised in favour of low earners.

(6) A minimum wage which was high by international standards, not far below the average wage, and indexed to the average wage.

(7) A supplementary benefit system providing everyone not other-

wise provided for with an indexed income related to the
minimum wage (for couples equal to 100 per cent of the
minimum wage).

(8) Earnings-related payments in the event of unemployment, illness or inability to work. In the event of illness the payment was
100 per cent for one year (with thereafter an entitlement to an
unfitness-for-work pension of 80 per cent till retirement age), of
unemployment 80 per cent for six months and 75 per cent for the
next two years, and of inability to work 80 per cent for six months
and 75 per cent for the next two years, and of inability to work 80
per cent (indexed) till retirement age.

(9) A generous indexed old-age pension system (equal for a couple
to the net minimum wage).

(10) A generous indexed child benefit scheme.

(11) Inability to work pensions based on the 'no-fault' principle. A
former employee certified as 'unfit for work' due to industrial
injury, health problems, a car crash, accident at home, etc., etc.,
was entitled to 80 per cent of his/her former income (indexed) till
pension age. Anyone (i.e. including self-employed, casual workers, very part-timers, etc.) above a very low income level who
became 'unfit for work' was entitled to a pension (for a couple
equal to the net minimum wage) till pension age.

(12) Widows' and orphans' pensions, with the pension for a widow
equal to a single person's old-age pension.

The achievements of this system were very great and can be summed
up briefly as follows.

First, the financial insecurity of a market economy was abolished.
Sudden shocks (e.g. accident, illness, unemployment or death of the
breadwinner) had no adverse income effects. Predictable income
losses (e.g. old age) were financially well provided for. Sudden or
arbitrary dismissal was impossible.

Second, the basic needs (housing, education, medical care,
minimum income) of the entire population were provided for.

Third, poverty was virtually eliminated. According to one study
(Abel-Smith 1983, p. 16) when the poverty-line was set at a disposable
income of 50 per cent of the average, then in 1975 the Netherlands had
the lowest proportion of households below the poverty-line (4.8 per
cent) of any EEC country. (The second lowest was the UK with 6.3 per
cent.) According to another study, using the Leiden poverty measure,
poverty in EEC countries in 1979 was as set out in Table 11.1.

TABLE 11.1 *Poverty % in country A according to the poverty-line of country B*

Poverty % in	Poverty-line of Belgium	Denmark	France	West Germany	UK	Ireland	Italy	Netherlands
Belgium	12.33	10.53	17.58	2.57	4.94	1.73	3.06	11.48
Denmark	25.06	23.13	32.84	11.19	17.18	10.05	14.07	23.18
France	19.98	18.37	27.10	8.01	13.53	7.69	11.37	18.93
W. Germany	10.54	9.54	16.98	3.13	6.57	2.70	3.83	9.96
Ireland	44.59	42.69	55.96	26.08	32.63	26.13	30.76	44.68
Italy	17.10	15.21	24.70	7.31	11.16	6.76	9.47	16.59
Netherlands	6.84	5.03	13.74	0.56	1.63	0.56	1.03	5.89
UK	22.40	19.78	30.38	10.58	13.85	10.85	12.48	21.42

SOURCE B. van Praag, A. van Hagenaars and J. van Weeren, 'Armoede in Europa', *Economisch Statistische Berichten*, 16 Dec. 1981, table 4.

Table 11.1 shows that, using the Dutch definition of poverty, there was only 6 per cent poverty in the Netherlands in 1979. It also shows that, using *any* of the EEC national definitions of poverty, the proportion of the Dutch population living in poverty in 1979 was the lowest in the EEC. (It also shows, however, that the proportion of the population living in poverty in the Netherlands according to the Dutch definition is higher than the proportion of the population living in poverty in West Germany according to the West German definition. This results from the higher Dutch idea of what constitutes the minimum consumption necessary to keep people out of 'poverty'.) The table also shows that, according to the Dutch understanding of 'poverty', in 1979 one-fifth of the UK population lived in poverty.

Fourth, a relatively equal income distribution was achieved. Meaningful international comparisons are notoriously difficult to make in view of different definitions of 'income', differences in the population covered (e.g. earners only, earning couples, all inhabitants), different demographic situations, different accuracy of the data and the variety of possible measures of inequality. For what it is worth, a comparison of OECD countries about 1970 showed that when post-tax incomes standardised for differences in household size were considered, by most measures the Netherlands had the most equal distribution of income of all OECD countries for which more or less comparable data were available (Sawyer, 1976, p. 19). Since policy in the Netherlands in the 1970s was of an egalitarian kind, it seems likely that a similar study for 1980 would produce a similar finding.

Fifth, support for Socialism and Communism were undermined. This was particularly important for Christian Democracy.

Generalising, one can say that between 1960 and 1980 the Netherlands made a transition from a society where the secondary income distribution was based mainly on performance to one where it was based mainly on need. This dramatic change took place in only twenty years amid almost universal approval in the first decade followed by growing alarm in the second.

4. PROBLEMS OF THE WELFARE STATE

The main problems of the welfare state are its financing, its effect on the labour market, its effect on profitability, its controllability and its effect on migration.

The difficulties of financing the welfare state under current

economic conditions are the dominant policy concern of the government, directly effect the entire labour force (via the growing burden of
social insurance premiums), and threaten the viability of the system.
Public expenditure has been rising faster than national income for
many years. Hence public expenditure as a proportion of total expenditure has been rising for many years. Some data are set out in Figure
11.1

Figure 11.1 shows that government and social insurance expenditure is about 20 per cent higher (as a proportion of the GNP) in the
Netherlands than in the UK. This discrepancy has increased sharply
since 1975. Simple extrapolation indicates that it will increase further

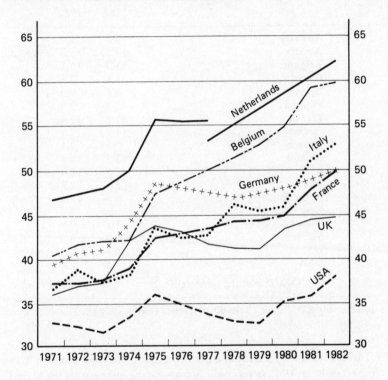

SOURCE   *De Nederlandsche Bank Jaarverslag 1982* (Deventer, 1982) pp. 49.
The break in the series in 1977 is a purely statistical phenomenon
reflecting a change in that year in the methodology of the national
income accounts.

FIGURE 11.1   *Public expenditure as a % of the GNP in a number of OECD
countries*

during the 1980s. The main cause of this discrepancy is the large and growing volume of transfer payments (i.e. the benefits listed under (7) to (12) in Section 3 above. According to the OECD, *Public Expenditure Trends* (Paris, 1978) p. 25 in 1972 income maintenance expenditure in the Netherlands as a proportion of gross domestic product (GDP) was far greater than in any other OECD country and more than double that in the UK. Some data are set out in Table 11.2.

TABLE 11.2   *Income maintenance expenditure as a proportion of the GDP in the OECD (in %)*

	1962	1972
Australia	4.7	4.0
Austria	14.1	15.3
Belgium	11.7	14.1
Canada	5.4	7.3
Denmark	6.5	9.9
Finland	6.7	9.9
France	11.8	12.4
Germany	11.9	12.4
Greece	6.0	7.1
Ireland	5.3	6.4
Italy	7.5	10.4
Japan	2.1	2.8
Netherlands	8.6	19.1
New Zealand	7.6	6.5
Norway	5.1	9.8
Sweden	6.0	9.3
UK	4.4	7.7
USA	5.5	7.4
OECD average (unweighted)	7.3	9.5

SOURCE   OECD, *Public Expenditure Trends* (Paris, 1978) p. 25.

Table 11.2 shows the rapid expansion of income maintenance in the Netherlands. In 1962 it was only just above the average for the OECD and significantly exceeded by four countries. In 1972 it was double the average and greater than any other country. (In both years the UK was below the average.) By 1978 persons received in transfer payments 29 per cent of the domestic value added, a figure higher than any other OECD country and more than double the UK figure (Eije, 1982 p. 23). By 1981, if 'transfer payments' are interpreted in a broad sense to include price subsidies and interest payments, the personal sector received 38 per cent of the national income in transfer payments (*Miljoenennota, 1983*, p. 22). By 1982 the number of persons living off state pensions and other transfer payments (in Dutch terminology the number of economically 'inactive') was 70 per cent of the number of employees plus self-employed (in Dutch terminology the number of economically 'active'). The number of the inactive rose by $5\frac{1}{2}$ per cent in 1982 and further significant increases are anticipated in the future. The number of the active is falling. On present trends the number of the inactive will exceed the number of the active before the end of the decade. It already exceeds it in the 50–65 age group. The conflict between active and inactive has become a central issue in Dutch politics. The active are interested in high real wages, low social security premiums, and an end to the growth in transfer payments. The inactive are interested in maintaining and if possible increasing the present level of benefits. Whereas in the UK this struggle has been largely won by the active (due to the British electoral system, the absence of Christian Democracy in Britain and the absence of a centralised socially conscious labour movement in Britain), in the Netherlands up till now the relative position of the inactive has been much better protected.

How has this increase in expenditure, quite out of line with developments in other OECD countries, been financed? The main sources of finance for this increase in expenditure have been natural gas revenues, borrowing, and social insurance contributions. This can be seen from Tables 11.3 and 11.4.

Table 11.3 shows that between the late 1960s and 1982 state expenditures rose by 12 per cent of the national income. This was mainly caused by an increase in transfer payments (7 per cent) and interest payments (3 per cent). This increase in expenditure was not financed by taxes, which remained about level (although there was some redistribution of the tax burden from companies to households). It was financed by increasing gas revenues (6 per cent) and increased bond issues (5 per cent). To finance further increases in state expenditure in this way will not be easy. Gas output is now over the peak and on a declining trend. Sales may recover temporarily from their sharp drop in 1982 if the home and overseas economies recover, and revenue may increase if there are further dramatic price increases on the world market. Nevertheless it seems most unlikely that in the future there will be a structural increase in natural gas revenues above the 1981 level of 6 per cent of the national income. The increase in gas revenues,

TABLE 11.3   *State sector accounts 1965–82 (in % of the national income)*

	1965/9	1970/4	1975/9	1980	1981	1982[a]
Expenditure						
(1) Consumption (wages and materials,	16.7	17.5	19.0	19.2	19.2	18.7
(2) Interest	3.0	3.3	3.4	4.1	4.9	5.7
(3) Price subsidies	1.0	1.5	2.3	2.7	2.5	2.5
(4) Transfer payments	3.5	4.3	8.4	9.5	9.9	10.5
Current expenditures	24.2	26.6	33.1	35.5	36.5	37.4
Capital expenditures	9.1	7.6	6.8	8.1	8.5	7.9
Total expenditures	33.3	34.2	39.9	43.6	45.0	45.3
Income						
(1) Taxes (excluding corporation tax on gas companies)	26.8	29.0	29.4	30.0	28.7	27.4
(2) Gas	0.2	1.0	3.2	4.5	6.0	6.1
(3) Other income	1.7	1.7	1.9	2.1	2.6	2.7
Current income	28.7	31.7	34.5	36.6	37.3	36.2
Deficit	4.6	2.5	5.4	7.0	7.7	9.1
of which, financed by medium or long-term borrowing[b]	3.8	3.7	3.6	5.2	7.9	9.2

[a] Estimate. For gas, receipts in 1982 as a proportion of an national income turned out to be below the 1981 figure.
[b] The balance is financed by short-term borrowing from the banks.

SOURCE   *Macro Economische Verkenning 1983* (The Hague, 1982) pp. 71 and 70.

a temporary source of revenue, has been spent on transfer payments, the recipients of which now regard them as a right to be maintained indefinitely. This has stored up trouble for the future when the revenue will have been used up but the corresponding income claim will still be there. The same mistake has been made in the UK with respect to North Sea Oil and gas revenues and will in due course give rise to serious difficulties for UK public finances and/or the living standards of the unemployed. In both countries the failure to convert the income from temporary natural resources into investment, but to use it to accelerate deindustrialisation and finance transfer payments, was a serious policy error. As for the issue of bonds the government is committed to *reducing* sharply the Public Sector Borrowing Requirement (PSBR) in order to allow scope for the private sector to borrow. Under present conditions of abundant private savings, a large current account surplus and deepening depression, emphasis on the need to reduce the PSBR is inappropriate. Due to the depression, industrial firms have little interest in capital market issues to finance investment. On the other hand, it is probably true that the high share of the state in available savings is one of the factors that has depressed the second-hand housing market (where average values fell by about one-third in 1978–83) and hence ended private house-building. Furthermore, if the demand for finance for business investment were to revive, the large government demand for finance would be a problem. The government is also worried about the effect of government borrowing on the level of interest rates (the real rate of interest is at the freakish level of 6 per cent), although international factors appear to influence them more. Moreover, the increase in government borrowing in recent years, combined with higher interest rates, has created its own financing problem. Interest charges take up a significant and rapidly growing share of the budget. In addition, there is a danger that a further increase in borrowing will undermine the government's credit rating. At the moment this is high because of the strong balance-of-payments position (the result of the internal depression), the high level of personal savings, the high level of interest rates and the low level of inflation. If its credit rating were to decline, e.g. because of balance of payments deficits, the government might be forced to introduce major cuts in expenditure in an emergency package, as has happened many times in the UK.

Because in the Netherlands the social insurance system is regulated by the state but administered jointly by employers and employees, its income and outlays were not included in Table 11.3. The relevant data are set out in Table 11.4.

Table 11.4 shows that between 1965 and 1982 social insurance benefits as a proportion of the national income increased by 12 per cent. This was financed by increasing contributions from employers and employees (by 10 per cent) and from the government by 2 per cent. Since 1980 the government has reduced its contribution (this results from its own financial problems). It intends to continue this policy. Hence in 1981, 1982 and 1983 contributions from employers and employees have had to be increased by more than the increase in benefits to allow for the reduction in the government contribution.

TABLE 11.4   *Social insurance system accounts*
(in % of the national income)

	1965	1970	1975	1977[a]	1978	1979	1980	1981	1982
Income									
(1) Contributions (employer + employee)	12.4	16.2	20.3	18.7	19.0	19.7	20.2	21.3	22.5
(2) Government contribution	0.8	1.1	2.0	2.3	3.3	3.5	3.9	3.2	2.8
(3) Interest	0.3	0.3	0.3	0.3	0.3	0.3	0.3	0.3	0.2
Expenditures									
(1) Benefits	12.5	16.2	21.1	20.7	21.8	22.6	23.5	24.2	24.7
(2) Costs	0.6	0.6	0.7	0.7	0.7	0.7	0.8	0.8	0.9
(3) Balance	0.4	0.7	0.7	-0.2	0.1	0.1	0.2	-0.3	-0.1

[a] The apparent decline in the relative size of the social insurance system in 1977 is a statistical illusion resulting from a change in the method of calculating national income in 1977. As a result the figures for 1977 and later are not comparable with those for the earlier years. (For comparability the pre-1977 figures should be reduced or the later figures increased.)

SOURCE   (a)   for 1965, 1970 and 1975, the *Statistisch zakboek* for 1966, 1971 and 1978.
(b) for the remaining years, *Macro Economische Verkenning 1983* (The Hague, 1982) p. 67.

Table 11.4 also shows that the cost of administering the social insurance system now absorbs almost 1 per cent of the national income (this excludes the administrative costs which fall on the employers and employees themselves)! If present regulations governing entitlement to benefits and the administration of the system remain in force, the burden of employer and employee contributions will grow steadily during the 1980s. This seems, however, an implausible and dangerous scenario since the number of employees in the market sector has been falling since the mid-1970s (in 1982 the fall was $2\frac{1}{2}$ per cent), profits in the non-energy and non-financial market sector are poor, real wages have been falling for several years and the national income has been falling since 1980. The government is convinced that these dangerous adverse trends cannot be halted without checking the rapid rise in social insurance contributions. Hence it has been proposed to reduce significantly the (past) income related benefits. It is proposed to do this by reducing the percentage of past income which recipents may receive and by reducing the length of the period for which entitlement to benefit runs. It is to be expected that from 1984 the benefits outlined in Section 3 (8) will be significantly reduced.

The labour market effects of income transfer programmes have attracted much attention in recent years. These effects are of two kinds, on the supply of labour and on the demand for it. As far as the supply of labour is concerned, both *a priori* expectations and empirical work suggest that the supply of labour will be reduced by income transfers that reduce the pain of the economic whip. There appear to be no Dutch studies of the effect of social insurance benefits on the supply of labour (Muysken and van den Burg, 1983, p. 19). Danzinger, Haveman and Plotnick, 1981 (pp. 996–9) suggest that in the USA income transfer programmes equivalent to c. 10 per cent of the gross national product (GNP) reduce the supply of labour by the recipients by about $4\frac{1}{2}$ per cent of total employment. *If* the Dutch programmes of c. 30 per cent of the GNP had three times the effect of the US ones, that would suggest a reduction of the labour force by c. 13 per cent. (These people would appear in Dutch statistics in the inactive, among the recipients of inability to work pensions, sickness benefit and unemployment benefit.) This is a guess for the impact of the benefits alone, and excludes any effect of the burden of social insurance premiums on the supply of labour. The US estimates also suggest that income transfers are a diminishing returns sector in the sense that increases in the programmes produce a disproportionately low reduction in poverty and improvement in income distribution and a disproportionately high loss of employment and output. On the other hand, as Pen (1981, p. 60) has observed, under present conditions of insufficient demand for labour, it is doubtful if voluntary inability to work/illness/ unemployment is a major brake on production. It probably just substitutes one group for another among the unfit for work/ill/unemployed. The high tax and social insurance contributions burden also reduces work motivation among the employed, leading to lower effort and reducing the effectiveness of organisations. Both the black economy and speculation (there is no capital gains tax in the Netherlands) are heavily stimulated by the present system and are financially attractive relative to employment in the white sector.

As far as the demand for labour is concerned, this depends on the extent to which companies are unable to pass on social insurance premiums to their customers so that they actually fall on the profits and continuity of the firms. Against this has to be set the effect of the increased net demand for labour generated by the net additional demand of the recipients of the benefits (i.e. additional demand of recipients less reduction in demand by payers of higher social insurance premiums.) In the internationally competitive sector cost increases are difficult to pass on except when they effect all countries equally. For example, an increase in world oil prices, is easy for the Dutch internationally competitive sector to pass on since it also affects competitors. An increase in social insurance premiums confined to the Netherlands, however, is quite a different matter. The adverse employment effects are increased in the Netherlands by the fact that social insurance premiums are levied on the wage bill and that above a certain point the relationship between premiums and the wage bill is regressive. As Douben (1983, p. 193) has observed: 'Thus the system of collecting premiums has given rise to a quicker increase in labour costs for labour-intensive activities. That as a result there are negative effects on the volume of employment can scarcely be doubted. Indeed there exists a possibility of a vicious circle which goes from higher social insurance premiums via higher labour costs to higher unemployment and higher social insurance premiums. When it is borne in mind that the height of the percentage benefit of the income-related benefits certainly does not stimulate the working of the labour market, the conclusion can be drawn that the system of social insurance in the Netherlands is partly the cause of the existence of economic difficulties in the welfare state.' Hence it seems reasonable to suppose that part of the rapidity of the deindustrialisation process in the Netherlands, part of the decline in total employment in the market sector, and part of the increase in unemployment (both official and hidden), have been caused by the social insurance system.

At the present time, profitability in the Dutch non-energy non-financial market sector is poor, balance-sheet ratios have deteriorated, investment is low, employment is falling and bankruptcies are an everyday occurrence. There are many possible reasons for the erosion of profitability which has taken place (OECD, 1983, pp. 20–1). Clearly the decline in real wages and the fall in total demand which have taken place in the last couple of years are important factors. Another significant factor is the high level of interest rates. There can be little doubt, however, that the large and increasing burden of the transfer payments system, financed as it is by deductions from the gross pay of employees, payroll taxes on employers, and other taxes, is a factor. Under conditions of weak demand and international competition it has been impossible to pass on fully the costs of the system.

It is not an accident that it was in the Netherlands that the possibility of a negative balanced budget multiplier was first extensively discussed. In traditional Keynesian analysis the balanced budget multiplier is positive. This means that an increase in government expenditure financed by a corresponding increase in taxes, raises total output. If the balanced-budget multiplier is negative, then an increase in government expenditure financed by increased taxes reduces output. This possibility was widely discussed in the Netherlands in the mid-1970s and reflected a situation in which profits (not wages as in Keynesianism) were the residual element in the economic system. Increases in taxes on wages or employee social security contributions were passed on by organised labour to the employers who responded to the increase in labour costs and squeeze on profits by shedding labour at home and switching production to cheap labour countries.

When the balanced-budget multiplier is negative, fiscal policy (other than increasing the PSBR) to increase employment requires, either a reduction in government expenditure with a corresponding reduction in taxes, or that organised labour ceases reacting to tax increases by wage increases. In the UK fiscal policy aims at the former, in the Netherlands at the latter. The Dutch choice was possible for the Netherlands but impossible for the UK because of the existence in the Netherlands of a centralised labour movement prepared to trade-off real wage cuts against the maintenance of welfare benefits. (Dutch experience has shown that the expected positive supply side effects of accepting reduced real wages can be wiped out by the negative demand side effects of the international depression, high exchange rate and high interest rates.)

An important topical problem is the controllability of welfare expenditures (Wolfson, 1981). Contributions rise every year and are a bigger and bigger burden on employees and employers, despite the fact that they are already much higher than was envisaged when the relevant laws were passed (le Blanc 1982) and everyone is agreed that they are already too high. Sometimes the social insurance system seems like an angry out-of-control giant that will destroy the entire employment intensive internationally competitive sector of the economy. Although in the short run the social insurance system is a built in stabiliser, protecting effective demand from sharp falls in employment, in the long run the social insurance system has become a built in destabiliser, preventing employment from stabilising, let alone recovering. It is a built-in destabiliser because of its supply side effect of increasing costs and squeezing profits and thereby reducing employment and output. Reasons for the apparently uncontrollable increase in expenditures are, *inter alia*:

(1) the rapid increase in unemployment,
(2) the open ended character of the relevant laws, so that anyone who meets certain criteria (pensionable age, unemployment, etc.) is entitled to the relevant benefits,
(3) the indexation of benefits,
(4) the granting to third parties (e.g. employers and workers and doctors working for them) the right to decide whether someone meets the criterion (e.g. 'unfitness for work') for receiving benefit, and
(5) the lack of connection in the public mind between benefits and costs, the idea that benefits are 'free' because they are free when used.

In the last few years, considerable effort has been devoted by officials to bringing welfare expenditures under control, so far with a singular lack of success.

The high average living standards, combined with the welfare state, has had a major impact on migration patterns. All inhabitants of the Netherlands are entitled to welfare benefits which ensure a standard of living which is high by the standards of most of the world. From the end of the Second World War to 1960 the Netherlands was normally a net emigration country. From 1961 onwards it was normally a modest net immigration country. In the 1970s the immigration became significant relative to the natural increase of the population. In most years net immigration was about one-third of the natural increase. In the peak immigration year 1975 net immigration exceeded the natural increase of the population. Gross immigration has exceeded the natural increase of the population in every year since 1973.

5. THE CURRENT DUTCH ECONOMIC SITUATION

Employment in the Netherlands fell by 1.3 per cent in 1981 and 1.8 per cent in 1982. It is expected to fall further in 1983. The labour force is rapidly rising due to demographic and social factors. Hence unemployment is rising rapidly. In 1981 it was still below the EEC average and well below the UK level. In 1982 it overtook the EEC average, but was still below the UK level. In 1983 it rose sharply above the EEC average, exceeded the UK level (this happened in April) and reached one of the highest levels in the OECD.[1] It seems likely that by the end of 1983, unemployment in the Netherlands according to the Dutch statistical conventions will have reached at least 16 per cent and that the Netherlands will have been firmly established as one of the unemployment black spots of the OECD.

Real wages in the private sector have been falling steadily since 1980. They fell by about 10 per cent in 1980–3. In the state sector the fall began earlier and has been bigger.

Real GDP fell in both 1981 and 1982 (by 1.2 per cent in each year). Prospects for growth are poor since domestic consumption is stagnant, investment weak, the outlook for net exports obscure, and real interest rates very high (the yield on government bonds exceeds the rate of inflation by about 6 per cent). The OECD expects a further fall in real GDP of 1.4 per cent in 1983.

The government's finances are out of control. Despite repeated attempts to reduce the PSBR as a proportion of the national income, it is steadily rising. It rose from 5.3 per cent in 1979 to 9.5 per cent in 1982 and will be still higher this year. This failure to bring the PSBR under control, despite repeated attempts to do so, compares unfavourably with UK experience. It partly results from the generous income maintenance system. Dismissal of staff by private employers increases social insurance and government outgoings and dismissal of staff by the public sector produces net savings much below the gross savings. Only a resumption of economic growth, or significant cuts in public sector salaries, or a drastic cut in income maintenance programmes, or radical and effective work-sharing, or some combination of these, will radically improve the public finances.

All in all the Netherlands is now in a serious situation. Although the decline in national income is insignificant compared with 1929–32, the unemployment figures will soon be comparable with the 1930s. Within a few years the Netherlands has changed from a country with an enviable rate of economic growth and level of economic and social development to one which has one of the worst recent economic records in the OECD.[2]

It would be a grave mistake to blame the welfare state for the current situation. The depression is a world-wide phenomenon, affecting West, East and South, welfare states or not. Furthermore, the welfare state has performed a valuable role in protecting the victims of the depression from extreme adverse economic consequences. Nevertheless the current miserable situation has directed attention to adapting the welfare state to conditions of depression rather than boom.

6. ADAPTING THE DUTCH WELFARE STATE TO THE DEPRESSION

According to the prevalant Dutch orthodoxy, in order for the current depression to facilitate the restructuring of the economy and to contribute to a new burst of capitalist economic growth in the late 1980s and 1990s it is necessary that:

(a) costs of production are cut,
(b) labour discipline and the ability of managers to restructure production, is increased,
(c) the supply of labour to the market sector is increased,
(d) incentives to work in the market sector are increased,
(e) taxes which fall on profits and the regulatory burden on firms be reduced, and
(f) technical progress creates profitable new investment opportunities.

Although some people in the Netherlands are opposed to economic growth altogether, and others to capitalism, the authorities are concerned with creating the conditions for a new upswing in capitalist accumulation. As far as the welfare state is concerned this implies:

(1) cutting the level of welfare benefits, the minimum wage and average earnings,
(2) reducing the protection given to workers in cases of the reorganisation of production by labour legislation and the welfare system,
(3) facilitating increases in the female participation rate,
(4) cutting the relative pay (and benefits) of those in the state sector and those receiving welfare benefits,
(5) cutting employers' social security contributions and corporation tax, and deregulation.

All these measures are now under way. The government plans to reduce the level of earnings-related benefits. The real minimum wage has already been reduced (as have the reduced minimum wage levels for young people from 17 to 22). Real wages are steadily falling. Instructions have been given that when new employers take over bankrupt firms they will not have the same obligations to the labour force as the previous owners. Increasing the female labour force has become an important policy objective with its own institution (the Emancipation Council). Cuts in the real pay of those in the state sector have been greater than those in the private sector. Official bodies are looking into deregulation. The corporation tax is being cut and social insurance premiums transferred from employers to employees.

Whether these measures will be intensified in the future, and how successful they will be, depends primarily on external factors. The Netherlands is a small foreign-trade-dependent country. All that the government can hope to do is to adapt the economic structure in such a way that the country will respond favourably to a new upswing in the OECD – if and when one happens.

A striking feature of the Dutch scene by British standards is the co-operation between the government, trade unions and employers in adapting to the depression. For example, work-sharing is officially supported. Similarly, the trade unions accept that, under conditions of negative growth and rapidly rising numbers of welfare-benefit recipients, real wages must fall significantly to finance the welfare benefits.

7. CONCLUSIONS

In the post-Second World War period, especially between the mid-1950s and the mid-1970s, the Netherlands developed one of the best, perhaps the best, welfare states in the whole world. It provided for the basic needs of the entire population, eliminated poverty, liquidated the financial insecurity of a market economy and greatly reduced inequality. It turned out, however, that the Dutch welfare state was like a bank, which in the well-known phrase, provides umbrellas when it is sunny. At the present time, when the Netherlands is one of the unemployment blackspots of the OECD, and the time is fast approaching when the number of persons living off state handouts will equal the working population, the prospects are for substantial reductions in the most attractive (earnings-related) benefits. The longer the depression persists the more the welfare system is likely to be reduced. In the short run a built-in stabiliser, in the longer run the welfare state appears as a built-in destabiliser, hindering attempts to get capital accumulation going again.

In the great boom of the 1950s and 1960s, many writers described 'modern' or 'transformed' capitalism. It was frequently stated that the creation of the welfare state marked a decisive break with the 'old' capitalism of financial insecurity, mass poverty and unemployment. At the present time we can see that this was partly true and partly false. On the one hand, the development of the welfare state did dramatically reduce the financial insecurity of the market economy. The financial lot of the unemployed is better now than it was in the 1930s. In addition, poverty and inequality have been sharply reduced. These are important gains and major improvements relative to the pre-welfare state situation. On the other hand, the welfare state did not, and could not, end the subordination of social and economic policy to the imperatives of capital accumulation. In a period of reconstruction of capital, such as we are now in, the latter are such as to reduce substantially the benefits provided by the welfare state.

NOTES

* I am grateful to G. Reuten for helpful comments.

1. See OECD, *Main Economic Indicators*, August 1983 (Paris, 1983). The most recent figures given here are for June 1983, when the Dutch unemployment rate was still below the Belgian and Spanish.
2. Although the balance of payments is in enormous surplus and inflation has fallen to 3 per cent, these are not unambiguous achievements. The former basically reflects the domestic recession, and the latter is unwelcome to debtors, both firms and families.

REFERENCES

B. Abel-Smith (1983) 'Assessing the Balance Sheet', in Glennerster.

L. J. C. M. le Blanc (1982) 'Economic en sociale zekerheid', in J. A. H. Bron (ed.), *Sociale zekerheid en recessie* (The Hague: Instituut voor Onderzoek van Overheidsuitgaven).

S. Danzinger, R. Haveman, and R. Plotnick (1981) 'How Income Transfer Programs affect Work, Savings and the Income Distribution', *Journal of Economic Literature*, pp. 975–1028.

N. H. Douben (1983) 'Sociale uitkeringen: omvang, groei en consequenties', in M. Brouwer and M. Ellman (eds), *De collectieve sector in de crisis* (Deventer: Kluwer).

J. H. von Eije (1982) *Geldstromen en inkomensverdeling in de verzorgingsstaat* (The Hague: Wetenschappelijke Raad voor het Regeringsbeleid).

H. Glennerster (1983) *The Future of the Welfare State*, ed. H. Glennerster (London: Heinemann Educational Books).

I. Gough (1979) *The Political Economy of the Welfare State* (London: Macmillan).

A. O. Hirschman (1980) 'The Welfare State in Trouble', *American Economic Review Papers and Proceedings*, pp. 113–16.

J. Muysken and H. van der Burgh (1983) 'Te beroerd om te werken?', in *Beleid en Maatschappij*, vol. X, nos. 1–2 (January–February).

J. O'Connor (1973) *The Fiscal Crisis of the State* (New York: St. Martin's Press).

OECD (1981) *The Welfare State in Crisis* (Paris).

OECD (1983) *Netherlands* (OECD Economy Survey, Paris, January).

J. Pen (1981) 'De crisis van de verzorgingsstaat', in *Preadviezen*.

Preadviezen (1981) *Overlevingskansen van de verzorgingsstaat*. Preadviezen van de vereniging voor de Staathuishoudkunde (Leiden and Antwerp: Stenfert Kroese).

M. Sawyer (1976) 'Income Distribution in OECD Countries', *OECD Economic Outlook*, Occasional Studies (Paris, July).

G. M. J. Veldkamp (1976) *De crisis in de nederlandse sociale zekerheid anno 1976* (Amsterdam).

G. M. J. Veldkamp (1978) *Inleiding tot de sociale zekerheid* (Deventer) vol. 1.

D. J. Wolfson (1981) *Naar een beheersbare collectieve sector*, ed. D. J. Wolfson (Deventer: Kluwer).

Index